Leading a Church to Maturity in Love

A Theological and Practical Guide to Church Leadership

— DAVID R. TOMLINSON —

Sacristy
Press

Sacristy Press
PO Box 612, Durham, DH1 9HT

www.sacristy.co.uk

First published in 2019 by Sacristy Press, Durham

Bible extracts, unless otherwise stated, are from the *New Revised Standard
Version Bible: Anglicized Edition*, copyright 1989, 1995, Division of
Christian Education of the National Council of the Churches of Christ in
the United States of America. Used by permission. All rights reserved.

Every reasonable effort has been made to trace the copyright holders
of material reproduced in this book, but if any have been inadvertently
overlooked the publisher would be glad to hear from them.

Sacristy Limited, registered in England & Wales, number 7565667

British Library Cataloguing-in-Publication Data
A catalogue record for the book is available from the British Library

ISBN 978-1-78959-023-4

Foreword

Many books on church leadership are written by those who hold so-called senior positions in the Church. They have been vicars and rural deans in the past, but this is a leadership responsibility that is remembered wistfully, and sometimes through spectacles whose glass is not as clear as it could be. Or else, because they are writing from such a different perspective, their conclusions are not necessarily as germane as they think they are. I plead guilty to the authorship of such books myself, though I hope they are relevant and accessible!

What is striking about this book is that David Tomlinson writes not as someone who used to be a parish priest, but he leads the parish church of St Mary the Virgin in Saffron Walden, which is a member of the Greater Churches Network and a thriving Team Ministry, and he is Area Dean. It is forged in the crucible of his considerable experience. He is writing from right inside that complicated matrix of responsibilities and opportunities that is the day-to-day lived experience of parish ministry. He is not just remembering how it used to be. It is this that gives his book energy and authenticity.

Neither is he concerned about the overall shaping of a diocese or a denomination. This book is about the local church and how to lead in the local church. It offers timely inspiration and wisdom on how to lead in ways that are humble, resilient, relational, consultative and collaborative.

Jesus said, "Blessed are the meek, for they will inherit the earth" (Matthew 5.5). Like many of the Beatitudes, this saying of Jesus is misunderstood. We're not sure what the word "meek" means. It sounds a lot like "weak". However, Jesus is just about the one person you can't call weak. He embraces weakness, but he reveals it to be God's greatest strength. His leadership is marked by servanthood. Therefore "meek" must mean something else. It must be that quality of facing testing situations and challenging people, of dealing with conflict, of being prepared to have difficult conversations, of striving to mediate and seeking peace that David explains here in great depth. It is about being obedient to an agenda higher than your own. It flows from that poverty of spirit which is the first Beatitude, and which David movingly describes in leadership terms as serving people with true humility. It bears fruit in inheriting the earth, meaning the Church becoming a community that can lead the world to maturity in love.

This book will be particularly instructive and helpful for clergy, but its vision of leadership will be relevant for many other people as well. It may even remove your fear of melons. But to understand how that works, you are going to have to read the book . . .

Stephen Cottrell
Bishop of Chelmsford
January 2019

Preface

I enjoy conducting weddings and, especially, preaching at them. The couple's love is a natural springboard into talking about God's love and the commitment that they are to make in the vows that follow the sermon. I usually draw upon the reference in the preface to the service how in marriage each member of the family is "to grow to maturity in love" to highlight how the inevitable irritations and conflicts of a shared life are all opportunities for love to deepen.

In the common life of the first disciples of Jesus, there is dissension and conflict. These flashpoints become stepping stones for Jesus' followers into a greater understanding of who he is and how God's mission is being realized through him. Through this tortuous process, the community around Jesus Christ learns what it means to love God and to love others. This is seen in sharp relief in the journey Peter undertakes. One notable episode from John's Gospel is depicted in the image on the front cover of this book. When it is Peter's turn to have his feet washed by Jesus, he is affronted. Jesus insists that Peter must allow him to serve him if Peter is to be a disciple. Peter with gusto, declares that in that case he would like his "feet and his head washed as well". Now this is a typical Johannine passage laden with symbolism, but the point that I want to draw from it is that out of the clash of expectations, Peter learns something about being a disciple and what it means for the community gathered around Jesus to "love one another". Their final encounter is by the Sea of Tiberias when the Risen Jesus asks Peter three times "do you love me?" Peter, chastened by his three denials of Jesus in the events leading up to the crucifixion, and trusting that Jesus can again see into his heart, answers each time "you know that I love you". Jesus, then, affirms Peter's maturity in love by foretelling his vocation as pastoral leader in the Church and a martyr's death. Like Jesus, Peter will lay down his life. Learning to love like Jesus Christ is what it means to "grow to maturity in love".

Christians see God's love revealed in Jesus Christ. In the life of Jesus, we have an insight into the dynamic interplay between the three persons of the Trinity. Reflection on the Gospels leads to our triune understanding of God, whereby we discover how divine reality is constituted by difference. Each person of the Godhead moves towards the others in self-giving, seeking to nourish, and letting the others find space in them. Thus, the Father is the Father not only because he is distinct but also because, through the power of self-giving, the Son and the Spirit dwell in him. The same is true of the Son and the Spirit. They are mutually constitutive of each other. Yet, the love that they share is dynamic and inclusive. God's love is infinitely giving, infinitely receiving, infinitely desiring to draw others into the ever-expanding circle of love. In the foreground, there is a space at the table, a symbol of divine hospitality. Here is an invitation for us all to come and participate in divine love, in eternal life.

Made as we are in the image of God, we are called to imitate this divine hospitality by making space, room for the other, without constraint or judgement. The offer to come and be, and to bask in love, is unreserved and generous.

Likewise, our common life is to be modelled on the Holy Trinity. Eternal life is the reality and paradigm for our corporate life together as brothers and sisters in God's family. Living in the Trinity, in the fullness of the Spirit, we live in love. God's love is white-hot, purging us from all that is mean, vain and calculating. Divine love stretches and expands our capacity to love the stranger, to embrace others and to offer generous hospitality.

In our life together, we repent of immature and destructive patterns whereby we fail to see others as distinctive, with their own unique contribution, and we come to know that we need to give them space in order that they may flourish. This process of self-emptying, *kenosis* (Christ's self-emptying in incarnation is instructive), is fundamental to life in community. Making allowances and being tolerant are the prerequisites for a much deeper acceptance of others. Respect is not enough. Affirmation should characterize any Christian community. This demands a graceful openness to the other, and a willingness to subvert our own preferences in order for the other to thrive. Within the Christian community, the mutuality of this demand is vital. As we all put ourselves at the service of others, the community is built up. In so far as we need to adapt to the others, we do. Yet, we are only saying "no" to ourselves in order to hear "yes" to who we are from the rest of the community. Our individual aspiration is shared: it is to be ourselves in a way that helps others to become more truly themselves.

The whole story of creation, incarnation and incorporation into Christ's Body demonstrates that God loves us and delights in us. The Church should order her life to reflect this truth: each of us is loved and an occasion of joy.

The presence of the Risen Christ, who transcends all human boundaries, impels the Church to be catholic. Diverse and embracing of each individual, culture and nation, the Church cannot take sides. In fact, the Church is to avoid side-taking and to seek actively to undermine the logic of bifurcation, of splitting people into protagonists and antagonists.

In her internal disputes, when often there are entrenched parties contesting an issue, every effort must be made to bridge these divisions. Opposing camps that can appear to be deaf and dismissive of the arguments of their opponents must be urged to engage with each other. Often there might be agreement about the truths that inform the divergent positions. In the debate about human sexuality there might be common ground in the recognition of Jesus' generous welcome of the outsider, in the requirement for faithfulness in sexual relationships and in the call to holiness. There might also be agreement that in Western society it is counter-cultural to regard sexual activity as an expression of and a means of deepening emotional intimacy and commitment. There could also be a shared understanding that integral to Christian discipleship is a common recognition that our bodies like our whole lives are to be hallowed: a common appreciation that being holy and chaste is fundamental to living out our faith faithfully. In so far as there is some common ground, debate can be sustained. Moreover, it is in the hope that in the dialectic of clashing positions that a greater truth might emerge.

Jesus, though he confronted the religious authorities for their abuse of power, sought consistently to avoid taking sides. While he gives the oppressed hope, he also requires of them radical change as he does of the rich. The choice implicit in the statement "You cannot serve God and mammon" has universal application. Therefore he tells both the rich and the poor to "love your enemies". Here is his critique of the envy and enmity that can so easily have the poor in their grip. Unless both rich and poor can let go of their drive to accumulate more and their tendency to put their trust in material prosperity, even at the expense of others, then the dominant values will prevail. Even if the rich are usurped by the poor, the culture will still be essentially covetous and the community riven by the division between the "haves" and the "have nots".

Max Warren, a general secretary of the Church Mission Society, memorably stated, "It takes the whole world to know the whole Christ." The rich diversity of humanity, even those with whom we fervently disagree, is under the providence of God. To ignore this truth is to be out of touch and to allow ourselves to be impoverished: to embrace the whole breadth of our global village is to be enriched and to grow in our knowledge of the Risen Christ who inhabits and judges, yet is never contained, by every culture.

Each individual church is catholic in the sense that it includes a variety, a range of people. Even the most homogeneous church is composed of unique individuals who, despite their apparent uniformity, are different from and strange to each other. Whatever the make-up of a church, the goal, in terms of her common life, is the same. The differences between people should be celebrated and not reduced to some colourless sameness. Engineering some artificial, and essentially false, unity is a denial of the value and contribution of each individual. Seeing the differences between people is an outworking of listening carefully to the individuals who belong to the church. Each individual brings a unique contribution. By valuing individuality, the church's life is enriched, if, sometimes, through the challenge of sustained loving relationship when there is sharp disagreement.

Nonetheless the other extreme is also unattractive and less than a catholic vision of church. Calling ourselves a church means that there is something we have in common. Our very reason for being there is what we share. If, rather than abolishing difference, we are fixated by it, then we become merely a conglomerate of individuals, an association of independent, distinct individuals connected only by proximity and sharing a sacred space.

By seeing that our identities are only discovered in relationship, we avoid this highly individualized understanding of human interaction where we are each free-floating and disconnected from those around us. Instead, we recognize that our commitment to each other in Christ holds us in relationship but also demands that we let others be who they are. We need to affirm and give them the space to discover their identity through their relationship with us. This affirmation and generous giving of latitude to develop and grow is reciprocal. What I offer, I, in turn, receive.

There is no such thing as pure identity or pure otherness. Identity and otherness are mutually constituted. They are mutually dependent and mutually mediated. In authentic relationships, there is an exchange of meaning to one another: I learn more about you and myself, and you do likewise. There is never any attempt to deny or mask difference. Instead difference is reasserted and sustained throughout each encounter, and in the continuity of an ongoing relationship.

There is a restless quality about relationships. They never stand still; no final harmony is ever reached. Constant negotiation is required. Besides the interplay between concession and acquisition, we cannot erase our identity or seek to control the other, or deny the difference between us by contriving some kind of final resolution. That means relationships are characterized by ebb and flow. When we are open to each other, there is an endless give and take. That's not to say that there cannot be agreement or an acceptance of disagreement, but there is value for both sides in the exchange. On particular issues the conversation might lead to a resolution. For example, when I was leading a church building project in a church in South Essex, there was broad agreement about the plans, but there was someone who had an alternative vision. Rather than add a new frontage to the church with an office, toilets, and servery, she argued that it made more sense to attach the back of the church to the old church hall at the rear of the building. I was keen to hear her reasoning and to see if we needed to think again. Our conversations were robust and my arguments tested. Whereas I could not convince her, our exchanges were helpful to me and left me even more sure that what we intended to do was right. I thanked my conversational partner for being prepared to challenge me and the view of the majority, and asked her to do likewise if she disagreed in the future. We started our dialogue and finished on good terms, and our relationship deepened. In the dynamic of engaging with our different perspectives, we learn and the church's life is strengthened. By keeping an appropriate distance and speaking from opposing positions, individuals flourish, relationships become stronger and the church moves forward with greater conviction.

Given that any church's members are at dramatically different stages of understanding, maturity and responsiveness, relationships are often marred by self-assertion or self-denigration. That is why the church's life must be marked with patience. Thankfully, God is committed to the Church and to the slow and sometimes painful process of growth and transformation. In short, the Church is a work in progress.

Christ's resurrection, his Risen Life, means that our flesh and blood are open to God's presence and the medium of God's love. Furthermore, the reality of Christ in our midst is the promise that the Church is the prototype of a new community. The Church is a pilot project for the whole of humanity. God chooses people to come together—to be a people "called out"—for the benefit of those who do not yet belong. To change the analogy, the Church is a "rough draft" of the new humanity, with the Spirit as the relentless author, who continues to write until the work is complete. Therefore in our corporate life we patiently bear with our experiences of failure and immaturity, ever hopeful and trusting in the graceful persistence of the Holy Spirit. Our life together demands of us a hard, patient labour of love, as we each grow to maturity in love.

The Church is the community in which we are fashioned into agents of social change. By our experience of our life together, ambiguous as it sometimes is, we slowly but assuredly learn to envision and to create a harmonious community, born of humility and truth. Through it, we can play our role in wider society in creating just, thankful and peaceful societies. This is the rationale for and ultimate goal of the Church, a universal renewed humanity, centred on the risen Christ. Driven by this vision of the Church, leaders need to model and facilitate the creation of this radical, catholic community. This task of leading the Church into maturity is what this book is about.

It starts with a theological understanding of the Church, grounded in the biblical story, and centred on the revelation of God's purposes in Christ. The Church is the community centred on the risen Christ, present by the Holy Spirit. Those in the community are drawn together by Christ, who seeks to shape the community's life and to help her to grow in love.

Chapter 2 draws upon the wisdom of "systems thinking". After all, whilst far more than an organization, the Church is one. Insights from this field can offer insights that cannot be gleaned from elsewhere.

Chapter 3 explores the importance of vision. Without vision, the leader and the community they lead do not know where they are heading. A clear, comprehensible vision sets the leader and community on a course of transformation that should impact every day and on every decision.

Chapter 4 centres on "servant leadership". The mentality of the leader is integral and determinative to the leadership that will be offered. If the picture, the model of leadership inside their heads, is based on Jesus' example encapsulated in that memorable statement that "the Son of Man came not to be served but to serve", then the community will be under inspired leadership.

Chapter 5 explores what it means for leaders themselves to keep on growing: if they want to lead a church into maturity, then leaders need to grow too. The leader's individual development and the church's journey are ongoing: the state of maturity is never reached. Progress will only be made, nevertheless, if the leader is moving forwards.

Communication, the subject of Chapter 6, is fundamental to establishing and maintaining good relationships. The leader needs to be exemplary. Besides leading by example, they need to help others directly to modify how they speak to each other, in order to facilitate good and constructive relationships. Listening in depth is essential to good leadership and again, by modelling this careful attention to the other, the leader sets the standard for the church.

In any church there will be people who, because of their upbringing and life experiences, struggle to relate well to others. There are also likely to be factions with their own agendas, battling to get their way. Dealing with difficult individuals and groups, the topic of Chapter 7, is integral to sound leadership, and helping them to be transformed is essential to leading a church into maturity.

Team building is vital in church life. Working effectively in teams is a constant and crucial feature of our life together. The character and skills that are needed for the leader to lead teams successfully are also critical to building up the corporate life. Chapter 8 considers team formation and building up the church's common life.

Chapter 9 explores how leaders can engage with conflict. In any healthy, honest relationship, there is bound to be conflict from time to time. Alongside the normal rough and tumble of human reactions, any process of change will elicit different reactions and generate tension and disagreement.

Whereas inclusivity is a laudable goal for a church, this does not mean that "anything goes" in terms of how people relate to each other. There will be good safeguarding practices to maintain and a virtuous culture to defend. When the boundaries are transgressed, it is the leader's task to take action. Chapter 10 examines the imperative to confront and how best to do it.

When people fall out, they often need someone else to help them to talk together about their sense of grievance and, if they can, discuss how to resolve their disagreement. Mediation is the theme of Chapter 11.

Many different organizations—and the church is no exception—are, as a result of diminishing resources, seeking the benefits of collaboration. Although there are drawbacks to working together with other churches or other agencies, significant gains can be made by doing so. Chapter 12 considers the pros and cons of collaboration, and how to calculate when the benefits outweigh the costs.

Chapter 13 looks at how forgiveness is central to the Christian faith and what that means in practice. As human beings we, inevitably, sometimes get it wrong, and consequently hurt others. A mutual recognition of our shortcomings should mean that we are gracious and gentle with each other. Knowing our own selfishness and clumsiness, we should be both swift to seek forgiveness and to forgive.

The final chapter is a reflection on the cross of Christ. Jesus' death is central to our faith and to our Christian discipleship. This kind of leadership is demanding, costly and stretching. To keep our eyes fixed on the crucified Christ is instructive and inspirational for those who seek to lead. In the words of Isaac Watts' famous hymn, "Love so amazing, so divine demands my soul, my life, my all."

In talking about leaders, I have avoided using gender specific pronouns but have used the second-person singular form instead. By this means, I have got around the rather awkward alternate use of the male and female pronouns.

The matrix of this book is my 25 years of ordained ministry in the Church of England. Throughout that time, I have sought to learn, and to develop my leadership skills. Reflection and experience have given me some deep convictions about how to lead a church into maturity. I owe a debt of gratitude to Bridge Builders, an independent charity that seeks to transform the culture of the church in relation to how leaders lead and the way conflict is handled.[1] As a participant in its courses I assimilated wisdom about myself and ministry, especially about the importance of getting the processes right in change management and the perhaps counter-initiative imperative to engage with conflict, rather than flee from it..

I also need to thank my colleagues whose expertise, affirmation and support have been a great gift. I am grateful to Anna Martin, Kate Ollerenshaw, Gordon Smith and Cath Stuckey who proof-read my text and offered suggestions. I am also indebted to Natalie Watson for her knowledge and insight. However, I have learned most about love from my wife, Jenny, and our two wonderful daughters, Clare and Rebecca. I increasingly love and appreciate them.

I have been working on the book for some time. During its genesis my thinking has evolved, and will, I am sure, continue to do so. What you read here is what I think at present, and I hope that it is some use to you. My goals are to speak some truth, and for you to find stimulation to lead you to further thought and maybe into dialogue with someone else. At the heart of this book is the belief that the quality of our relationships in our churches matters profoundly. Through them others can glimpse the foot-washing depicted on the cover. We are called to offer to all people the hospitality of God, as we are summoned to come to sit and eat with God, with our brothers and sisters, and with all whom God invites.

Contents

CHAPTER 1

The Church—An Inclusive Community

A warm welcome

Many Christian communities aspire to be inclusive and to offer a warm welcome to all. However, aware that the Church is seen by some as exclusive and liable to judge those who do not conform to the popular stereotypes of followers of Jesus Christ, some churches and cathedrals feel the need to spell it out. Here is the "welcome statement" of Coventry Cathedral which makes explicit that everyone without exception is welcome:

> We extend a special welcome to those who are single, married, divorced, widowed, straight, gay, confused, well-heeled or down at heel. We especially welcome wailing babies and excited toddlers.
>
> We welcome you whether you can sing like Pavarotti or just growl quietly to yourself. You're welcome here if you're 'just browsing,' just woken up or just got out of prison. We don't care if you're more Christian than the Archbishop of Canterbury, or haven't been to church since Christmas ten years ago.
>
> We extend a special welcome to those who are over 60 but not grown up yet, and to teenagers who are growing up too fast. We welcome keep-fit mums, football dads, starving artists, tree-huggers, latte-sippers, vegetarians, junk-food eaters. We welcome those who are in recovery or still addicted. We welcome you if you're having problems, are down in the dumps or don't like 'organized religion.' (*We're not that keen on it either!*)

> We offer a welcome to those who think the earth is flat, work too hard, don't work, can't spell, or are here because granny is visiting and wanted to come to the Cathedral.
>
> We welcome those who are inked, pierced, both or neither. We offer a special welcome to those who could use a prayer right now, had religion shoved down their throat as kids or got lost on the ring road and wound up here by mistake. We welcome pilgrims, tourists, seekers, doubters . . . and you!

The humour adds to a sense of a warm, all-embracing welcome. This commitment to everyone who comes through the doors represents the catholicity of God's Church and the generous love of God. This inclusive community is the fulfilment of the biblical narrative and an outworking of the statement in Genesis 1:27 that "God created humankind in his image, in the image of God he created them . . . "

The Church's vocation is to fulfil humanity's calling to live as people made in God's image, reflecting God's all-embracing love. This matrix for understanding of what it means to be God's people is grounded in the story of God's people, often known as salvation history. Woven through the Bible is a recurrent summons for God's people to care for the poor— the widow, the fatherless and the foreigner (Deuteronomy 10:18)—and to ensure that they do not oppress the weak. As they have experienced tyranny and genocide in Egypt, and have been refugees and exiles in Babylon, they are not to repress or subjugate anyone among them. Exodus and Exile are the two seminal events of the theology of compassion and the two definitive experiences for God's people in the Old Testament, who are called to give expression to this theology. By including rather the rejecting the weak, the stranger, and those who are victims of violence, God's people are to reflect God's inclusive love.

God's concern for victims of violence

God's concern for victims of violence is seen early in the biblical narrative. In Genesis 4, Cain's murder of Abel draws a stinging question, as God asks pointedly, "Where is your bother, Abel?" By his defensive, rebellious retort, Cain distances himself from his brother, "I do not know; am I my brother's keeper?", and, of course, the answer is "Yes, you are." Heavy with anguish and distress, God's words reveal Abel's demand for justice, "What have you done? Listen: your brother's blood is crying out to me from the ground."

Later in Genesis, we find the story of Joseph and his brothers. While Joseph is younger than his brothers, apart from Benjamin, he is his father's favourite. His own naivety, allied to a streak of arrogance, further accentuates his brothers' jealousy. They gang up on him and thrust him out of the family, selling him to Midianite traders; as he is taken away, they expect never to see him again. When they go to Egypt to plead for food in response to the famine ravaging their land, Joseph is in a position of power. He engineers a similar scenario that had resulted in his expulsion from the family: they must decide whether to abandon the youngest child, Benjamin, falsely accused of stealing one of Joseph's silver cups. Unable to face his ageing father without him, Judah speaks up and offers himself in place of Benjamin: "please let your servant remain as a slave to my lord in place of the boy, and let the boy go back with his brothers. For how can I go back to my father if the boy is not with me? I fear to see the suffering that would come upon my father" (Genesis 44:33–34). This redeeming act stirs deep emotion in Joseph, and he cannot maintain the pretence that he does not know them. He weeps loudly and reveals that he is Joseph, whom they sold as a slave. Thus Joseph repudiates revenge, breaks the cycle of violence and forgives those who have wronged him. He is reunited with his family and they come to settle in Egypt.

God's rebuke of Cain and God's vindication of Joseph demonstrate God's commitment to the victims of violence. In God's censure of Cain, the sanctity of life is underscored. Through God's redeeming action, God works to rescue and prosper Joseph, bringing the family back together and taking forward the plans that God has for the descendants of Abraham (Genesis 12:1–3). From the patriarch's family, God is to constitute a people that will be the "light to the nations" (Isaiah 49:6). These seminal stories help to shape a people called to eschew violence, embrace social justice and care for the marginalized.

Exodus—the formative experience for God's people—determining their self-understanding as a people who are not to oppress and victimize others

God's rescue of Abraham's descendants (Genesis 12:1–3), when they are exiled and tyrannized in Egypt, are formative events for the nation that declared that they were "God's people". Through this nation, God works out his plan for the reconstruction of a united human society, not formed and maintained by violence or pride, one that is not based on the murderous jealousy of Cain (Genesis 4:8) or the arrogance of Babel (Genesis 11:1–9). Integral to God's plan is the giving of the law (Exodus 20:1–21). Through keeping these commandments, Israel gives expression to the special relationship between God and God's chosen nation. In response to God's rescue from bondage in Egypt, Israel is under an obligation to respond with unequivocal loyalty: "I am the Lord your God, who brought you out of the land of Egypt, out of the house of slavery; you shall have no other gods before me" (Exodous 20:1–3). These laws demarcate their distinctive corporate life, identifying them to the world as God's people. Their vocation is to represent God, reflecting God's characteristics in their corporate life and in their relationship to their neighbouring nations.

As the Exodus demonstrates God's concern for the oppressed, Israel is to mirror God's commitment to those who are victims of the abuse of power through subjugation or neglect. In the same way that God saw their misery and heard their cries, and liberated them (Exodous 3:7–8), God's people are, likewise, to have compassion on those who are burdened by poverty, and release them from their plight. Israel is set free in the Exodus, and as a result the nation is called to be radically different, distinctive. The Exodus constitutes the calling of Israel out of Egypt into a unique relationship with God: "When Israel was a child, I loved him, and out of Egypt I called my son" (Hosea 11:1). Summoned to escape oppression and bondage, to escape servitude, they are given a vocation: they are to be a nation that, unlike any other, does not victimize anyone. Conscious of their ill-treatment by those in power in Egypt, they are to show compassion to the weak and vulnerable. The rationale is clear and based on empathy: you have experienced oppression, don't put others in that position when you have power. On the contrary, because you were powerless and defenceless in Egypt, you must take care of the widow and the orphan: "You shall not deprive an immigrant or an orphan of justice; you shall not take a widow's garment in pledge. Remember that you were a slave in Egypt and the Lord your God redeemed you from there; therefore I command you to do this" (Deuteronomy 24:17–18). The golden rule—treat others as you would like to be treated—is the rationale for the summons not to mistreat the foreigner in their midst, and it is given emotional impetus by their experience of being refugees living in a foreign land. Again, they know what that is like, for they were a minority from a distant land in Egypt. "You shall not wrong or oppress a resident alien, for you were aliens in the land of Egypt" (Exodus 22:21). This emphasis on compassion for the powerless as a defining feature of God's people is ignored in the brutality of battles and their aftermath, as the Promised Land is entered and claimed (e.g. Joshua 6:21).

This strong biblical emphasis on caring for the poor conflicts with the view that the poor should be blamed for their poverty. The tension between those who line up to blame victims for their troubles and those who compassionately look to help is illustrated in the book of Job. The central character faces a succession of devastating disasters that are not his fault, and ends up destitute, sick and grief-stricken. Three of Job's friends, known ironically as "Job's comforters", overlay the multiple tragedies that Job has endured with guilt and shame. Job rejects their analysis, aware of his innocence, and pleads for his vindication. Beneath Job's longing for a public restoration, and an intimate encounter with God, is a deep confidence in God's faithfulness. His protestations are informed by a robust faith and a profound awareness that God is alongside those who are victimized and not on the side of their tormentors. "For I know that my Redeemer lives and that at the last he will stand upon the earth; and after my skin has been thus destroyed, then in my flesh I shall see my God whom I shall see on my side, and my eyes shall behold, and not another" (Job 19:25–27).

Exile as God's judgement on God's people's failure to fulfil their vocation to be a "light to the nations" (Isaiah 49:6)

The halcyon era in Israel's history was the reign of King David. Under his leadership, Israel became a mighty nation. Militarily powerful, Israel's territory expanded, and David was recognized as the ruler of a vast swathe of land. He was internationally respected, and, with the country's boundaries secure, the people felt safe. Internally, David consolidated the nation by curtailing the independence of the tribes and fostering a sense of nationhood. A great military commander, a shrewd politician and a visionary, David was the idealized king and his time on the throne the golden age.

During the reign of David's successor, Solomon, Israel reached the high point of her wealth and influence. Solomon orchestrated the building of the great Temple. His reputation for wisdom and opulence was known in the surrounding countries and beyond, and his people enjoyed peace and prosperity. "Judah and Israel were as numerous as the sand by the sea; they ate and drank and were happy" (1 Kings 4:20). "During Solomon's lifetime Judah and Israel lived in safety, from Dan even to Beer-sheba, all of them under their vines and fig trees" (1 Kings 4:25).

This propitious state of affairs did not last. In order to maintain his extravagant lifestyle at court and his lavish building programme, Solomon had to extract high taxes from the people and enlist a vast army of forced labourers. It is not surprising therefore that the people's instruction to Rehoboam, Solomon's son and successor, was "lighten the hard service of your father and his heavy yoke that he placed on us, and we will serve you" (1 Kings 12:4).

Rehobaom decided to do the opposite. His threat to increase the people's burdens provoked the ten most eastern and northern tribes to declare their independence from the dynasty of David, thereby splitting Israel into Northern and Southern Kingdoms. After a history of unfaithful kings, the Northern Kingdom came to an ignominious end, when in 722 BC, Samaria, the capital, was captured by the Assyrians. The Southern Kingdom continued for a further 135 years.

In the line of kings, there were two that bucked the prevailing trend of reigns characterized by idolatry and injustice. At the very beginning of his reign, King Hezekiah (*c.*715 BC) renovated and reopened the Temple. Allied to this momentous event was a systematic purge of all the rigmarole and paraphernalia of idol worship introduced by his father Ahaz. When Hezekiah also led a revolt against Assyrian suzerainty, the King of Assyria set out to quash the rebellion. He toppled the fortified cities of Judah and laid siege to Jerusalem. Despite overwhelming odds, the capital of Judah held out. Eventually, a calamity struck the Assyrian camp and, having sustained numerous deaths, the foreign foe retreated. Hailed as a marvellous act of divine deliverance, this inexplicable and unexpected victory renewed the kingdom's confidence in God.

Following Hezekiah's death, Manasseh came to the throne. He kowtowed to Assyrian hegemony, and, with Judah reduced again to a vassal state, he decided to pursue a policy of religious syncretism. The nation became largely apostate with diverse cults and even child-sacrifice to foreign gods.

The next godly king was Josiah, who reigned from 639 to 609 BC. He inaugurated thorough reforms, removing all the idolatrous objects of Assyrian and Canaanite worship and closing down the associated sanctuaries. Having prohibited Spiritism and human sacrifice, he renewed the nation's covenant with God. Notwithstanding this dramatic transformation in the political sphere marking the renewal of the national life, Jeremiah, the prophet, longed for and looked for a deeper renewal, whereby each individual would have God's law "written upon their heart" (Jeremiah 31:33).

Josiah's radical reforms were rapidly undone by his successor, his son Jehoiakim. Having enlisted slave labour to build his palace, Jehoiakim incurred the ire of the prophet Jeremiah, who launched a series of scathing attacks, accusing him of exploitation and violence. The prophet warned the king that his misrule and victimization of the poor were under God's judgement: Judah faced the threat of invasion.

After 200 years of dominance, Assyrian rule was challenged by an emerging power, Babylon. Caught up in political manoeuvrings, Jehoiakim aligned Judah with the Babylonian king, Nebuchadnezzar. However, when the Babylonians suffered a set-back because they failed to defeat the Egyptians led by the Pharaoh Necho in a battle on the Egyptian border in 601 BC, Jehoiakim withheld the tribute money due to the Babylonians, an act that was tantamount to rebellion. Jehoiakim died in 598 BC, and the Babylonian backlash came a year later, when the new King Jehoiachin was on the throne. Jerusalem was besieged and captured, and 3,000 of the nation's elite were taken captive to Babylon, along with the Temple treasures (the first swathe of the Babylonian exile).

Nebuchadnezzar appointed Zedekiah, another of Josiah's sons, to the throne of Judah. Weak and indecisive, the new king was easily swayed by his advisors who counselled him to look to Egypt for help. He did not heed the wisdom of Jeremiah, who presented an alternative but unpopular strategy: the nation's only hope of survival was submission to Babylon. Expecting Egypt to come to his aid, Zedekiah revolted against Babylonian oversight in 589 BC. But without Egypt's support, Judah was soon overrun and the Babylonian army again surrounded Jerusalem. Although the eighteen-month-long siege with its ensuing famine took a heavy toll, Jeremiah's pleas to surrender fell on deaf ears. In 587 BC, the city's resistance came to an end when the walls were breached. Retribution followed: the walls were reduced to rubble, and Solomon's magnificent Temple was razed to the ground.

The Babylonian exile lasted about fifty years. Spiritually bereft, far from Jerusalem and without a temple for worship, the people found reassurance in Ezekiel's vision of the "glory of the Lord" (Ezekiel 11: 23) amongst them: God had not abandoned them. In the crucible of exile, the theology of God's people was reshaped.[1] No longer was God viewed as territorial, located and limited to a particular land or city. Rather God's people discovered, or perhaps rediscovered—after all, they had been rescued from Egypt—that God was with them far from home.

King Cyrus ascended to the throne of the nearby Persian kingdom in 559 BC. Through his military skill and prowess, the Persian nation expanded into an empire. Amongst the Jewish exiles, there was a sense of hope that Cyrus might defeat Babylon and be the means of their deliverance. This hope found fullest expression in the book of Isaiah in which Cyrus is described as the agent of God's liberation of the exiles, whereby they can return to their homeland. "Thus says the LORD to his anointed, to Cyrus, whose right hand I have grasped to subdue nations before him and strip kings of their robes, to open doors before him— and the gates shall not be closed" (Isaiah 45:1). In referring to Cyrus as

God's anointed, God's agency was seen in deliverance for God's people through Gentile kings and their armies. By finding Cyrus to be the Lord's "anointed", Jewish theology is further refined: God is understood to be the Creator who reigns sovereign over all the nations; even a heathen king can be an instrument of his purposes for Judah.

In 539 BC, Babylon fell into the hands of the Persians. Cyrus authorized the Jewish exiles to return and to rebuild their Temple, in line with his enlightened understanding of empire. A year later, the first and main party went back to Jerusalem and embarked on the rebuilding. After a significant delay because of opposition from the Samaritans, who were refused permission to work on the project, the Temple was finally completed in 515 BC. The next stage of reconstruction was the re-establishment of Jewish law under the leadership of Ezra, a priest and scribe, who returned in 458 BC. Thirteen years later came Nehemiah, who was sent by the Babylonian King Artaxerxes I to rebuild the city and in particular the walls. Despite opposition and threats the task was accomplished in 52 days. To mark this great achievement and to signify its importance, God's law was read and expounded to a vast public assembly. Convicted, the people confessed the nation's sin and renewed their covenant with God (Nehemiah 9—10). As the rebuilt wall was dedicated, there was great rejoicing and feasting (Nehemiah 12:27–43).

As Israel's history unfolds, its theology develops in the crucible of exodus and exile. In their rescue from slavery in Egypt, God is on the side of the Jewish people, a tribal deity. As they establish themselves in the Promised Land, as the kingdom of David accrues kudos, riches and power, they see the God of their ancestors as supreme, the God who is above all other gods. Through defeat, banishment and return from exile, they learn that the God of their ancestors, the God of the kingdom of David, is the one and only, the universal God. This insight gives added status and responsibility to God's people and their calling to be the "Light to the nations" (Isaiah 49:6) is renewed.

Jesus Christ fulfils the calling of God's people to the "Light to the Nations" by forming a new community around him characterized by self-giving and generous love

Jesus Christ gathers disciples around him who are to fulfil the calling of God's people to the "light of the world" (Matthew 5:14). Through his teaching and his example, his followers learn the importance of rejecting violence and including those who have been ostracized. Notoriously, Jesus mixes with those who are typically excluded: prostitutes, tax-collectors and publicans (Luke 15:1–2). By enjoying their hospitality, Jesus signals the radically inclusive love of God.

Jesus' critique of how power is used and abused by the political and religious authorities provokes a backlash. His prophetic action in the Temple in Jerusalem, when he rails against exploitative practices, inflames their anger and makes his death inevitable (Mark 11:15–19). Yet, through his death, we gain conclusive insight into his own understanding of his vocation, the new community that he came to establish, and the all-embracing love that was his sole motivation.

Throughout the Scriptures, we see the prophets castigated, rejected and beaten. This typical reaction to these exceptional people is at its most vivid and sharp in the crowd's demand that Jesus be crucified.

Persecution of the prophets and the murder of the Messiah have their roots in the dark recesses of the heart where lurk pride and envy. Once these malevolent desires to eradicate those who challenge us are let loose, violence ensues. As the dark deeds are perpetrated, there is some measure of release; with aggression expressed, anger vented, the status quo returns.

In terms of the biblical narrative, it is Satan who deceives the mob and convinces those in power that abandonment to these pernicious thoughts and malign motivations is right, sometimes in the guise of a greater good that is supposedly being served. Caiaphas, the high priest, articulates this alluring counterfeit philosophy eloquently, "it is better for you that one man die for the people than the whole nation perish" (John 11:20). As the object of dark forces beyond their knowledge and control, those who conspire against Jesus are swept along. With the protagonists in the grip of this evil, their plotting and scheming gains a sinister momentum. Some of the hordes in Jerusalem become the playthings of those in power, manipulated and urged to collude in Jesus' crucifixion. Caught up in the belligerence against Jesus, they bay for his death. Culpable as they are, there is evil at work, and they are in its tight, suffocating grasp. Jesus retains his poise; while he accepts the aggression and violence, he resists the prevailing mood and engulfing darkness. "Father, forgive them, they do not know what they are doing" (Luke 23:34). From his perspective, Jesus sees the deeper reality of what has happened. As well as failing to recognize Jesus as the Messiah, the authorities and the crowd calling for his crucifixion are also caught up in ancient and abiding patterns of persecution. Expelling the "troublemaker" releases the tension and resolves the conflict. A "sacrifice" is made, relieving the distress, and the god of a pseudo-peace is satisfied. The status quo returns, and "all seems well again". In short, victimization prevails again! In the conspiracy to have Jesus killed, we recognize that he becomes a scapegoat. This is an insidious and evil phenomenon. In the political and religious tension swirling around Jerusalem, heightened by the imminent celebration of the Passover festival and the swelling crowds, the Roman and Jewish authorities collude together. The baying crowds who call for Jesus' death are caught up in a maelstrom of fear and frustration. In addition to the plotting by those in positions of power, there is a swirl of collective anger centred on this reputed Messiah. The escalating tension is unleashed. By having him killed, the threat Jesus poses to the status quo is eliminated, and catharsis is achieved for the city and nation.

John the Baptist declares that "Jesus is the Lamb of God who takes away the sin of the world" (John 1:29). In this profound Christological statement, there are echoes of Old Testament ideas. Jesus as the Passover Lamb is a recurrent motif in the New Testament, reminiscent of God telling Moses and Aaron in Egypt:

> Tell the whole congregation of Israel that on the tenth of this month they are to take a lamb for each family, a lamb for each household . . . Your lamb shall be without blemish . . . You shall keep it until the fourteenth day of this month; then the whole assembled congregation of Israel shall slaughter it at twilight. They shall take some of the blood and put it on the two doorposts and the lintel of the houses in which they eat it . . . The blood

shall be a sign for you on the houses where you live: when I see
the blood, I will pass over you, and no plague shall destroy you
when I strike the land of Egypt.

Exodous 12:3–13

As the Lamb's blood daubed around the door identifies the Jewish homes
and marks them out for deliverance from death, Jesus' blood shed on
the cross brings salvation from sin and death. Resonances with the
symbolism associated with the goat sent out into the wilderness on the
Day of Atonement feature:

When Aaron has finished atoning for the holy place and the
tent of meeting, and the altar, he shall present a live goat. Then
Aaron shall lay both his hands on the head of the live goat, and
confess over it all the iniquities of the people of Israel, and all
their transgressions, all their sins, putting them on the head of
the goat, and sending it away into the wilderness by means of
someone designated for the task. The goat shall bear on itself all
their iniquities to a barren region: and the goat shall be set free
in the wilderness.

Leviticus 16:20–22

By imposing the nation's sins on the goat, the burden of guilt is lifted from
the people. The nation's relationship with God is restored as the animal
is banished. As the goat wanders into the wilderness and towards death,
the people's offences are expiated.

The "suffering servant" depicted so vividly in Isaiah 53 reverberates
in this idea of Jesus as the Lamb of God. The servant's vicarious suffering
presages Jesus' crucifixion and the Christian interpretation of his death's
significance: "He was wounded for our transgressions, crushed for our
iniquities; upon him was the punishment that made us whole, and by
his bruises we are healed" (Isaiah 53:5). Jesus' quiescent demeanour, his
courageous passivity in face of hostility and wanton violence, and his
excruciating death, evoke the comparison with this passage: "He was
oppressed, and he was afflicted, yet he did not open his mouth; like a
lamb that is led to the slaughter, and like a sheep that before its shearers

is silent, so he did not open his mouth" (Isaiah 53:7). The Festival of the Passover is essential to the self-understanding of Israel. It keeps the formative event of the Exodus at the heart of the people's life. Recalling the historical period when they were an oppressed and victim people shapes their world-view, and enshrines the values of compassion and justice. Derived from this experience of slavery and tyranny, and their deliverance from bondage, come a concern for those who are victims, and an ordering of society that seeks social inclusion.

However, Jesus' interpretation of the Passover serves as a critique of Israel's failure to learn from her experience of victimhood and to be a victimless people (Mark 14:12–21). Although the Law and the Prophets reflected a deep concern for the marginalized and vulnerable, expressed in the injunction to care for "the widow, the orphan and the alien in their midst",[2] an ethnic and national superiority insidiously infiltrated the nation's culture. In particular, some factions began to follow an agenda informed and energized by an understanding of Israel as over, and ultimately against, others. A radical, inclusive moral attitude to the weak and those who did not belong was usurped by an identity based on exclusion.

Jesus' death means that our relationship with God is centred on the victim, Jesus himself. In identifying with all victims, Jesus renders redundant any notion of God as exclusive or tribal as redundant. His death is for all people everywhere and throughout time. The Cross demonstrates that the God of Abraham, Isaac and Jacob, the Father of our Lord Jesus Christ, is the universal God. As this Cross definitively expresses God's all-embracing love, there is no longer any justification for forming an exclusive community in the name of God. Without the need to assert an identity over and against others, to exclude or as a corollary to create victims, this community can give a welcome to everyone. This revolutionary approach requires everyone to repent of a self-understanding and pattern of behaviour that produces victims of any kind. By extension, it involves learning how to relate to and be in solidarity with those who have been cast out or are excluded by wider society.

A recurring theme in Jesus' teaching—which is brought into sharp focus in the Beatitudes—is the antithesis between relationships based on dominance and those founded on a gracious reciprocity. Jesus advocates that in all our interrelationships we should be gracious, with the other person's wellbeing uppermost in our minds. Thereby our relationships are marked by self-giving, sacrificial love and signify our rejection of violence.

Jesus takes on himself the antipathy and violence of the people and God's judgement on all life-denying ways of living. He is God's promise of a new covenant, a new relationship between God and God's people and within God's people.

As Jesus seeks to gather a people around him, defined only by their allegiance to him, and by nothing else, he castigates those who exclude—they have sinned and incur God's wrath. Those who object to the grace Jesus offers, his joyful inclusion of those considered by many, and especially by the religious leaders, as unclean, unworthy and unfit to belong, are labelled as "blind". With penetrating insight, Jesus knows that there is grave danger in the act of exclusion: the protagonist's underlying blindness deepens and intensifies—it becomes harder for them to see.

As the Holy Spirit is poured out at Pentecost, God's project to shape a people in God's image, foreshadowed in Israel's history and heralded by the prophets, finds fulfilment. Set against attempts to build a unity over and against God, as seen starkly in the enmity of Cain and the pride of Babel, this new humanity receives her life and unity from God. The supreme sign of this venture to renew humanity is a Church that is centred in its worship on the Risen Christ.

The Church's mission

After the resurrection of Jesus Christ, a resolute community gives a different verdict to the unanimity of the persecuting crowd screaming for Jesus to be crucified: "Jesus is Lord" (Romans 10:9), they proclaim. Full of the Holy Spirit, those who belong to this body of believers, who claimed that God had raised Jesus from the dead, could withstand the authorities' desire to quash their nascent movement. When they faced persecution and were confronted by those in positions of power, they were able to give a good account of themselves. The Paraclete, "the defender of the accused",[3] enabled them to give a robust defence of their faith in and to witness to Jesus Christ.

Reflecting on Jesus' life, teaching and crucifixion, and enthralled by their new life in the Holy Spirit, Paul and other early Christian theologians conceived the idea of Church in opposition to identities built on exclusion, violence and victimization. They recognized that in the raising of Jesus Christ from the dead, God gives us generously, gratuitously his whole life and his death on Good Friday. From this act of giving flows our experience of "knowing Jesus", and we express this encounter and our knowledge of his continuous gracious, challenging presence as "having a personal relationship" with him.

It is the resurrection that generates our language of meeting Jesus in the here and now, and it is the resurrection that is the criterion for assessing our experience of the Risen Jesus. The resurrection opened the way for Judaism to be turned into a universal religion. In this momentous, far-reaching event Jesus Christ, the archetypal victim, is vindicated. Through the Risen Christ, a new way of being together becomes possible; no longer does a sense of identity need to be generated by exclusion. Instead, everyone from whatever background or culture can gather in worship of the One who is the Victim. Rather than a collection of individuals holding their position over against others, or groups defining themselves in opposition to other groups, this singular community looks to be inclusive. By rendering no one a victim, this community becomes a model for a new society shaped around the Christ who welcomes all and binds this community to the Great Commandment "to love". "Love each other as I have loved you" (John 15:12) is the new commandment, defining the internal life of this community as inspired and shaped by the self-giving, sacrificial love of God. The Church, thereby, is this new community, centred on the self-giving, sacrificial love of the Son of God.

The characteristics of the Church

Committed to individual and corporate transformation

Belonging to this new community demands that the individual members undergo a profound conversion of heart, in order to ensure that their response to everyone reflects the defining love of the community. No longer can the individual seek to build their own security on the premise that others are inferior or plain wrong or to formulate their close relationships on the basis that others must be excluded. This narrow, separatist approach diminishes the human heart. By contrast, as everyone is seen as a potential friend, as someone invited to be a child of God in God's family, the individual is summoned to love more deeply and broadly. Maturity is a commitment to and an increasing realization of the goal to find common ground with the rest of humanity.

Pursuing the quest for unity

Typically, human beings tend to construct their own sense of identity, individual and social, on the basis of who is excluded. Notwithstanding that it is the dominant approach to self-definition, Jesus offered a sharp critique of those religious practitioners who thought and acted in this way. Those who bolstered their own status and fostered elitism by denigrating others met with Jesus' judgement. He criticized vehemently the religious groupings that saw themselves as superior and rejected those who fell short of their own high standards. Jesus refused to ignore this kind of exclusion. He confronted and objected. In contrast, Jesus gathers and seeks to establish a community, the source of whose life is grace.

With the recognition of the importance of caring for the outcasts, those victimized by social exclusion, Israel's prophets stress the centrality to authentic worship and a dynamic relationship with God of responding generously to the "orphan, widow and alien" in our midst. This emphasis set before Israel the challenge to craft a sense of identity that did not create victims.

Rather than a self-understanding constituted over and against others, their distinctiveness was to be found in a respect and sense of kinship with all. This ideal is fulfilled in Jesus Christ and is given expression by the community centred on him. Through the resurrection, we can encounter and orientate our lives on the Risen Christ. His gift is a unity derived from and sustained by his Risen Life. No longer do we need to find security and our identity by differentiating ourselves from and by degrading others. On the contrary, focused on Christ, we are delivered from self-absorption and any competitive rivalry with those around us. The Risen Christ shows us by his wounds, now glorified, God's profound and ultimate subversion of those who misuse power to abuse and subjugate others. Yet, for those who approach the Risen Christ in humility and love, grace and forgiveness abound.

To be justified by faith in Christ is to be brought into a relationship with all the others who have put their trust in him. Through this relationship with Christ, and with our brothers and sisters in Christ, the Church is called to model the unity that transcends all boundaries and encompasses everyone. The Church is to offer this unity, beautiful and shocking, for the whole of humanity to imitate. As the Church embodies and inculcates this inclusive unity, it becomes a source of hope to the world: historical wounds and deep divisions can be overcome.

Accordingly, anyone whose primary allegiance is to Jesus Christ, and as a result is committed to God's mission, cannot belong to any other social, cultural or religious group uncritically. In 1933, when the National Church Synod in Germany took the decision to include what was known as the "Aryan Paragraph" in its constitution, thereby excluding Jews from key positions in the Church's life, Martin Niemöller recognized this discrimination as an affront. In response, he established the "Pastors' Emergency League", the forerunner of the Confessing Church. In 1934 the Barmen Declaration, which was drafted by the famous theologian Karl Barth and adopted by the Confessing Church, declared that the Church was accountable to Christ as her Head, and not the leader of the State, the Führer. Dietrich Bonhoeffer, a leading member of the Confessing Church, was a notable critic of the national church and the state, and was arrested and executed shortly before the end of the Second World War for his opposition to the Nazi regime. Those whose first loyalty is to Jesus Christ, and his mission of sharing God's inclusive love, cannot offer unswerving commitment to any other group, and must, when there is a clash of loyalties, be prepared to take a stand.

The example of the Confessing Church in Germany reminds us that Christians need to be prepared to critique what is happening within the Church's life. The Church is never perfect, and it is vital that those in positions of authority listen to the critical voices. We should be wary of aligning ourselves with a particular group within the Church on the basis of theology or for any other reason. There is an intrinsic danger that any sub-group can take on the trappings and characteristics of a faction. It can become defined by its dissent. Its internal unity is sustained by setting itself over and against someone or some other group. As such, they undermine, to varying degrees, the drive for a unity centred on the Crucified and Risen Victim, an inclusive unity. To align oneself with these groups comfortably and wholeheartedly would be to subvert God's goal in Jesus Christ. Knowing Jesus entails a gradual, but necessary, liberation from a sense of identity shaped by various tribal loyalties to one formed solely by allegiance to Jesus Christ; this sense of self is given to us, derived from what Jesus Christ has done for us and our participation in Jesus Christ's life. Rather, any body of people who want to challenge what is happening in the Church should offer their criticism and recommendations in solidarity with the rest of the Church, unless the Church is taking steps, as in the case of the National Church in Germany in the 1930s, to undermine the Church's witness to God's universal love.

Any faction or group established on the basis of social or religious conflict, has, by definition, forged its identity by opposition to another faction or group. At best, this can only be an interim state of affairs: it is contrary to our understanding of the Church. On the other hand, if a community derives its life from God's grace in Jesus Christ, then it is properly ecclesial. Any clash with or critique of the culture and other groups in its locality stems simply from its commitment to Jesus Christ and is not intrinsic to its life.

Correspondingly, there is a question mark about homogeneous churches, those which do not reflect the make-up of their locality but are, by contrast, uniform in terms of class, stage of life, their understanding of how to interpret the Bible, ethnicity. It should be noted that it is easier to recognize the commonality in another church rather than in your own. It can seem as though they are illustrative of and reinforce the fragmentation of modern life. Indeed, it could be argued that they are giving at least tacit approval to the segregated lives most people live and, at worst, solidifying the status quo: alienated groups remain apart. Besides the rather limited and stunted experience gained by only relating to "people like us", the ability of the Church to be self-critical is vitiated—no contrary opinions are likely to be heard.

Conscious that the Church's unity in Christ is the fundamental and abiding truth of our common life, we learn not to distance ourselves from others, or to see others as rivals: modes of behaviour motivated by a competitive attitude are divisive and contrary to God's purpose for his Church. Rather we are called to stay deeply engaged with each other and to seek the best for each other: relationships within the Church are to be characterized by mutual respect and love. In order to establish and nourish these reciprocal, respectful and generous relationships, everyone has to be committed to and abide by the disciplines of peacemaking.

The template for relationships within the Church is God's gracious relationship with us. God's gratuitous giving is seen in the whole act of creation through which a relationship based on the generous love of God is established with humanity. In this love, each individual's autonomy is revered, for without it God's intention to ask us to respond freely to the invitation to share in the life of Creator is undermined. God has no ulterior motive, no hidden agenda. God's offer is straightforward and God allows us the space to decide for ourselves; God's grace precludes any attempt to manipulate or control or dominate. Alongside the utter value given to our individuality, in order for our response in love to God to be authentically our own, there is an allied responsibility—we must take our freedom seriously.

One of the first signs of the presence of sin is the readiness with which responsibility is denied and others blamed. In the story of the Fall, the Lord God asks, "Have you eaten from the tree of which I commanded you not to eat?" The man said, "The woman whom you gave to be with me, she gave me fruit from the tree, and I ate." Then the Lord God said to the woman, "What is this that you have done?" The woman said, "The serpent tricked me, and I ate" (Genesis 3:11–14). This refusal to take responsibility militates against mature and deep relationships rooted in truth. Indeed,without a willingness to acknowledge our sin there can be no repentance and no forgiveness. Being wrong can be forgiven, whereas insisting that we are in the right, when we are wrong, confirms the power and hold of sin. Moreover, living in denial, effectively perpetrating and maintaining a lie, obviates any hope of renewal and transformation. Relationships are marred and fractured. For authentic peace to be restored, falsehood needs to be recognized and confessed.

Depending on God's grace and mercy

Coming to Christ humbly, ready to receive grace and mercy, rules out any trace of self-justification. Without the need to secure our own position and bolster our status by defining ourselves over and against others, a new way of relating to those around us becomes possible.

Equally, there is no scope within the orbit of the Risen Christ for sectarian attitudes. As the impetus to separate ourselves from others derives from self-justification, there is no longer any desire or energy to divide the community into "them" and "us".

An authentic relationship with Jesus Christ results in profound and continuing transformation. This conversion of life is to be clearly observed in a changing attitude and interaction with others. The pattern of relating commensurate with knowledge of Jesus Christ is characterized by compassion in the context of the deep challenge to shape an inclusive, unified community. Correspondingly, those who are more likely to be excluded, namely the poor and vulnerable, should be given special attention and actively embraced.

Our dependence on Jesus Christ is nourished through prayer and worship, and by obedience to God's word to us in the Scriptures and by receiving the sacrament. Along with these spiritual disciplines, there must be a conscious commitment to model our relating to others on Jesus Christ. Our determined and thoughtful dedication to craft a life that imitates Jesus Christ in our service of others and our concern for the vulnerable is a validating feature of our discipleship. As Jesus said, "It is by their fruits that you shall know them" (Matthew 7: 20).

Our knowledge of Jesus Christ is evidenced by service of others. By actively engaging with other people compassionately, we encounter

Jesus Christ and share more profoundly in his life. Thus our lives can be integrated. In every moment, every encounter, every action, we meet and know Jesus Christ. This is a dynamic relationship too: the greater our knowledge of Jesus Christ, and through him, the deeper our intimacy with the Father, the more aware and alert we are to what we are being asked to do in the present. As our attention and orientation shift slowly, gradually but surely to Jesus Christ, we see more clearly what we are to do at home, at church, in the community or in the workplace.

In this transformation, our desires are sanctified. As Jesus repeatedly emphasized, our attitudes and actions are shaped by what we long for in our hearts. By seeking to centre and model our lives on Jesus Christ, we are increasingly formed by his generous, gracious and humble way of life.

Centred on the Eucharist

In the Eucharist, we encounter the Risen Christ and relive his betrayal and death. His crucifixion makes us suspicious of all theories and ways of viewing the world that create victims or legitimize injustice.

We encounter the Risen Christ in the sacrament and in God's word to us. By discerning the biblical emphasis on caring for the vulnerable and the victim, and the prophetic challenge to the systems that victimize, we see Jesus' life and the events leading up to his death in a distinctive way.

Through the formative and habitual encounter with Christ in Word and Sacrament, this new identity is realized. This reality is expressed succinctly and in a particular way by Augustine of Hippo (354–430 AD) in his Sermon 227, "We eat the body of Christ to become the Body of Christ."

Other ideologies and belief systems claim to provide a route to peace and contentment: in so far as they exclude others, they are fallacious.. Christianity and her practitioners are liable, however, to face accusations of hypocrisy, for the Christian Church has sided and colluded with those who denigrate and ostracize others on the basis of gender, race, history, beliefs or behaviour. (It must also be recognized that it is a human trait to label someone and some action as unacceptable if it allows us to condemn our neighbour and to escape censure ourselves.) This connivance with oppression, allied to a woeful lack of compassion, makes the Christian Church vulnerable to this charge. At its most virulent, this can amount to an organized and orchestrated campaign to portray the Christian faith and Christian morality as outdated, overbearing and repressive. Maligned as regressive, espousing Christian morals is castigated as judgemental on those who do not live according to these standards. The stark alternative is an amorality that is driven by the misplaced and dangerous conviction that happiness lies in a slavish pursuit of our own gratification. Consumerism is one symptom of the falsehood that the "accumulation of possessions" is the route to happiness. The reality is that the more we have the more we want; we are held in a perpetual state of unfulfilled desire. This restless pursuit of individual gratification results in chaos and confusion, seen in the breakdown of families, promiscuity, widespread debt and cruel circus games in various guises serving as mainstream entertainment.

The Christian Church needs to be robust in her defence. She can no longer afford to be timid. While the Church has been tardy in siding with the victims of oppression and has been embedded in cultural patterns of subjugation, it has also been at the forefront of prophetic and progressive movements, and in the vanguard of reform. In the modern world, the Church frequently offers a sharp critique of cultures and systems that victimize people, and stands alongside the victims, caring for them and highlighting their plight. Churches were at the forefront of the civil rights movement aimed at achieving equality under the law for African Americans in 1960s. More recently, the Trussell Trust and the network of food banks began when a Christian couple responded to a particular plea from a mother: "My children are going to bed hungry tonight—what are you going to do about it?" What began with a store of food in their garden shed and garage has resulted in hundreds of food bank centres. Besides providing emergency food and support to people in crisis right now, the Trussell Trust also seeks to campaign at local and national level to end hunger and poverty in the UK. Allied to a compassionate concern for individuals and families facing hardship is a determination to challenge injustice. Locally, I chair the board of trustees for Uttlesford Food Bank. In this rural and relatively prosperous area, the number using the food bank is not high, but for those who do it is a lifeline. At present, there is concern about the impact of universal credit. Through my chairing of the Local Strategic Partnership Children and Families Group, I am able to work with the District Council to monitor the effects as universal credit is rolled out and to help those struggling as a result.

Pressingly, the Christian Church needs to act radically and decisively to ensure that there are no victims of her own culture and praxis. Otherwise, her legitimate claim to be a community of mutual respect and to proffer a modus operandi with reconciliation at its heart will be undermined. Moreover, the Christian Church's transforming analysis of human society arising out of salvation history will be ignored. For the Judaeo-Christian worldview is the origin of the modern emphasis on the victim which has brought enlightenment and provided the impetus for change. The Church should be the community of peace par excellence, as the ultimate and supreme victim has been slain and the Lamb's benign reign of peace has begun:

> They will hunger no more, and thirst no more; the sun shall not strike them, nor any scorching heat; for the Lamb at the centre of the throne will be their shepherd, and he will guide them to springs of water, and God will wipe away every tear from their eyes.
>
> *Revelation 7:16-17*

As Christians, we should be committed to challenging any social order in which the act of showing compassion for others is under threat. This involves a resolute commitment to understanding and bringing to light the hidden sources of conflict. Besides this revelatory dimension, a genuine resolve to pursue peace means protesting against any counterfeit peace based on pretence and deception. Seeking truth is integral to the life and witness of the Christian community.

In Jesus' utter refusal to respond in kind to his adversaries' aggression, we see God's rejection of violence. God is love, and this truth is eloquently revealed in the passion of Christ, the self-giving of Jesus to death. As the tension escalates, and the level of violence inexorably rises, Jesus eschews force, and meets brutality with a robust passivity. Under the severest provocation, Jesus does not let his heart harden or label those attacking him as his enemies. This determined and generous response, evinced as he empathizes with his opponents and meets their ferocity with grace and forgiveness, reaches its zenith *in extremis* as he pleads for God to have mercy on those who have tortured and killed him (Luke 23:34).

In the light of Jesus' example, the classic means of producing peace by expelling those whom we hold responsible for our conflicts should not be a feature of church life. Furthermore, to exclude those with whom we disagree is to offend God's generous grace and to impede our own experience of God's mercy. It is a great spiritual truth that we can only be recipients of God's grace if we are prepared to be agents of God's grace: what God has given us is to be shared with others. This exchange features in Jesus' parables, most forcibly in "the parable of the unforgiving servant" (Matthew 18:23–end). In several comparisons, Jesus highlights that God's relationship to us is a paradigm for our relationships with each other, "Love your enemies and pray for those who persecute you, so that you may be children of your Father in heaven; for he makes his sun rise on the evil and on the good, and sends rain on the righteous and the unrighteous" (Matthew 5:44). This dynamic, whereby we have to be channels of grace in order to be recipients of grace, is integral to Christian prayer, and is expressed in the best-known, the Lord's Prayer: "Forgive us our sins, as we forgive those who sin against us."

Having been reconciled to God and each other, those people who constitute a church are bound by what God has done for them to be reconcilers, those who seek peace. Closely allied to this drive for peace is the commitment to forgiveness. It is the working assumption that in all our relationships in church forgiveness should be readily offered and received. This is not to ignore the struggles that there can be when the wound caused is deep and still open but to recognize that whatever the grievance, the avowed goal is forgiveness. In the stark choice between accusation or forgiveness in our relationships, we must choose forgiveness.

By making this search for authentic peace within the community our priority, churches can become countercultural communities. In competitive cultures, individuals are set one against another. This means that others are viewed as rivals and conflict is endemic. Adversarial ways of thinking and behaving are the norm. As a result, issues become polarized and the outcome of any conflict is analysed in terms of "winners" and "losers". As a contrast, churches are to be communities that challenge this combative approach to conflict and offer the world an alternative model of handling disputes.

With this in mind, instead of conflicts appearing to be a distraction from the real work of the Church, resolving them is vital to the life and witness of the Christian community. When people encounter the Church, they intuitively know how honest and close the relationships are. Therefore, the internal dynamics of a church have a direct bearing on her mission. That is why it is imperative that churches are committed to maintain the disciplines of peace: simple and direct speech, attentive and deep listening, and inclusive consultative processes. Then the Church will have a distinctive praxis to offer the world as a model of how to engage with conflict healthily and graciously.

Reflecting God's all-embracing love

Jesus changes for his followers the perception of the "other". Instead of seeing others as rivals and seeking to secure our own survival or advantage by excluding them, we are challenged to create a community that is inclusive.

After the resurrection, those who had earlier denied and deserted Jesus—especially Peter—are penitent in Jesus' Risen Presence. Their contrition is met with forgiveness. A new community is formed, constituted by forgiven disciples drawn together by the risen Jesus. Founded on the inclusive grace of God, the Church continues to be dependent on God's mercy; as such there is no scope to return to the old ways of competition and exclusion. Since Jesus Christ, the ultimate and definitive self-giving victim, has been vindicated by God, and is at the heart of the Church's life, the Church must guard against victimization. Exclusion and rejection on the basis of identity can have no place; they are antithetical to the Church's origin and mission.

The temptation, of course, to revert to an adversarial mind-set, shaped by a "them and us" mentality, is there. Bifurcation features in much political discourse. Stark alternatives are presented, "in or out", "for or against", "pro or anti". However, being enmeshed in competitive relationships is destructive and life-denying. Following Jesus means refuting this perspective. Instead, we are to imitate Jesus. We must be concerned with everyone's wellbeing and try to make no one our victim. Responding compassionately to the "other" becomes central to our common life. By giving the "other" primacy, generous attitudes and gracious service begin to characterize our relationships. By emulating Jesus' self-giving concern for the "other", the Church represents the generous love of God to a world often oblivious to God's providential care and God's presence. Salvation history interprets the historical events depicted in the Bible as revealing God's personal redemptive activity to bring about his goal of a global community united around the Risen Jesus: the Church. With Jesus, the Lamb of God (John 1:29 and Revelation 5:6), at its heart, no one is excluded. Jesus, the universal and eternal victim, has been vindicated and raised, and shows us the way towards an inclusive unity, derived from the primacy of compassion and sustained by a culture of peacemaking.

Being a church leader with compassion and courage

While the cross is the pinnacle, the zenith of Jesus' self-giving to the Father and to the world, it is the culmination of a life of self-offering too. This pattern of sacrificial love is constant at each and every stage and becomes a more deeply ingrained feature of his character as he faces and meets each new challenge. His life of grace and service is to be the template for our own and the model for our corporate life.

Within the Church, there is no scope for rivalry. Competitiveness distorts relationships. When people are jostling for position and fighting for approval, they become locked into a destructive nexus of relationships. Imitation rather than mutually fostering discipleship becomes a means of gaining an advantage. Learning, instead of being inspired by the call to holiness, becomes motivated by the quest for success. Whilst appearing at times to be strong and energetic, this culture is unhealthy: the source of its strength and the origins of its energy are in human selfishness. At its worst, everyone is reduced to an enemy. Locked into this network of relating in which everyone is "out to win", all are losers. Stuck in these destructive patterns, the individuals and communities are in the grip of death. This acquisitive way of relating is the origin and the outworking of the Fall (Genesis 3) in which humanity seized its own identity, instead of receiving it thankfully from God.

Living in a Christian community is bearable when at its heart and pulsing through all its relationships is compassion. God's grace and an awareness of our common humanity inspire a generous, mutual acceptance. Our individual capacity for self-delusion gives us a conviction that the truth should be sought vigorously but humbly. Every relationship, indeed each encounter, should be characterized by giving attention to each other, allied to a respect and even delight in each other. Grounded in reciprocal relationships of depth, compassion and truth are the shared goals of Christian community.

The journey from a fearful to a loving community is made in small, gentle steps and is marked by compassion. Leading a community through this transition demands a gentle wisdom and an instructive empathy.

A salutary story

An old Sufi tale tells of a man who strayed from his own country into the world known as the Land of the Fools. He soon saw people fleeing in terror from a wheat field. "There's a monster in that field!" they shouted to him. He looked, and saw the "monster". It was a watermelon. He offered to kill the "monster" for them. He cut it from its stalk, carved a slice and began to eat it. The effect: the denizens of the Land of the Fools were now more terrified of him than they were of the watermelon! "He'll kill us next!" they shouted. And so they drove him away with their pitchforks.

The next day, a woman strayed into the Land of the Fools, and the monster story was related to her. But, instead of offering to help them with the "monster", she agreed with the Fools that, yes, it must be dangerous. So she led them away from it on tiptoe and, by so doing, gained their confidence. She then spent time—a long time—in their houses, until she could teach them, little by little, the basic facts that would enable them not only to lose their fear of melons, but even to cultivate them for themselves.[4]

The Church: More Than an Organization, but an Organization Nonetheless— Insights from Systems Thinking

Learning to lead systematically!

Churches are set in complex contexts, both ecclesiastical and societal. Often each individual church is related to a number of others in multi-level structures. By way of example, within the Church of England, there may be up to six levels—parish, team, deanery, episcopal area, diocese and national.

From a civic standpoint, there could well be a town council and a district council, and, of course, there will be numerous other agencies and organizations that will have some connection with the church, and they will have certain expectations about the relationship.

Given this multifaceted setting, and the subtle and various relationships that need to be negotiated, drawing upon wisdom from systems thinking is essential. Let's start with a definition.

My working definition of a system is "a group bound together and working towards some common aims". Families, churches and most organizations clearly fit this description. Seeing your church as a system can offer some insights that will influence how you lead.[5]

Systems thinking is used in management and leadership theory to help those in positions of responsibility to see the connections in the organization of which they are a part and to consider how their actions are likely to affect those they oversee over time.

It also has application within the field of family therapy, when a therapist works with an entire family rather than with its individual members. The underlying assumption is that the behaviour of one individual is related to how the family functions as a whole. For example, if one member of the family is behaving badly, instead of responding to the unacceptable behaviour by focusing solely on the difficult individual, systems theory would indicate that some attention should be paid to the individual's network of relationships, with a special emphasis on those primary relationships within the family.

Systems thinking draws our attention to the connections in any system—an organization or family, for example—and helps us to see the consequences of our actions in the longer term. By understanding how we lead in the light of these insights, we can discern what is going to work best in both now and in the future..

During 25 years of ordained ministry, I have watched how plans for transformation and church growth, initiated from the centre of the diocese, struggle to influence what is happening in the parishes. They typically flounder because not enough emphasis is placed in the connections within the structures, between the senior leadership—the bishop and archdeacons—and those working at parochial level. It appears that the Church of England is understood to have the classic three-tiered structure of senior management, middle management and worker on the shop floor, when it is much better conceived as a system. With a systems approach, we are likely concentrate more on how to communicate effectively at the points of connection. Within the Church of England that would mean working harder at persuading area deans and lay chairs of the merits of any new initiative, and then working with these key players in convincing the clergy on the ground. A greater awareness of how systems work would also encourage a more careful and methodical approach to the processes whereby change is achieved. This would lead to fewer central edicts about how the Church needs to be transformed and greater concentration on helping those who lead local churches to implement some general aims in their context. Systems thinking would lead those in senior leadership to give more energy and time to how the strategy connects with the parishes. The outcome would be fewer yet more coherent initiatives aimed at transforming the local church but each would prove to be more effective, adding up to significant and enduring change.

In addition to seeing your own church as part of a larger system, anyone involved in church leadership can benefit from the insights of systems thinking. Looking at the wider network of relationships as well as the individual concerned enlarges your understanding of any pastoral situation. When handling change, you are likely to pay more attention to your own role and actions because you know that the emotional intensity and reactions around the changes will heavily influence how you respond to the pressures involved. When an issue becomes divisive, you will have a greater appreciation of your role as a focus of unity, holding the church together.

Systems thinking demands that we take into account the generic characteristics of systems in interpreting what we observe about church life. Therefore, we need to be aware that systems have a number of consistent features. This insight means that as we seek to make sense of what we see, so we bear in mind these truths.

Looking beyond linear causal chains to the wider context to explain results

Most of us are predisposed to think in terms of linear causes i.e. "A" caused "B" caused "C". Often the reasons for an outcome are more complex. For example, if a church leader failed to visit a significant church member when they were sick, it would be easy to point the finger at the leader and complain about their lack of care. Taking trouble to look at the whole picture would reveal that the leader's son has been seriously ill for two weeks and that the church has had to make the leader's secretary redundant because of financial constraints. Both these developments have placed the leader under considerably more pressure, cutting into the time he used to have available to carry out pastoral visits. Seeing an individual's wider context helps us to understand them, and to know what might need to happen to bring improvement.

Focusing on the emotional processes that are causing the presenting symptoms

We have all been at meetings where the mood is heavy and plodding. As every point is contested and all feel the need to have their say, progress is laborious. Working sluggishly down the agenda, energy and enthusiasm drain away. People leave at the end mildly depressed and shaking their heads. As well as muttering angrily, they wonder why, with so many good and gifted people in the room, it is always like that. Now, in trying to make things better, you might look at the externals; for example, the composition of the agenda, the ability of the person in the chair, seating arrangements. Yet you might be missing the fundamental reason. Beneath the content of the discussion, there is fierce competition fuelled by personality differences and a battle for status. Only when these emotional undercurrents have been addressed can the group begin to function better.

Paying attention to the whole system and looking beyond individual dysfunctional parts

The functioning of any part of the system is shaped, at least partially, by its position in the system rather than just its own nature. This dictates that attempts to tackle any pressing issue include consideration of how the system might need to be modified.

Typically, when a minister or another church worker is unable to withstand the pressures of their position or to deal with the workload, they eventually move somewhere else, and a new person fills the post. It is only when this pattern becomes repetitive that alarm bells start to ring. However, by then, several people have left feeling emotionally bruised and with nagging doubts about their own abilities. Thinking systemically makes us aware of the structures, relationships and stresses which have a bearing on the individual in the post, and enable us to consider whether these need changing as opposed to replacing the post-holder at regular intervals. If a congregation is killing off its leaders, do not blame the corpses! This change of perspective is like looking at *Gestalt* pictures, those clever black and white pictures which reveal a beautiful young woman or a crabby old witch, or a candlestick or two heads facing each other. What you see depends on where your focus is, and shifting your focus enables you to see the alternative image. In this case, you need to see the system, as well as the individual.

The predictive value of systems thinking

By reflecting not on the personality or skill of an individual but on their place in the system, vital information can be gleaned. When seeking to predict the results of any decision, due attention should be paid to the system. The current system is shaped by its history: our exploration of what is impacting the current system needs to extend back into the past, even beyond the preceding generation. Indeed, the nature of relationships in the present can have more to do with the emotional processes that have been successively reinforced for many generations than with the logic of the contemporary connections. For example, an engaged couple might usefully spend some time exploring their relative position in and experience of their families of origin, alongside taking into account their personalities, interests and their overall compatibility.

Interrelatedness: everything affects everything else

Systems thinking is about interrelatedness. The discipline of it is to recognize that within organizations, families and teams there are complex patterns of interaction. With elements of a system linked through a web of relationships, a linear interpretation of events is not appropriate. Everything affects everything else and if a problem lies within a system to which we belong, then we need to acknowledge that we too are contributing to it.

One of the conclusions of recognizing the interconnectedness in any network of relationships is that everyone should take responsibility for a part in the faults and failings of the system. A search for a scapegoat will only take us up a blind alley! Those within a system share responsibility, in both culpability and credit, for how it is functioning.

The positive side of this systemic truth is that we can all equally be part of the solution. Certainly, if we transform our contribution, the whole pattern of relationships will be affected. Consequently, any action we take has the potential to improve or be deleterious to the functioning of the system. For example, many of the leaders in a church are feeling unsupported, because the senior leader doesn't seem very interested in what they are doing. Whenever they get together, this is a topic of conversation. The issue is analysed at great length with everyone having a story to tell. Even so, unless they decide to make their observations and conclusions known to the senior church leader, then they are colluding and playing their part in maintaining the status quo.

When the outcome of our action determines our next action, this is defined as a feedback loop. For example, how I approach a difficult matter with those affected leads to a series of exchanges, each building on the preceding one. Thus, if I start with a leading question, this is likely to result in a defensive reaction. Then I have to decide how to respond to the impasse. I could either reflect on my own behaviour and learn a valuable lesson or blame those who are stonewalling. Reflecting and learning could lead to a more open approach whereby future conversations are likely to be more productive. By contrast, impugning those we have challenged is a self-defeating response. Our capacity to improve our interactions is diminished, and there is an attendant danger that the relationship would deteriorate further. Whatever approach is taken, a cycle is set up. Reflection, accompanied by learning and growth, leads to a propitious cycle. Denouncing our conversational partner as obstructive produces a destructive circle that is likely to become increasingly vicious!

Cause and effect are not usually closely related in time and space

Feedback loops—one action dictates the next—can be hard to see, because they influence behaviour over time, and there may be long delays between cause and effect. There may also be differences between the short-term and long-term consequence of any course of action. Despite these difficulties, learning to work out the possible ramifications of the various options when a decision needs to be made is a key leadership skill. By rigorous scrutiny, we reduce the risk of unforeseen consequences when any decision is taken. Being aware that every choice has intended and unintended results, both positive and negative, can help us to see the whole picture more clearly.

For example, consider the following scenario:

> A church committee has to decide whether the local operatic group should have its concert in the church or the parish hall. The strong and stated preference of the operatic group is that the concert should take place in the hall as it is much easier to serve refreshments there. A swift decision is made by the church committee, because it does not seem to be a major issue, and everyone is informed that the concert is to be in the parish hall.
>
> Close to the event, the operatic group arranges two rehearsal dates when it wants to use the stage in the hall. Unfortunately, the stage doubles up as a place for storage and is full of toys, books, a snooker table and many other assorted things used by the various groups that meet in the hall during the week. Removing and replacing the equipment before and after rehearsals is a taxing undertaking and finding volunteers to carry out this task is known to be difficult. As a result, at the subsequent church committee the original decision is reversed: the operatic society is then told that the concert will have to take place in the church.
>
> The person in charge of the publicity for the concert does not hang about and is on the phone. All the posters and tickets have been produced and now advertise the wrong venue. An irate email arrives the same day from a church committee member who has been asked to rig up a sound system in the hall for the concert and has spent several hours of their spare time doing this.

In summary, the consequence of a fast decision without careful consideration of the implications results in much time being lost and a significant fall-out. A longer decision-making process, including a proper assessment of the options, would undoubtedly have saved time in the long run.

Once we recognize the delay between cause and effect and the law of unintended consequences, we can see the merit in slowing down the decision-making processes. Indeed, our maxim becomes "faster is slower". In addition to an agreed and careful consultation process generating better decisions, it is also likely that there will be support for its outcome. Despite the impression that planning the process before starting may be unnecessary and laborious; it will, in most cases, actually speed up implementation and increase the likelihood that intended goals will be reached. Typically, rushing through decisions is counterproductive; it actually costs time in the long run. Aesop's famous fable about the hare and tortoise seems instructive here. The old adage "the more haste, the less speed" applies.[6]

Quick fixes can backfire

Once groups recognize the law of unintended consequences and how they often result from short-term thinking, the advantages of "going slow to go fast" are acknowledged. What is true for organizations is also true for individual conversations. Strong advocacy without genuine inquiry may create resistance or non-compliance in the long run, even though at the time it might seem that you are winning the argument. Also, in group work, whilst a strong leader might be getting results by correcting mistakes or completing tasks, there is a danger that they are debilitating the group. Alongside the goal of fulfilling the set tasks, developing the capacity of the group must also be an aim. Otherwise, in the long term, the leader is at risk of being overwhelmed with the issues that are not addressed. Furthermore, only by increasing the ability and expanding the scope of the system can problems be prevented from simply shifting around the system.

Small changes can produce big results, but where you will get the highest leverage is often hard to see

As Archimedes said, "Give me a lever and a place to stand, and I will move the world."[7] Frequently, the facet of the system creating the problem is complex and hard to see. Consequently, there are multiple explanations for any situation. The leverage needed to bring significant change through well-focused actions is often found in structural intervention rather than direct action on the immediate and obvious event.

Before you decide where to make changes, it is worthwhile doing a comprehensive analysis of the system. We need to look at the following five areas:

- Which events happen each day and on a weekly basis?
- Are there any patterns in these events and the way they happen?
- What is the hierarchy among those involved; how do they work, and how does information flow between them?
- What are the deeply embedded assumptions and generalizations that determine how we see our role and work and influence our action?
- What is the vision, the shared picture of the future to which people are committed?

Before you can begin to analyse what should be done, you have to be able to get beneath the presenting events to the underlying structures. As we move from observable patterns in the outcomes, to external structure, to the mental models and to the overarching vision, there is an increasing opportunity to initiate lasting and effective change to the system. For example, switching from a view of healthcare as "treating illness" to "creating wellbeing" is a fundamental shift in emphasis and would have a radical impact on every part of the system: a simple but instrumental change. In a church context, changing the congregation's thinking from "what I can get" to "what I can give" can have a transformational effect on the ethos of the church and on every relationship within it.

In group work, addressing the mental models informing people's behaviour rather than highlighting how the ground rules are repeatedly contravened will have a greater impact. Likewise tackling how an organization reacts defensively to developmental feedback instead of scrutinizing the areas of poor performance brings a more notable improvement in the outcomes. Typically, a structural intervention will take more time in the short term, but bring marked benefits over the long term.

To summarize: the structure is generative, the patterns of behaviour responsive and the event reactive. Changing the structure will produce different patterns of behaviour. As a corollary, it is the structural explanations of the current situation that are going to generate the more significant and long-term plans for change.

Dividing an elephant in half does not produce two elephants

Systems have their own integrity. It is only through seeing the whole system that you can make incisive judgements about what needs to be done to improve performance. That is why it is so important, when devising a planning process for a facilitation or consultation, to have representatives of the whole system present, and certainly from every part of the system that is likely to be affected by an impending decision. The alternative method of seeking to divide the system into its constituent parts, in order to analyse the impact, is futile. Only a distorted impression of minimal value will emerge. It requires multiple perspectives to garner enough valid information to make decisions that are going to lead to long-term propitious change.

You can have your cake and eat it too, but not all at once

What appear to be mutually exclusive goals can be compatible over the long term. Dilemmas such as central versus local control, contented and committed employees versus competitive labour costs, rewarding individual achievement versus everyone feeling valued, are the result of static thinking. They only seem to be either/or choices because we only think of what is possible at a fixed point in time. Over the longer term, there are other options. What is required is determination to achieve your goals and careful planning. Then you can have accountability at the centre combined with local autonomy. A profitable, dynamic company with committed, well-paid staff becomes possible. Teams in which individual achievement is valued by all because it contributes to the collective aims can be developed. In church terms, the leader can seek and make plans to mould a strong cohesive community that is also open, hospitable and welcoming. The leader should be encouraged: what might seem to be alternatives can become two goals that are within reach, as a result of creative, careful thought.

System thinking and leadership

In order to integrate systems thinking into your leadership, you need to be aware of the insights this discipline offers and take time to reflect thoughtfully on what is happening. Often what you will see will be complex and could be bewildering, certainly at first. Consulting with others could well add to your understanding.

The constant temptation is to act swiftly. Given the frenetic pace of life and the rush for action—"something must be done"—we tend to make a decision about the right course of action precipitously. Making the wrong decision, though, slows everything down in the long term. As a business consultant once told me, typically companies have insufficient time to carry out a consultation process properly, but they do apparently have enough time to do it twice. After the first attempt has been bungled, a second one is required.

Systems thinking should make us cautious. Wary of getting it wrong, we must ensure that we glean as much information as possible, attempt to understand how everything interconnects, explore the options, and then decide what to do. There is no excuse for inertia, but careful thought and being, at least, aware of the convoluted and intricate nature of systems should lead to better decisions.

CHAPTER 3

On Being a Consultative Leader

The family wants to go out for the day! You could just tell them what they are going to do: "We're off to London Stadium to see the football." You might just let everyone make a bid, in which case you'll probably end up with four distinct and irreconcilable options—"shopping", "a film", "hang-gliding" and "the football". Unless everyone is up for dashing from one to the other and ending up exhausted, you now have a problem.

If, on the other hand, you begin with what each individual wants— "time together", "excitement", "something to see" and "the opportunity to buy a shirt"—there might be scope for discovering an event that just about works for everyone. To go down this longer and more time-consuming route demands a commitment to collaborative decision-making.

Likewise in church, perhaps especially when it comes to building projects, it pays to consult with all the interested parties within and outside the church. As much as it is possible, you seek clarity about the aim. Why are we doing this project? Then you strive for consensus on what is going to be done.

You

Values and visions are essential parts of the same strategy. Unless your vision is consistent with your values, your leadership will not achieve the desired results. If integrity, honesty and compassion are important to you, you need to ensure that the process you design for discerning the vision matches up to these values. Nothing that is done in the church is ever incidental: it either reflects these core values or it does not. That is true both about what is done and how it is done.

The aspiration of the leader to develop as an individual by embracing the required disciplines drives and resonates with the church's ethos. Individual flourishing should inform and shape the culture and the activities. It is a key aspect of the leader's role to provide the conditions whereby everyone can lead the most enriching life possible. As a result, the community's capacity for mission and ministry will be enlarged.

A key starting point for the leader is how we view other people. Do we meet people assuming the best we can about them? Do we meet each person intrigued and determined to discover more about them? Do we approach them with compassion and curiosity? Do we engage with them expecting to glimpse an aspect of God's character?

If the leader relentlessly encourages by example every individual's personal growth, then the church's culture begins to be aligned with this goal. If a church is a community where people are inspired to imagine future possibilities, where enquiry and commitment to the truth are the norm, where current reality is embraced and where challenging the status quo is expected, then its common life will be characterized by energy and vitality.

When I led a church in South Essex, the porch at the front of the church was in a poor state. Instead of simply replacing like with like, there seemed to be an opportunity to do something exciting and radical. In the light of our vision, the church worked on how the front of the church could look if we were bold and innovative. A renowned architect produced some plans. The frontage was spacious, bright and modern with a glass roof. It included toilets, an office, an area from which to serve refreshments at services and events, and a large space that would be good for mingling after services but would also make a warm and inviting meeting venue. After we had worked out the costings, sought grants, held some fundraising events and had a Gift Day, we were still £150,000 short.

One of the churchwardens, Denis, was a builder by profession. He had come to faith quite recently and was finding his position challenging, but I was seeing his faith deepen and watching him thrive in this leading role in the church's life. As I worked closely with him, I was encouraged to see him grow in confidence as his leadership developed. Faced with what looked an insurmountable gap between the money we had and money we needed. Denis proposed to me that we could do a lot of the building ourselves, highlighting that we had bricklayers and others with building expertise in the congregation. As Denis warmed to his theme, he thought of another member of the church who had recently retired and could be our site foreman. Many could be labourers, and others could make cups of tea and bacon sandwiches. I could feel his sense of exhilaration at this route through the current impasse, but I wanted to test whether this was genuinely feasible. There were some aspects that we would need to contract to the experts, notably putting up the metal frame for the glass roof, the flooring and the plumbing. When we had rigorously scrutinized the costings and subtracted the work that we would do ourselves, we found that we had just enough money to complete the project. It looked possible.

Vigorous discussions in the Parochial Church Council followed about the merits of this new proposal, exploring the risks and the advantages. Alongside this scrutiny of this new plan, we needed to check that the church was prepared to make the necessary commitment. It was going to entail a huge sacrifice of time, especially by those individuals who were going to play a major part. Eventually, everything seemed to be in place to take a decision. Before the climactic vote at the PCC I asked Denis, who was going to oversee the work: "Denis, do you think we can do it?" I remember his smiling face and his confident, "Yes, I'm sure." His faith that God had provided this opportunity was rock solid. I was convinced, and told him, "Denis, if you're sure, so am I. Let's do it."

An arduous and at times difficult year followed, but there were many high points too, knocking down the old porch, laying the foundations, seeing the walls go up, and the roof winched into place, to name a few. When we had finished, we all knew that we had invested an immense amount into the wonderful new church frontage, which was eye-catching as people passed. "Our blood, sweat and tears" had gone into it, and we all shared in the satisfaction of a job well done. The church's faith had flourished, and the church's capacity had increased beyond all recognition. The church now grasped what could be achieved and had a greater appreciation of the contribution each individual made to her life. The church had also felt and seen the strength of her commitment to God's mission and her life together. This new-found confidence was a springboard into the plans for a new church centre behind the church.

Before I left, plans had been drawn up for a state-of-the-art centre, and it was envisaged that the church would again do most of the work on the building themselves. This enterprise took some time to complete but now the church is benefiting from a visually attractive and purposeful centre for church events and groups, and which serves the individuals and groups of the parish.

Your context

In a project such as this, you need to have a rigorous determination to understand reality accurately. You need to know something of the church's history. When it comes to the present, you must find out the facts, both harsh and benign. You should be aware of any constraints, things that limit your options. Then you need to consider what resources are available, including financial (how much money does the church have and where does it come from?), people (who can help make it happen?) and their gifts (what can each individual contribute to the development of the church?).

This taking stock is a precursor to working out where you need to go. This gap between where the church is now and where you think that the church should be generates a tension. This dissonance is uncomfortable, it disturbs the status quo. But through it, some impetus for change develops.

Your approach

How do you approach discovering and shaping a vision? How inclusive are you going to be in this process? How can you make sure that you draw out all the wisdom that is on offer? How can you consult and make decisions in a way that builds trust and confidence in your leadership? How you handle this stage will impact directly on the success of the venture, and any future consultation and decision-making process will be enhanced or dogged by people's memory of how it was handled this time.

By devising the process carefully and seeking agreement for it, you will exemplify how the church's values should affect everything that is done. For example, if it is important for you and your church that everyone should know that they are valued, the processes that you initiate and lead should put this aspiration into practice. By ensuring that everyone is consulted, paying particular attention to those who are usually ignored, you help to establish an inclusive ethos. As a result of listening to everyone's perspective, you create an atmosphere. Everyone feels that they are important and that their views are worth hearing. These consultative processes are then seen as a community enterprise through which growing and learning begin to emerge as distinct opportunities for all those who belong.[8]

In order to gain all the benefits of working together on discerning the vision, all participants must exercise the discipline of suspending their assumptions. This practice opens up the full range of possible solutions. Debate must be characterized by respect for each other and each other's perspective. Your task is to facilitate these exchanges. You must also guard against the discussion becoming too serious; it militates against creative thinking. Injecting some humour can help to keep anxiety levels low: your aim is to keep the mood a little playful without being flippant. If it all becomes too heavy, this becomes a stumbling block to meaningful exploration of the issues. Though there might still be some measure of disagreement at the end of the discussion, there is a need for an agreed course of action. In these circumstances, having had an open and robust exchange of views, the leader needs to acknowledge that while there might not be unanimity, there needs now to be unequivocal support for what has been agreed and commitment to its implementation.

Modelling and fostering an attitude of reflective openness

The practice of reflective openness does not come easily to most people. Transparency about our own thinking, questions and failings as leaders is crucial to good and trustworthy leadership.

Unless you take this risk, superficial listening and conversation result. To create a culture of true open-mindedness, leading by example can help to win the trust of those with whom we work. By so doing, you can help others to grow and to establish transformative relationships of trust and mutuality.

Integral to my role of training incumbent, I have regular supervisions with the curates I am helping to train. The worth of these conversations is directly related to their level of openness and honesty. For my part, when we are discussing topics I seek to invite a genuine exchange of views. Therefore, I share the thinking behind my opinions, and ask what they make of my arguments. Equally, I want to know their perspective and their underlying assumptions. Having a mutual exchange, expressing both what we think and why we think it, whereby we are curious, interested and keen to learn from each other, fosters good relationships that are likely to strengthen over time.

For the leader of the Christian community, shaping a culture and ethos where nurturing relationships are fostered is fundamental to their work. Where relationships improve, the quality of thinking also improves. We need to listen carefully and give attention to facing and resolving underlying conflicts. Bringing tensions and rumbling disagreements to the surface for exploration gives scope for relationships to deepen. This, in turn, strengthens the intellectual capacity of the team and, consequently, their performance.

Collaboration and discovery, rather than solutions and plans, should be our way of working. Deep listening in the context of a clear vision releases people's potential. The servant leader knows that people have much to offer, and it is the leader's responsibility to nurture people's gifts and to empower people to use them. This feature of servant leadership is integral to the position of priests in the Church of England. They are given this mandate in their ordination service: "Guided by the Spirit, they are to discern and foster the gifts of all God's people that the whole Church may be built up in unity and faith."[9] By contrast, mechanistic and hierarchical approaches constrain, instead of setting people free to offer the full range of their gifts, and thereby to engender the organization's development.

The pictures inside people's heads: paying attention to the mental models

The ideas that shape our thinking need to be uncovered. Otherwise, they remain unexamined, whilst affecting our behaviour. At worst, the gap between our mental models and reality makes our actions unproductive. Ideally, the organization to which we belong and the ambitions we share need to be acute, in line with reality. Equally, our actions should be in accord with our interpretation of reality and aligned to the direction of travel. To journey towards this level of integration, where our thinking and actions are consistent, and seek to take us and the organization of which we are part from present reality towards our vision of a better future, demands that we are determinedly rigorous with ourselves.

The models can be simple generalizations—"people are untrustworthy"—or they can be complex theories, such as an explanation of the dynamics within our families. Whatever they are, they are active: they shape our interactions and our actions.

Deeply entrenched mental models can impede development drastically, militating against any systemic insights that suggest that fundamental change is necessary. Unless the mental models are brought to the surface and examined, they undergird and maintain the status quo.

In general, unexamined assumptions can often lead to inefficiency, bad decisions and inappropriate responses. If we long to be effective, we must be prepared to scrutinize our thinking and our behaviour. This entails paying close attention to our mental models. If we desire to become aware of our mental models, our ways of thinking, and how they relate to our behaviour and what we do, there are some key disciplines to which we need to adhere:

What are the differences between our espoused theories (what we say) and our theories in use (the implied theory in what we do)?

- Are we making "leaps of abstraction" (noticing our jumps from observation to generalization)?
- Are we prepared to explore the assumptions and judgements which underpin what is being said but are not articulated?

Balancing advocacy and enquiry

Conversations become more productive if we learn to strike the right balance between advocacy and enquiry. The opportunity for collaborative learning is enhanced through the process of stating your position and the reason behind it, and then seeking the other's point of view. This can be described as "reciprocal enquiry". Making our thinking explicit and subject to challenge helps to foster an atmosphere of genuine openness.

Through combining advocacy with enquiry, we display a willingness to expose our thinking and the possible flaws in our understanding. This is a vulnerable approach: we run the risk of being wrong and being seen to be wrong. In order for our interlocutors to be aware that our position is contingent—that we are prepared to change—we need to tell them. We could say something like this, "This is the way I see it". Beneath this approach is a determined curiosity: we are authentically interested in what others think.

If our aim is to seek genuine dialogue over an issue, then we are set free from any compulsion to impose our view on someone else. Indeed, the occasions when we will need to persuade or convince will be fewer. Moreover, when there is a clash of opinions, resorting to enquiry as opposed to advocacy reduces the heat generated by the conflict. "What is it that leads you to hold that position?" and "Can you illustrate your point for me?" are two useful questions.

Inculcating a culture in which it is the norm to state your position on any presenting topic, explain your reasoning, and be receptive to questioning and challenge is a central task for the leader. In this culture, any consultation process will feel open and engaged, and generate energy and commitment to the process and the outcome.

By allowing all the participants to have their say, the final outcome of the process will, typically, have their support. Even those who hold a view that does not prevail, as long as the decision has been reached through an inclusive process that has been handled with integrity.

In his book *The Lions* Ian McGeechan, head coach of the British Lions Rugby Union team on four tours, underlines the importance of rigorous, open, no-holds-barred debate in reaching a decision that everyone can support:

What we need is uniformity of thought and complete understanding. We won't always agree as a coaching team, but I know this much: we'll be honest with each other. If someone has a problem—and this goes for the players as well as the coaches—there must be no innuendos, no whispering and no hiding in corners. I want it out in the open like a shot. Only by being prepared to talk things through will we reach the answers we need.[10]

Building a shared vision

"Being a visionary leader is about solving day-to-day problems with my vision in mind."[11] The idea of vision is closely related to the concept of "mission" and the "core values" that inform all that we do. While our mission is our *raison d'être*—why we exist, the vision is the picture of the future we are seeking to create.

The "core values", such as honesty and integrity, help us to fulfil our vision. Progress in pursuing the vision gives everyone involved renewed enthusiasm. Besides being bolstered by success, aspiring towards a goal provides all participants with opportunities to learn and grow.

Rather than imposing a vision on a church, the leader's task is to be attentive and discern "pictures of the future" which have authentic support. Indeed, it can be counterproductive to try to impose a way forward. No matter how passionate the leader is, and how good the plan, this approach is likely to provoke resistance.

The leader's task is to articulate a coherent way forward that will elicit commitment. Equally, the leader needs to be aware of the potential limits to progress and how they need to be addressed.

For themselves and for their church, leaders need to work at gaining a coherent and compelling vision. Before people can know what they need to do to move towards their vision for their church, and themselves, they must have a firm grasp of their current context. This means that leaders need to be constantly curious and to be unremittingly inquisitive. They must be committed to seeing reality with increasing accuracy.

Arriving at a shared vision demands a dynamic, interactive method. This cohesive picture of the future emerges through candid discussion, and through the leader's discovery of where the available opportunities resonate with their own personal motivations and goals. By continually sharing their own thoughts and hopes, the leader sets the tone whereby others are prepared to do likewise. As the leader has to hold the vision, it is imperative that the leader plays their part in shaping it. Unless the leader is comfortable and confident with the vision, then any moves forward are likely to be hindered by the leader's lack of resolution and indecisiveness.

Remember: it is what a vision does, not what it is, that counts. Without a shared vision, everyone is prone to petty preoccupations. To lift people's eyes from the routine and the mundane, leaders must articulate a long-term aim that is worthy of deep commitment.

Aligning people's vision and values

Effective and significant change arises out of the leader's acute understanding of the identity of the organization, awareness of its history, present strengths and weaknesses, and aspirations. Gaining this knowledge will entail listening to all the organization's stakeholders. Once the organization's identity has been grasped, the leader is in a position to begin to mould its vision—the aims for the future that shape its current life and values—the characteristics that define its corporate life, every relationship and interaction.

Over the first six months or so after starting in a new parish, I have visited the key individuals in the church in their homes, including the churchwardens, the PCC, and other lay and ordained colleagues. Then I have widened the circle to include as many others as time allows. Given the purpose of the visit is to establish a relationship, I am looking to learn about their families, priorities and interests. In particular, I ask about their faith journey by opening up an exchange about their church connections. "Have you always been involved in church?" is a straightforward, introductory question. As I am also looking to learn about the history of the church, I will also inquire about when they started coming to the church and how it has changed since they first came. When I arrived in Saffron Walden, where I am currently working and where there is a church school and a strong civic ministry, I went along to see the head teacher and the Town Clerk in my first week. From this positive start, I then moved on to other stakeholders like the Mayor, the head teachers of the other schools in the town, and my ecumenical colleagues. In these early stages, I was trying to understand the history of the church and town, to establish relationships with individuals and to begin to discern the priorities for my own ministry in the first year.

Inherent power is released if people share the same vision and values. It is worth reiterating that an organization's vision and values can seem coherent and meritorious in themselves, but their worth should be judged by how much impact they have. They must influence each decision. Therefore they should be a daily feature of the organization's life. They are tools for mobilizing and focusing energy. The criterion for judging them, regardless of how they are defined, is "What impact do they have?"

If a direction has been determined through an inclusive and consultative process, then everyone will, on the whole, move forward together. Even if there is some measure of dissent, then, as long as everyone has been properly heard, the church can work successfully to make the vision a reality. Building into the process time for reflection, after the decision has been implemented, enables everyone to see if the changes proposed have achieved their intended goals. Moreover, it helps for those opposed to see that their concerns have been taken seriously and will be revisited.

Hopefully those who contend against the current direction can express their view in this kind of way: "Look, we talked about this, and I had a different perspective. You heard my perspective, and we agreed to do this. We are committed to implement this decision, but we'll have a checkpoint to make sure these actions are achieving the results we intend."

The example of the leader is crucial for holding the church to its avowed vision and values.

"Be the change, you wish to see"—Mahatma Ghandi[12]

Underlying this shift is the leader's own personal journey. If the leader is intentionally and determinedly seeking to reflect, explore and to become more open, then these attitudes will start to permeate the whole community. Confucius said, "To become a leader, you must first become a human being." The desire to serve is the core motivation of great leaders, and the growth of people under their charge is the best indicator of greatness. The test of what might be called a "servant leader" is: "Do those served grow as persons? Do they become healthier, wiser, freer, more autonomous, more likely to become servants themselves?"

Depth of commitment, the clarity and persuasiveness of their ideas and the extent of their openness to learn more continually further define outstanding leaders. While they are prepared to admit that they do not necessarily have the answer, they are able to instil through their own inner confidence the conviction that together, "we can learn whatever we need to learn in order to achieve the results we truly desire".

Through this open approach, this willingness to learn, the leader sets the tone for the whole organization. The atmosphere is changed, and a renewed hope about the future is instilled.

The goal of learning from an organizational standpoint is to enhance the learners' capacity, individually and collectively, in order to produce the desired results. It is worth noting that building capacity, whereby greater knowledge is gained and skills enhanced, takes time, often considerable time. Patience is vital.

Alongside the quest to be more open, ready to learn, committed to serving, the leader must be determined to be responsible and to yearn for adventure. This prayer of Sir Francis Drake conveys this questing attitude born of a profound trust in God. It is a fitting conclusion to this second part, and acts as a bridge to our next section about the goal of "becoming a great leader".

Disturb us, Lord, when we are too well pleased with ourselves,
When our dreams have come true
Because we have dreamed too little,
When we arrived safely
Because we sailed too close to the shore.

Disturb us, Lord, when
With the abundance of things we possess
We have lost our thirst
For the waters of life;
Having fallen in love with life,
We have ceased to dream of eternity
And in our efforts to build a new earth,
We have allowed our vision
Of the new Heaven to dim.

Disturb us, Lord, to dare more boldly,
To venture on wider seas
Where storms will show your mastery;
Where losing sight of land,
We shall find the stars.
We ask You to push back
The horizons of our hopes;
And to push into the future
In strength, courage, hope, and love.

This we ask in the name of our Captain,
Who is Jesus. Amen.[13]

The desired learning will increase the learners' capacity, individually and collectively, to produce results they truly want. One of the most reliable indicators of a team that is learning together is the presence of robust and open conflict. For this to happen, defensive strategies must be rejected, assumptions must be revealed and challenged, and there must be an established pattern of reflection and mutual enquiry. Alongside a determination to challenge opinions, it is helpful if there is a light, playful and exploratory feel to discussions.

The leader needs to ensure that the team meets regularly and often enough. This is fundamental: getting people together and talking together creates a whole set of possibilities that are not there prior to the meeting.

Setting, enforcing and adhering to the ground rules establishes and sets the ethos and the working practices for the team. Amongst the ground rules should be a commitment by everyone to suspend assumption and to pursue the truth of the current reality rigorously. Consequently, the team members must be encouraged to raise the difficult issues. In order to gain a better understanding of the current situation and, as a result, achieve improved outcomes, conflict must be recognized as helpful and productive.

In any team that is functioning well, individual accountability will be fostered, and reflection on one's own work and behaviour will become routine.

As teams, in various guises, are the basic building blocks of most organizations, these teams need to be able to learn. Otherwise the organization's ability to improve its performance will be severely hampered. In short, unless the internal teams can learn, the organization cannot.

Over the last 25 years, I have led an all-age worship team which has had the task of planning and delivering a service at least monthly. The goal is an act of worship that has something for people across the age-range from a young child to a nonagenarian. Currently I lead a team producing a "Family Service" monthly. At every meeting, we review together the last service, on the basis of three questions: "What was good?", "What could have been better?" and "What can we learn?" When we are planning the next service, we also apply the "child-friendly test", checking that there is something that is going to connect with the children. Our ability to learn from each service has meant that we have been able to improve what we do. One example is how we have more actively engaged the children present. We have an action song, and another for which the children can play simple instruments. We also include an item near the beginning called "setting the scene", which opens up the theme of the service and also involves the children. After the talk, there is a child-friendly response that everyone is invited to make which invariably involves movement, usually down the main aisle to the top of the nave. All these aspects are included to ensure that the service is child-friendly. One thing that we learned was that the children who had gravitated on arrival to Children's Corner by the font and near the West Door were distracted and hard to draw to the front to participate in those parts of the service specifically aimed at them. Therefore, we moved the toys, table and colouring books from the back to the top of the north aisle. Then whoever was leading the service or giving the talk could see them and address them directly. The journey to the front was also shorter. The pattern of reflecting and learning continues in our Family Service Team meetings. We accept that a new service is never perfect and that there is always something to learn or relearn.

High-performing teams have the capacity to grapple with complex issues and to initiate innovative and co-ordinated action. Teams develop by members sharing good practice with each other and learning together through dialogue. In the mutual exchange of views, each individual can become an observer of their own thinking and offer a critique of their point of view.

CHAPTER 4

Serving the People in True Humility

*So Jesus called them and said to them, "You know that among
the Gentiles those whom they recognize as their rulers lord it
over them, and their great ones are tyrants over them. But it is
not so among you; but whoever wishes to become great among
you must be your servant, and whoever wishes to be first among
you must be slave of all. For the Son of Man came not to be
served but to serve, and to give his life a ransom for many."*
Mark 10:42–45

*The wicked leader is he whom the people revile. The good
leader is he whom the people revere. The great leader
is he of whom people say, "We did it ourselves".*
Lao Tzu, D.533 BC[14]

The importance of humility

In his book *Good to Great*, Jim Collins describes how his extensive research
provides convincing evidence that the best leaders combine personal
humility and steely resolve. If you desire to be a great leader, then you
need to learn humility. Humility is expressed in self-forgetfulness. When
I asked my Dad, who was self-effacing, how he fostered this quality, he
told me, "I'm going to live three score and ten or maybe for a little while
longer. From an eternal perspective that's not long. I'm one of six billion
people on the planet. It seems reasonable to be humble about my position
in the great scheme of things." The other means whereby people acquire
the virtue of humility is by living a life of service. By focusing on the needs
of others, their attention has shifted off themselves and onto others. It

is, however, a characteristic only others can notice. You cannot notice it yourself. Moreover, you cannot be self-conscious about endeavouring to be humble. As you soon as you notice that you are humble, you no longer are! You cannot measure your progress; otherwise you run the risk of being proud of your humility! Humility only results from taking your attention off yourself and onto others by seeking to serve them. By focusing on the needs of the church and those around you, your attention is directed beyond yourself. Making your goal the wellbeing of God's Church, your attitude and actions are directed towards building up individuals and the common life. When something is achieved, you deflect attention away from yourself. You invest any credit in those with whom you work. You give the credit for any achievement to others. Your identity is invested in the success of the church. You consistently produce superb results, demonstrate unshakeable commitment and set the standards for everybody else. You meticulously scrutinize their own performance and hold themselves responsible for any failures.

The best leaders know that the starting point for progress in any organization is in facing the harsh facts of the current situation. You must strive to create a culture where the truth is sought and faced unswervingly and where crucial information cannot be ignored. Good leaders are able to ask penetrating questions. In one of the parishes in which I served, I noticed that talk of a possible building project seemed to make people jumpy. During the early exploratory steps, some members seemed suspicious of what was happening, as though they suspected that they were being kept in the dark. This led me to ask questions. It transpired that the PCC had not been kept informed about a previous project and had ended up paying a significant sum to the architect, who had been enlisted to draw up some abortive plans.

In my current setting, the parish's finances were not in good shape when I arrived. This was no surprise, because I had been quizzed about what I would do about the annual deficit in the interview for the post. I had some ideas about what to do but needed to find out what had been tried already, asking the hard questions about what had been done to encourage church members to join a giving scheme in the past. Raising the issue of an annual budget was met with some incredulity, initially. Then, to understand our financial situation further, I had to understand the nature of the various funds, and to be clear about what was restricted and could only to be used for defined expenditure, and what was not. I needed the answers to these questions to be fully in the picture.

Dialogue is the best way to discover the facts. It is important to analyse the situation without apportioning. Once the current position has been ascertained and assessed, your next tasks are to make people engage with what is actually happening and to identify the implications. Putting these hard truths on the table alongside the organization's vision means that you can draw up a coherent and cogent action plan. This should offer a step-by-step course identifying what needs to happen to move from the present reality towards the aims defined by the vision. To refuse to face reality is to appear out of touch. If you seem disconnected from the issues and the problems which those around them are facing daily, this will demotivate and sap everyone's energy. After an action plan has been put together, you need to pursue it single-mindedly. You and everyone else must be disciplined, attending to the agreed programme and ceasing activities, even if they are beneficial in themselves, which do not comply with it. Actually, what you decide to stop doing is as important as what you start to do.

In his book *A Failure of Nerve*, Ed Friedman identifies three popular, contemporary assumptions about leadership that are debilitating. With the speed of change and high levels of anxiety in society, an emphasis on accumulating as much information as possible has developed. The false premise underpinning this drive is that, if you have enough knowledge, you'll know what to do. In practice, the opposite is the case: lots of information, often contradictory, overwhelms and confuses. Rather than attempting to gain more and more facts, what you need to cultivate is an appropriate confidence in your own judgement and a sense of adventure. Otherwise there is a danger of "paralysis by analysis".

The second myth is that empathizing with someone's feelings will help them to mature. While there is a place for empathy without an accompanying challenge to take responsibility for someone's life and situation, it could simply leave someone where they are, or worse. Furthermore, feelings of empathy could stop the leader from taking a stand about invasive behaviour. The value of issuing a challenge, thereby stimulating courage and strength, is often underplayed.

The final delusion is that selfishness is a greater threat to a community than individuals losing their individual identity. Living in an anxious setting and a fretful age, there is a strong urge towards togetherness, an overemphasis on unity. At its worst, this tendency leads to a conception of a community as a bland uniformity. Of course, at the other extreme there is a similarly disturbing picture of a dysfunctional community, a collection of strong individuals each demanding their own way. The healthy ideal of a Christian community is of strong individuals committed to each other and working towards a common goal.[15]

Being a nurturing presence

In order to promote the growth of each individual, you need to care, support and teach in a way that helps people to achieve greater independence. Like a nurturing parent, the leader must practise support that fosters the other person's development in line with identity in the process. A sensitive and creative response with the appropriate balance of support and detachment, calculated to stimulate the individual's growth to maturity, is the leader's difficult assignment.

By nurturing through care, support and teaching, we facilitate the other person's growth towards greater confidence in their own identity. Steering a course between too much advice on the one hand and false humility on the other, you will be able to offer strong, unselfish encouragement. This statement summarizes the position of the nurturing leader: "I want you to grow to be independent of me. You'll decide together when you are ready to move towards greater independence."

Being one of the people

If you are to have an effect on the church's life, you must get connected. For any leader coming into a new church, this needs to be a top priority. Unless the leader becomes a member of the church family (gets "connected" to use family systems terminology), they will be a leader in name only. In short, until you belong, you will have minimal influence on the church's long-term health.

When I became curate-in-charge of St Mark's, which serves a more deprived part of Godalming, I was told by one of my predecessors that he had been told by the archdeacon, when he started, that "if he visited people in their homes and loved them, he would have a fruitful ministry". This seemed good advice, which I strove to put into practice. Likewise when I had moved into the house in Grays, the archdeacon came to visit and gave me a similar steer: "Do pastoral visits, and the people will love you back." In both settings, over the first few months, I systematically visited people to get to know them. Besides these visits—mostly pre-arranged, but sometimes I just called unannounced—I tried to make the most of every encounter to learn about my locality and to find out about the individual facing me.

There is no short cut. Somehow you have to establish significant one-to-one relationships with the church members. Without this grounding there is a danger that you will feel and be perceived as disconnected. This is essential and vital to any sustained ministry in a church. I cannot stress too strongly how important this is. Without the leader being and remaining connected, any attempts to lead the church in any direction will prove futile.

Also, whenever a new leader begins his or her work, they must have a strategy for integrating into the church community. Intrinsic to this approach will be "identification", adopting some aspects of the church's culture—their way of doing things. If this is allied to an explicit message of God's love and acceptance, then the leader's introduction into the church community can be a powerful symbol of God's embrace.

Learning about the church's history and paying particular attention to its formative events should give some insights into the church's sense of identity: how people see their church. Knowing something about the church's self-understanding will, in turn, shed some light on the current practices; they are expressions of identity. The most obvious examples of this phenomenon are to be found in the worshipping life of the church. "We are a smells-and-bells church" describes two features of acts of worship, but beneath there are, probably, other stronger and more significant messages about identity. These implicit statements of the church's self-understanding need to be heeded, otherwise what appear to be superficial changes could impinge on questions of identity and elicit very strong reactions. Be warned.

The opposite danger to being too detached is to be entirely connected, what might be described as "fused". The trap is that you become so connected that you merge with the church community, adopting totally its norms and values, and become indistinguishable from everyone else.

The ideal is to be connected whilst remaining self-differentiated. You need to strive to keep the focus on your own position and direction, whilst remaining in close relationship with others in the systems in which you move. Sometimes it might seem easier to withdraw, for example if you are under attack, but whatever the provocation, stay in calm communication with those who are opposing you. In a crisis, this takes on renewed importance and is an active process. You should do all you can to maintain meaningful relationships with all those involved. Alongside seeking people out, particularly those antagonistic to you, this involves keeping a check on your emotions. You need to be cautious about sharing your feelings, apart from with some selected individuals.

Trusting the people

A leader's ecclesiology, conceptually and in practice—there can be a distinct difference between the leader's articulated and actual understanding of church as revealed in how they lead—determines their approach to leadership.

There are leaders who are heavily influenced by the role of the prophet in the Old Testament. Along with the king and the priest, the prophet was imbued with the Holy Spirit, in order to live out his vocation. Typically, he had a direct and disturbing encounter with God through which he would be given an insight into God's plans and be commissioned for a particular task. The prophets can be seen as "rugged individuals". Those leaders who seem to model themselves on prophets like Moses fail, in my opinion, to take seriously the gift of the Holy Spirit given to all those in Christ.

If we take seriously that the Holy Spirit resides and is at work in and through each individual, and in the Church as a whole, then this has to dictate how we lead. Proper processes of consultation and shared decision-making must be put in place with the aim of gaining from the collective wisdom of God's people; this correspondingly improves the quality of decisions made. When people know that their views matter, their commitment and engagement to the corporate life of the church is deepened dramatically, and amazing possibilities come within reach! Conversely, and paradoxically—and it is true in all kinds of settings—the more that you use power to try to control people in church life, the less influence you have on them!

Don't be afraid to challenge

Integral to the leadership role is fostering a sense of responsibility. If people are acting irresponsibly, the dilemma is that, as soon as you intervene, you have assumed a measure of responsibility yourself and pre-empted them from taking the initiative themselves. Instead of, effectively, undermining people's autonomy by either telling them what to do or by taking over, it is better to confront people with the consequences of their actions or their inaction. This essentially means delegating anxiety. If you don't adopt this approach, then the anxiety becomes lodged with you. Then you find yourself stuck in a rigid triangle formed by you, the other person and their failure. The only means to escape this bondage, to break free, is to challenge the other person. Remember that they must take responsibility for their own actions.

The leader has a responsibility for the organization as a whole and for the individual members. If you are to help the organization to become and remain healthy, you must focus, perhaps counter intuitively, on yourself, your own character and behaviour. You have to take responsibility for your emotions and make no excuses. Rigorous self-examination, increasing self-awareness, along with a rigid determination to take responsibility for yourself, are fundamental to mature leadership. This entails learning to control your anxiety. You must examine yourself honestly, striving for integrity between your values and beliefs, and how they are demonstrated in your relationships and public life.

There is an irrefutable and simple logic at work: the integrity of the leader promotes the integrity of the church family. Equally, if the leader is self-differentiated, a clearly delineated person, with no blurred edges, and no shadowy outlines, then everyone in the church is encouraged by their example to discover and express who they are; each will become more autonomous, exhibit greater independence and become a more distinct individual. There is a clear correlation, even a causal relationship here, which no leader can afford to ignore.

Almost inevitably, there will be some people in the church community who seem unable to control their behaviour and who tend to be reactive. Their disruptive and difficult behaviour can cause significant hurt and distress. Confronted by this lack of self-control, the leader should respond by taking a stand. You must declare unequivocally where the boundary lies. Even if this is emotionally uncomfortable and could be labelled as "paternal", the leader must not shirk issuing this challenge for the benefit of the individual and the wellbeing of the Christian community.

Once, on returning from holiday, I discovered that there had been some physical interaction between two individuals at church on the preceding Sunday. This disturbing incident was first relayed to me, tangentially, in a prayer at Morning Prayer on the following Saturday, my next day back at work. Having clarified exactly what happened and liaised with the churchwardens, I went to visit the protagonists. They did not need me to tell them that their behaviour had been unacceptable, and it was necessary to make it clear that there was a boundary, and they had crossed it. Making these visits and taking this action was reassuring for the church that had been shaken up by the incident. In both conversations, we moved from the flashpoint in church to talk about the conflict between them and how we might move towards a resolution.

Keeping your distance too!

Church leaders are to be unifying figures in the church's life. As people of integrity who engender trust, individuals within the church invest their loyalty in them. They hold the community together and could be said to be at the centre of her life. They also need, however, to have the ability to step forward to be in front and ahead. From this position, they can challenge and ask questions that are aimed at drawing out a stronger response to God's love. There should always be something eccentric which literally means "out of the centre". The leader is sometimes like a familiar friend but sometimes like a stranger. Keeping some distance allows those around you to move forward and to discover more about who they are called to be.

Mature leadership includes feeling comfortable when people say "no" to us. Indeed, it is the leader's responsibility to make it easy for people to say "no". Unless people can decline, they cannot say "yes" freely and with conviction.

Similarly, leaders should not feel threatened when others distance themselves from them. Moving away relationally is an attempt to gain emotional comfort and safety, to re-establish a sense of self. It might feel like rejection, but the leader needs to contain the resulting anxiety. The person's sense of safety should be uppermost in the leader's mind. I have made the mistake of pursuing people who want some more distance, and this has proved counterproductive. The decision as to whether to seek further contact or to remain at a distance, risking the possibility that you appear uninterested, is a difficult judgement to make. Making the right decision is easier if you are aware of your own tendency. I know now that I am more likely, effectively, to chase someone away than to appear not to care. Thus I need to take this trait into account in my analysis. Obviously, if there is a repeated pattern of someone distancing themselves from you, you should not pursue them. Nevertheless, if you sense someone moving away from you, you could offer her an opportunity to talk if they want to do so. Listening to and seeking to understand them might make them feel safer.

Helping people to feel safe is an important aspect of the role of the leader. You should seek to create an accepting and welcoming culture whereby people feel comfortable enough to be themselves. In this secure atmosphere in which people feel loved for who they are, there should be scope for deeply held and distinct viewpoints to be expressed. This capacity to accept differences will be a boon to the whole church community.

The greater emphasis on Safeguarding in Church life in the last decade is aimed at ensuring that children, young people and vulnerable adults are protected. Safer recruitment of employees and volunteers is a protection against inappropriate individuals being put in a position of responsibility and care for others. Health and safety policies have become a requirement for churches, and risk assessments ensure that the leader of any activity or event considers carefully the physical and other dangers beforehand. These measures add to the Church's drive to be a welcoming community where everyone is cared for and safe.

Getting a reaction

Emotional reactivity is about feelings being expressed almost instantaneously. Perhaps this is best illustrated by drawing a parallel with a vending machine: push the button and the emotion comes out. The level of reactivity will vary according to the sense of threat perceived by the individual or the group. Unless we are prepared for this reactivity in others, there is a danger is that we will react similarly. Instead of pacifying the situation, we will escalate it, producing an upward spiral of volatility.

Negativity is one form of reactivity, but those who are criticized should be slow to label their critics as "against them". In particular, any strong reaction to a church leader is an indication of emotional investment. Whether people are being positive or negative towards you, they are interested in and want a relationship with you. This knowledge should make the leader more ready to meet with those most intensely negative church members. Giving them some time and engaging with their observations might well lead to some surprising developments.

Feelings are subjective: they are often more about us as a subject than about the reality we face. We need to be cautious about giving credence to our emotional reaction to events and circumspect about expressing them. We should be aware of the impact on the system of putting our feelings out into the open.

Creating an open and welcoming space around you

A leader who has a high level of self-differentiation is by definition confident about who they are and what they believe. This means that they know what is important to them, their own priorities and goals. They have a clear understanding of what they will and will not do. They have some definite boundaries in their relationships with others. Above all, they know that they are loved unconditionally by God. They will not feel threatened by people with different beliefs and identities. This makes it possible to begin to shape a nurturing and receptive church culture.

Once a course has been set for the church, she will be able to withstand any opposition because she does not need approval to feel OK about herself. The leader remains committed to the direction and pace of change. Whatever the resistance that ensues, they remain resolute. They do not withdraw under pressure but keep strong and open relationships with everyone involved, and particularly with those who are hindering progress. They put particular time and energy into keeping on good terms with anyone who was opposed to the changes that are being made. If they persevere, staying strongly connected to the church community, then eventually plans will be implemented and the community will be able to settle into new rhythms and routines.

Remember: if you hope to lead a growing, leading, maturing community, you need to seek to grow, to learn and to mature!

The maturity of the leader is fundamental to a church's wellbeing. This means that your ability to manage yourself is more important than your motivational skills. The effective leader has the capacity to take sharply defined positions and is not surprised by opposition and resistance. When conflict arises, you need to hold your nerve and stay connected with everyone, especially those opposed to you.

The church is an emotional system, and it needs a leader. Everyone deep down knows this is true. When there is no leader, a kind of power-vacuum develops, and the a community feels ill at ease. Anxiety levels will rise. Conversely, if the leader is good, then everyone is to some extent invested. They want it to work. That does not mean that there will not be conflict. What it does mean is that, if you stay calm, clear and connected, and you have properly consulted, then you can be confident that, more often than not, you will prevail. This truth is reassuring for the leader. In short, if the leader weathers the storm, eventually the church will rally around the leader's position.

Your task is to go on articulating your own position, based on the outcome of your consultation and your emotional connection with people. Providing that your position is reasonable and grounded in what is best for the community, you need to be prepared to explain where you "stand" and why. Do this well, and you are in a powerful position to lead and take the church in the right direction and also to foster the growth of those you lead. Rather than the leader feeling under pressure, it is now those who are dependent upon the leader who, in response, have to define themselves. This process challenges the church members to "grow up", to mature and to know where they stand on the current issue and why. If you take the trouble to work your own self-differentiation, this effectively acts as a provocation to the rest of the community to do likewise—to self-differentiate, to know what they think and why they think it.

Respecting individuality—making disciples of Christ, not clones of you!

If you label someone, your understanding of them is blinkered: we see them through the lens of our shorthand description and miss anything that may challenge our thinking. Our view of them is fixed. Should this practice be widespread, it will make the relationship tight and solid. Then there is no scope for flexibility, growth and change. The mood, as a result, becomes depressingly serious.

When you go a step further by defining the other person, by telling someone what they should think, believe or decide, then this is disruptive to the health of the community. If you notice that you are slipping into this pushy or, even worse, coercive approach, then you are probably feeling unsafe around them. In these circumstances, the advice is the same: define yourself. By resisting the urge to define the other, you are behaving maturely and creating enough space in the relationship for the other individual to begin to reflect on his own behaviour, and, hopefully, start to change.

In short, you must avoid pigeonholing people and resist any temptation to control them. Rather you must foster an ethos where individuality and boundaries are respected. It is healthy if we all know where our boundaries begin and end, and what, in terms of feelings and attitudes, is ours and what is the other person's: "This is my space and my stuff, and that is your space and your stuff," to put it bluntly.

Servant leadership enables a community to reach its goals and to foster the growth of each individual. If leadership is measured solely by whether certain tasks have been completed or targets reached, then it could be argued that a different style of leadership might be equally or even more effective. However, other approaches to leadership do not place such a strong emphasis on the development of the individuals who do the task. Rather the priority is on simply getting the work done. For churches the welfare and growth of those who belong can never be incidental.

Change, development and growth leads to a time of testing—being resilient under pressure

Whenever you orchestrate change, expect to come under pressure, because any challenge to the status quo may upset the interpersonal dynamics. Change makes people uneasy, and the resultant anxiety can become focused on you. You, as it happens, are, rightly, held responsible. You should expect a reaction. Steel yourself.

Your attempt to move the church in a particular direction is bound to bring you up against the forces of inertia and to generate some opposition. Given this resistance, you need to be determined and to persevere.

Making some progress does not signal the end of the battle. Rather those opposed to the change might renew their efforts to stop what is happening. Be alert. You must recognize attempts to sabotage but not be perturbed. You need to stay calm. By remaining resolute and simply restating your position, you stand up to the opposition. Insomuch as you hold your nerve, the change process will continue to move forward. Since you have not reacted emotionally and not withdrawn but stayed engaged and rational, you are well-placed to think carefully and speak straightforwardly in defence of the changes that are being implemented.

Servant leadership

One of the marks of a healthy church is that individuals discover and use their gifts, and grow to maturity. This is fostered by "servant leadership". An affirmative answer to the four questions below about those you lead would mean that you are this kind of leader.

- Are those you lead becoming more defined, more confident in who they are and they have to offer?
- Is their faith in God?
- Is their faithfulness in relationships with others deepening?
- Are they becoming servants themselves?

Some church leaders simply assert their authority to get their way in battles in the church's life. Besides positional power, leaders can muster allies or use force of personality to ensure that the church moves in the direction they want. While these methods can lead to what looks like progress, they are detrimental to the corporate life. They undermine relationships and jeopardize the growth to maturity of the individual members.

By contrast, if the goal of the leader is to strengthen the sense of community and to see individuals become confident people, sure of who they are and for what they stand, then the leader seeks to share responsibility and to support each individual's journey of growth. These features are linked. There is mutuality between belonging to a cohesive, loving community and individual maturity.

Indeed, individual transformation is nurtured through a community of grace. Reciprocally a gracious community is sustained and flourishes through individual transformation. Your task is to foster relationships that are characterized by loving, generous interactions. Through example and by challenging any attitudes or exchanges that do not enhance the church's life, you have an essential role. There are no short cuts. In so far as you model and demonstrate self-giving love and compassionate commitment, you are creating a nurturing culture, whereby the church community and her individuals can change meaningfully and for the long term. Leading this way is exciting and exacting. It is stretching but immensely worthwhile. A servant leader is what we should all aspire to be. This humble approach is both fulfilling and fruitful.

Ian McGeechan, head coach of the British Lions on four tours, exemplified servant leadership by investing passionately in the players, the staff and the concept of the four home nations coming together to go to one of major rugby playing nations in the southern hemisphere every four years His example inspired those he led to put the other players and the goals of the tour above their own individual ambitions. The best exemplar of this attitude was Jason Leonard who he describes as "his ultimate lion". He relates that when Jason was not picked for the Test team in 1997, he did not brood on the decision or wallow in disappointment but made sure that those chosen ahead of him had his support in the preparations for the match. Ian identifies this sacrificial attitude and behaviour is the key to a successful tour. " . . . to be like Jason Leonard, to hide your disappointment and help the cause: that's the ultimate. You might not be on the field the whole time to win a Test match, but you can help create the environment that helps win the Test match."[16]

Paying attention to the interior life

You are uniquely positioned to shape the community and provide the right setting in which individuals can flourish. Therefore, you need, regularly, to shift your vigilance from your outer life to your inner life. Observing what you are feeling, whether anger, joy, contentment or sorrow, honestly and fully, helps you to control your emotions. Thereby you guard against overreacting to events or encounters that put you under stress. Self-awareness is vital to remaining calm under pressure. You should acknowledge and process and, if appropriate, let go of any feelings inside you. By paying attention to your feelings, you understand yourself better. In turn, you are able to sift them, let go of what is false and hold on to what is true. This refining process enables you to behave with greater authenticity, and you avoid the roller-coaster of emotions that are generated by the ups and downs of relationships. Self-reflection can also help us to avert the Punch-and-Judy competitiveness that might lead you to be critical behind someone's back or to make personal attacks to someone's face.

A lack of self-awareness can leave us a prey to strong emotions. For example, some relatively minor setback can bring to mindhook an unresolved major issue from the past. In a way this cannot be helped. Your resulting emotion is then disproportionate to the incident. You might feel despair. You might regress and be reduced to feeling helpless and weak. Equally, if you are hiding from feelings of shame or inadequacy, then you can, unconsciously, transfer those emotions onto someone else. Of course, if, in turn, they unconsciously take on those uncomfortable stirrings, they might express your distressing emotions, presenting them as their own! If, however, you are aware of your own sensitivity, then you can contain your reaction.

Present conflicts can trigger past conflicts. When our reactions to disagreement seem to be stronger than they should be, it is worth asking oneself, "Of whom or what does this conflict remind me?" Our answer alerts us to unfinished business from the past that is still unresolved.

Although self-reflection can often bring some answers and some wisdom it is often beneficial, particularly in uncovering the unconscious stuff, to find a safe setting in which to take the risk of telling our story. In the act of telling and through the responses offered by the listener, new insights can be garnered. Once we have thoroughly engaged with this experience, gained the self-knowledge available and worked through any difficult aspects, we are then able to let it go.

Constructive feedback from someone you trust and whom you experience as being on your side is a genuine gift. Being told what they have perceived as they have listened to us and observed our body language or how our story has resonated with them can give us insights into our own experience. By contrast, advice or suggestions can be unhelpful, whilst criticism or personal attacks can often be destructive.

Whereas you might be able to dismiss particular feedback from one source, for example that you seem to be angry, if several people experience you as irate, then it would be worth reflecting deeply and searching inwardly for its origins. The working assumption must be that there is something behind this common response to you. Recognizing that you are holding, for instance, unresolved anger towards your parents increases your self-awareness, and can, if addressed, lead to some measure of healing.

Accepting what you cannot control

Homeostasis refers to resistance to change. Any set of relationships is deeply entrenched, fixated on the status quo. If any attempt is made to transform the current situation, the established pattern will adjust with the aim of keeping things as they are. Thus when you endeavour to bring change and to foster maturity, you are up against some powerful forces. Sometimes thwarted and occasionally sabotaged, you are bound to feel weak and ineffectual at times. Frustration can mount, and you can be assailed by defeatist thoughts. At these points you need some help. You can share your struggles with a friend. You should turn to God in prayer.

Besides looking to God to make a difference, praying through a situation can give you some emotional distance from the events. This will help you think more clearly, which, in turn, should lead you to a careful and considered next step.

Sleep and energy will be lost unless you can distinguish between what you can and cannot control. Learning to live with what is beyond your control is an important lesson for any leader. This is expressed simply in what is known as the serenity prayer written by the American theologian Reinhold Niebuhr:

> God grant me the serenity to accept the
>   things that I cannot change;
> the courage to change the things I can;
> and the wisdom to know the difference.

CHAPTER 5

Leaders who Enable Others to Grow Are Growing Themselves

As the leader, you mould the culture, the atmosphere of the church. You do this consciously and unconsciously. You need to recognize this reality and pay attention to it.

The next time you watch a choir conductor at work, notice how the choir mirrors the characteristics of their conductor. Timidity and flamboyance are both infectious. In the same way, the congregation reflects your characteristics. Therefore, if you want the people you lead to grow, then you must be growing yourself. Assuming you long for them to take steps towards greater maturity, then you must be developing too. Your own spiritual growth is integral and vital to your leadership; you must pay careful attention to your own relationship with God and to have someone to whom you are accountable. As it is your primary responsibility, it should be integrated into your rhythms and routines.

I have been an associate of a monastery at Crawley Down in Sussex, the Community of the Servants of the Will of God. I aim to go on retreat there for a couple of days twice a year. When I stay, I see the Superior Fr Colin to make a sacramental confession and to have a conversation about my prayer life. I have also agreed a "rule of life" with him, one of the commitments an associate makes. Besides regular retreats, I have promised to pray the services of Morning and Evening Prayer, and spend an additional 30 minutes each day in silent prayer. Although I do not always manage to adhere to these disciplines, they undergird my relationship with God. This pattern works for me, but each individual needs to find one that sustains them. In line with the wise saying "pray as you can, not as you can't", we need to find our own rhythm. Being accountable to someone is an important means of keeping your prayer and how you are faring to the forefront, and guarantees that your relationship with God will be examined periodically by you and whoever you choose to support you. Only if you are allocating time and energy to your own spiritual growth can you expect the people that you lead to do likewise. To nurture their growth, you must ensure that you are being nourished too.

Becoming the person God created you to be—not someone else!

Becoming more yourself is how you can become a better leader. Knowing and managing yourself needs to be your top priority. This might sound self-indulgent but it is not! Seeking to be a less anxious individual and becoming a more vividly defined individual are the two most significant functions of a leader.

You determine the emotional climate by the quality of your presence. If you can retain your equanimity under pressure, you protect the church from the contagion of anxiety. Should you inherit an uptight church, you should set yourself the task of helping it to relax. You engender this change of atmosphere by being relaxed and at ease, and through the careful use of humour, which serves to lighten the mood. As you set the right tone, your example reduces any tension and feeling of constraint, and frees everyone up to be themselves. A more prayerful and thoughtful church is the result.

Anxiety

Anxiety is the response to a real or imagined threat such as abandonment, not being cared for or respected. It can be like an electric current, flowing through a church. If you can contain your own anxiety, you can check the flow or, even better, be a circuit breaker.

When confronted with an anxious person, a great way to stay non-anxious is to be curious. Often anxious people can go on the attack. Your response must not be to counterattack or to defend yourself. The best way to defuse the situation is by listening and asking open questions. By being receptive and paying attention, you help to reduce the emotional temperature. Once the heat has dissipated, progress can be made.

One of the main advantages of a calm emotional atmosphere is that controversial issues can be discussed reasonably. There is a direct relationship between the intensity of one's emotions and one's ability to think clearly. By staying calm under pressure, you moderate everyone else's reactions.

When the atmosphere is saturated with anxiety, the leader is in jeopardy. Unless you can retain some distance, you are going to be the focal point for the swirling waves of anxiety, the eye of the storm. Now as the leader, you need to know that there is bound to be some anxiety in the church's life. The task for you is to distinguish between what rightly belongs to you because of your role and what does not. Providing you can distinguish between the two types of anxiety—anxiety that should rest with you because of your responsibilities and anxiety that should not—you can guard yourself against being overwhelmed.

Chronic anxiety can manifest itself in a church's life in many ways. Anxiety makes people feel uncomfortable. Significant dysfunctional behaviour is the result. People turning up late or not at all to meetings, the forming of cliques and factions, widespread apathy or multiple conflicts can all be indicative of a deeper malaise. They are all attempts to relieve anxiety by getting some emotional distance. Distancing is a feature of relationships where one of those involved tries to get some relief from the emotional intensity of the relationship by pulling back emotionally or by putting some physical distance between them and the other participants.

Physically withdrawing may appear an obvious route to emotional distance but it may not work. Alternatively, you can remain involved but achieve some emotional distance by hiding your real self. This is psychological withdrawal. Getting some distance, in either of these two ways, may only offer temporary relief.

Pushed to its limit, the quest to achieve some emotional distance leads to the relationship breaking down. Underlying this rupture will be chronic and acute anxiety. Albeit severing the relationship does bring some respite, it does have costly consequences. For both sides there will be some lasting emotional wounding, and this can have a negative impact on future relationships.

In the face of deep-seated anxiety, any attempt to tackle the issues is likely to be sabotaged. Rather than seeking to find solutions, it is better to start by facing the entrenched anxiety.

Your task is to track down the source of the anxiety. This begins by doing some research. Besides looking for answers, you are seeking to establish good relationships. Simply by getting to know people, you reduce the level of anxiety by bringing your own calmness to bear. Through conversation, you learn about the church's story and begin to discover the different perspectives on the current situation. Through gentle enquiry, you discover what is causing the anxiety. Your questions help everyone to achieve a measure of emotional distance. More detachment means greater insight. Thus, everyone starts to see reality more clearly.

A good starting point for your exploration is the history of the church's life. Draw up a chronological list of the significant events in the church's past, and focus on those that would have generated anxiety. These may include any noteworthy change of direction or contentious decision. Attention should also be paid to any unresolved issue lingering in the church's life.

Creating a less anxious church

Churches function well when their leaders are not threatened by adverse events. Anxiety is infectious; one person's anxiety can trigger another's. This process is multiplied many times over. Your task is to absorb anxiety and not to pass it on. By containing it, you stop the contagion in its tracks. This is done by remaining non-anxious. Reducing the level of anxiety in the emotional system is your work. It is essential to being an effective church leader. You need to manage your own anxiety. Through staying in meaningful contact with all those involved, your own calmness prevails.

One indicator of the level of anxiety in the church is how strong the pressure is to conform. Greater stress increases the collective need for togetherness and uniformity; diversity becomes less acceptable.

Who are you?

God is at work to make you into the person you were created to be. In every situation, God is shaping you. In trying to make you more Christlike, God looks for you to respond to every experience in repentance and faith. Whatever you are facing, God's goal is to form your character to be stronger and more loving. Becoming your true self is a liberating process; you are set free from what has bound you, held you back. This is spiritual growth. As the old saying goes, "Growing old is inevitable, growing up is optional." Honesty about what we need to change is essential. Courage to face ourselves and to endeavour to mature is fundamental. In all relationships, we must seek to live truthfully. This places us in a vulnerable position—we are on the line.

Increasing self-awareness and a greater readiness to take responsibility are two markers of personal development. Being confident about who we are and what we stand for enables us to be firm and decisive. Then we can let our "yes" be "yes" and our "no" be "no". Saying a categorical and simple "yes" or "no" is clear. Whereas equivocation creates uncertainty, the ability to be straightforward, even about what does not matter to us, creates an atmosphere in which everyone else is free to define themselves too. Knowing ourselves gives us the capacity for flexibility, whilst remaining firm and clear about its limits.

Marking boundaries

Healthy boundaries are founded on a strong sense of identity. Secure within those boundaries, you can be truly yourself in relationships and yet maintain your own values under pressure. Whatever the circumstances, you are then able to act in a way that is consistent with your deepest self.

With clearly defined boundaries, you are free to relate to others as you choose. You have the scope to express compassion without losing a sense of who you are. You are not overwhelmed by whatever needs or emotions are around you. Self-assured, you do not need to act to meet someone else's need, although you can choose to do so. Intact boundaries mean that you are less reactive. If others are anxious, you can stay calm. In your encounters with other people, you are able to define yourself. Similarly, you do not invade other people's boundaries. After a conversation, you should be able to say: I have not taken on anything that is not mine or given you anything that is not yours.

When boundaries are recognized and respected, everyone is allowed to express themselves and no one seeks to dominate anyone else. With blurred boundaries (I do not know where I end and you begin), a person swings from merging with others to being separate from them. The goal is to be connected and clearly defined at the same time. In other words, you are aiming to be comfortable in any relationship, yet always able to maintain your own identity while engaging freely with people.

When you are under attack, you should defend your boundaries. For example, if you are being patronized, you should refuse to be treated like a child. In taking this stand, you are maintaining your status; you are an adult and the dialogue should be characterized by mutual respect. Undergirding your position is a positive value: all people are of equal value, created in the image of God, and as such deserving of respect.

Knowing your own beliefs, wants, needs and intuitions can help you to understand how you relate to others. By paying attention to your inner life, noticing your reactions and reflecting upon them, you can deepen your self-awareness. When you have a strong reaction to someone, the reasons for it will be related to who you are. Be alert to any of these strong reactions. Any responses that surprise you by their intensity are worth further exploration. If you can discover what it is about yourself that has been touched, then you learn more about who you are.

Through a high degree of self-awareness and a strong sense of your own identity, you can retain healthy boundaries in every relationship. In a community where everyone has a good self-understanding and a clear sense of their core values, healthy reciprocal relationships in which everyone expects respect and treats others with respect are the norm. To foster this kind of community everyone needs to be more confident about who they are. Without this self-confidence, intimacy becomes problematic. Intimacy is dependent on both parties feeling secure and safe. It is hard to respect the boundaries of someone else if we are not sure about our own. When both people know who they are and can make free decisions about how much of themselves to share, then intimacy becomes possible. If the relationship is characterized by self-awareness and mutual respect, then both people can take the risk of being vulnerable with each other. Clear boundaries make it possible for us to be ourselves while also being in a close relationship with others.

Being aware of your own boundaries means you can spot when they are being challenged. When your boundaries are under threat, it can be a sign of some unaddressed anxiety that you or the other person feel. Having a high degree of self-knowledge should enable you to differentiate between the two.

Self-differentiation

Self-differentiation is the capacity of an individual to act according to their values, especially in the face of pressure to do otherwise. In short, it is the ability to say "I" when those around you are demanding "you" or "we". The self-differentiated individual will be able to say, "This is who I am, what I believe, what I stand for, and what I will do or will not do" in a given situation. They will not blame others for their own behaviour but will take responsibility for their actions.

Self-differentiation goes hand in hand with maturity. Martin Luther's famous speech in 1521 before the papal authority commission is the epitome of self-differentiation:

> Unless I can be instructed and convinced with evidence from the Holy Scriptures or with open, clear and distinct grounds and reasoning—and my conscience is captive to the Word of God—then I cannot and will not recant, because it is neither safe nor wise to act against conscience. Here I stand. I can do no other. So help me God.[17]

A caveat is necessary here. Whereas self-differentiation is defined by the taking of clear positions, this does not mean that you will not change your mind. Indeed, part of the rationale for self-differentiation is to engage in dialogue. In this exchange of views, you may gain new insights. Thereby the process of self-differentiation continues. It never stops.

You need to recognize that you can be mistaken, and that you need to go on learning. You offer your own position, not defensively but vulnerably. You enter discussion on the premise that you do not possess a total command of the issue under discussion. You accept that whatever position you hold is contingent. You concede that however firmly you hold your opinion, it is also wise to engage again on the issue. By checking once more the coherence and cogency of your argument, you go on working towards your definitive view. This approach is the basis of an honest exchange, whereby all the protagonists can learn something. This modus operandi means that everyone benefits and represents a commitment to go on learning. Thereby the iterative development of our thinking continues.

People who are confident in who they are and what they believe are able to be comfortably connected with others. A person with a high level of self-differentiation is less needy, and able to be distinct from rather than dependent on those around them. They are able to be themselves in company and to remain comfortable.

It is important not to think that self-differentiation is code for militancy or intransigence. Compromise remains possible but only on the basis of what makes sense to the participants, not as a result of pressure. In fact, a self-differentiated person will be entirely comfortable in changing their mind, if they have understood the necessity to do so. By contrast, someone who is not self-differentiated is more defensive and more likely to become firmly entrenched in their position when challenged.

In so far as each individual in church is confident in their own identity, they will be able to keep a close connection with each other, even in the heat of conflict. As a result, the church will be more cohesive in its common life with a greater depth of mutual caring. In any ongoing task or a project, the church will be better able to act as a unit.

An ability to regulate their emotions is a feature of individuals with a high level of differentiation. Consequently in churches where self-differentiation is encouraged, the passion generated by deeply held convictions is more likely to channelled into the ministry and mission of the church, rather than be dissipated in anxious interactions and petty squabbles.

Striving to become more self-differentiated is a vital task for any leader. Being a more clearly defined person will be of great benefit to your church, and, likewise, to any system to which you belong, including your family. It could also be argued that there is a theological imperative to work on your self-differentiation: you have a responsibility to develop into the person God has made you to be.

Helping the church to mature!

One of our aims for the churches with which we are involved is to foster the individual growth of its members. Mature Christians should:

- know more about what they believe and why they believe it;
- have a strong sense of the values they cherish and how their values should drive their actions;
- be clear about their long-term goals and their connection with the current direction of their lives;
- recognize their responsibilities and be determined to live them out faithfully.

This definition of maturity reflects insights from the world of "family systems" thinking.[18]

If you are relating to someone who holds a contrary view, then you will be impelled to state and defend your position. If you want to help those around you to become more self-differentiated, you need to be committed to raising your own level of self-differentiation. Insomuch as you increase your self-differentiation, you compel others to follow suit.

The healthiest communities have more individuality. Emotionally separate and autonomous people relate easily to others. They do not have an agenda of their own, beyond getting to know others. In interactions, they are looking for mutual exchange. Content with who they are, and comfortable in their own skin, they have no need to use the other for their own ends. They are not looking to control or impose themselves. Mutuality is their goal. Equal, affirming relationships are their aim. Strong individuals make for better, healthier communities.

Conversely, should there be pressure to conform within a community, then individuality is stifled. This attempt to deny individual differences is often founded on the error of making unity tantamount to uniformity. A coercive network of relationships that stifles individuality is the outcome. Stunted individuals are the damaging consequence.

Self-differentiation and being a calm leader

If you are highly self-differentiated, you are not likely to be swayed by the emotional climate around you. You will not be affected by praise or criticism. You will exercise self-control whatever the pressure. Far from reactive, you are free to choose when to express your emotions.

Conflict, however, does put you under particular stress. If you are to be effective in managing conflict, then you have to be able to control yourself. Self-control arises from self-awareness, from knowing and understanding yourself. Being aware of the powerful emotions stirred up by a tense situation, yet refraining from expressing them, is a sign of strength. By remaining calm, you help to moderate everyone else's reaction. In helping to keep everyone calm and clear-thinking, you facilitate rational discussion. Thereby the probability of finding some kind of resolution is increased.

Anxious systems

There is a connection between the leader's level of self-differentiation and the anxiety level of a congregation. There is reciprocity here; it works in both directions. Anxious churches tend to put more pressure on the leader not to differentiate, not be different. This emphasis on conformity is inhibiting; it acts against your efforts to bring about change and implement plans to develop the church. Similarly, churches led by people with a low level of self-differentiation are more likely to be anxious. A lack of clear and strong leadership creates a power vacuum. Others make a bid for power. Without a sense of direction, church life seems aimless and repetitive. Discontent follows. Grumbling and complaining begin to characterize the church's life. Understandably, everyone becomes more anxious; no one feels safe or secure.

Playfulness and paradoxical behaviour

When a church gets anxious, relationships become more serious. To counteract this prevailing mood, you can decide to be playful. Through humour, you can lift the heaviness that is blighting relationships and interaction. Acting playfully frees other people by forcing them out of their solemn "games".

Closely allied to playfulness is paradoxical behaviour. Whereas this has its dangers, it could be worth a try if every other attempt to bring change to the system has simply reinforced the current patterns.

Whether acting playfully or paradoxically, you challenge the status quo. You break free from any emotional dependency. You break out of the pattern of repetitive encounters. Shifting your position makes the other people in your relationship network behave differently; they have no choice. They have to adjust to the change initiated by you.

Emotional distance

"Emotional distance" relates to how much of our inner selves we share in our relationships. If we are happy to reveal something of who we are, and particularly what we feel, then people will feel connected with us. On the other hand, should you prefer to keep your distance, others will do likewise and keep theirs.

At its extremes, you can clearly see the impact of emotional distance on the church. If we keep too great an emotional distance, there is no connection of any depth between people. The church community becomes a collection of disparate individuals. On the other hand, if we are too close, we do not have enough space to relate as two distinct individuals. We merge. This results in a fused unity. Diversity has been lost. Stripped of the differences between people that would enrich the church, this unity arises out of uniformity and is a form of denial. This pretence leads to an underlying and destructive anxiety.

If you are confidently self-differentiated, you can choose the emotional distance between you and others. If you feel that you are being crowded, you can create some space by remaining in control of your emotions and by defining your position. This creates some space without severing the connection. If you would like to get closer to someone, you can share more of yourself, which provides an opportunity for the relationship to deepen. Yet this increased sharing needs to be exploratory, in order to guard against overloading the relationship.

The leader sets the tone, the emotional temperature of the church. The warmth or coolness of the atmosphere is noticed by those who come into the church community. This first impression is vital; it is hard to shift it. As leader you will influence and shape the emotional pitch over time. The longer you have been in post the more responsible you are for how the church feels to those who visit or look to join. If your ethos is warm, open and friendly, the church will gradually imitate these attributes, providing that you take the risk of sharing yourself. There is a balance to be struck here, however. You have to tread a fine line between being too reserved and overloading the community with your own emotions. By talking about how you feel, and what you think, you enable others to do likewise. This, in turn, creates an open atmosphere where everyone feels free to be themselves. If too much emotion is swirling around, and the level of intimacy is high, this is likely to feel uncomfortable to some. Certainly those looking to belong may find it too much, and a shade unsafe. This danger needs to be borne in mind.

Self-differentiation and clarity of thought

If you have a high level of self-differentiation, you will not be knocked off course by a strong negative reaction to a decision that may have been taken. When you do come under this kind of pressure, you need to exercise self-control, especially around how much of what you are feeling you reveal. The first task here is to monitor how you are feeling and to check that your own emotions correspond with reality. It is so easy to get things out of perspective or to be swayed by the experience of those close to you. Your feelings can easily get skewed by others' feelings or by other factors like tiredness. Asking others to give you feedback on whether your emotions match up to what is happening or not can be helpful. Sometimes it is hard to work that out on your own.

You need to discriminate between what they are feeling and what is actually the case. For example, a feeling of rejection does not mean that they are being rejected. Rather it could be coming from your past, a previous experience that has been hooked by a feature of your present relationships. It is important to ensure that the emotional coherence is retained—your emotions correspond to reality—and that you understand and stay in control of your feelings. Thereby you maintain the ability to choose to share and what to share of your emotions, instead of running the risk of losing your temper or dumping your emotions on someone. In the event that you do lose control, the emotional level around you will escalate unhelpfully.

Ideally, you need to remain unperturbed by any anxiety swirling around. Then you are detached enough to see the situation accurately. From this standpoint, and by calm analysis, you can identify the possible options before deciding what needs to be done. Remain calm and think clearly—this means that you can continue to be an effective leader, even when there is a strong anxious response to your leadership.

Mature leaders are not overwhelmed by the size of a problem or by the prevailing level of anxiety. On the contrary, they are prepared to be flexible, look at the different options on offer and make a considered decision about the best course of action. Their response is characterized by clarity and objectivity, in spite of the tension. Clear convictions will shape their thinking and their conclusion.

The aim of the leader's decision to define their position should not be to galvanize support. Rather it is to prompt others to define themselves, to do the work necessary to self-differentiate. The goal is for everyone in your church to know what they think and why they think it. Each individual's confident grasp of their own position, allied to an ability to explain their underlying reasoning, makes discussions constructive, whereby a mutually acceptable resolution more likely. Besides constituting a healthy response to the conflict, this approach, hopefully, avoids polarization.

Instead of a headlong rush to get others to join their "side", everyone is encouraged to determine their own standpoint first.

Test case: Paul, circumcision and the Early Church

Consider, by way of example, Paul and the Gentiles. Through his mission to the Gentiles, Paul came to the firm conviction that to insist that male converts must be circumcised in order to be included in God's people was mistaken. He believed with great passion that this rite was unnecessary— faith in Christ and baptism were sufficient—and an insuperable obstacle in the way of Gentile believers. With a tenable and zealous commitment to his position, Paul railed against his opponents, sometimes resorting to blunt and pointed advice; in his letter to the Galatians, he urges his "enemies" to go the whole way and emasculate themselves. Despite his somewhat injudicious expression, Paul did want to stay connected to those who, at times, opposed him and questioned his credentials as a "latter-day" apostle, a "Johnny-come-lately". In particular, the church in Jerusalem had, at times, lurched from apparent support to expressing legitimate concerns to actively undermining him. Yet, Paul desperately longed to maintain his relationship with the church there, the mother church, and to express the common unity between its Gentile and Jewish wings. This aspiration found tangible expression in the collection. Although it was inspired by the relative poverty of the church in Jerusalem and a pressing need, its symbolic significance was very important to Paul. It represented the strong emotional relationship between the new and emerging Gentile church with Jerusalem, where the nascent Christian communities had arisen out of the wonder of the resurrection and the joy of the outpouring of the Holy Spirit: they were one family, God's family. In terms of family systems, Paul strongly self-differentiates and, notwithstanding the seriousness and fundamental nature of the dispute, seeks to stay emotionally connected.

CHAPTER 6

Modelling and Facilitating Good Conversations

Each congregation is unique. Yet, all are working with a small set of core issues: mission and how to achieve it, bolstering strengths and mitigating weaknesses, how best to use resources, anxiety and how to manage it, and wholeness and how to maintain it.

Healthy churches have a sense of purpose. The questions "What is God calling us to be?" and "What is the meaning of what we do?" are constantly addressed. Discerning and articulating a clear direction and a coherent rationale for the shape of the church's life now keep the community focused and looking forward.

Once a vision has been determined, then the task of working out how to make it happen begins. When the church has the requisite gifts and energetic enthusiasm for the vision, then it will be able to journey towards its vision with confidence. There will be an accompanying sense of purpose and a belief in the community's ability to shape its own future.

Too wide a gap between present reality and the envisaged future can create some dissonance and affect the impetus behind putting the church's plan into action. Without a true grasp of present reality, any proposal about what needs to be done is bound to be based on false assumptions. Inevitably, unrealistic targets sap everyone's energy and are demoralizing. By contrast, a sound assessment of the current situation is a firm basis for planning for the future.

The ideal model of a church is that of a harmonious team where each individual's contribution is recognized and valued. Besides this basic tenet, each individual member should be enabled to be confident in who they are and what they believe, whilst remaining open to what other people have to offer. A mark of a healthy church is that people take responsibility for their own behaviour and for the tasks assigned them with a sense of purpose and gratitude.

Two key variables determine the health of a church: emotional maturity and the quality of communication. The level of emotional maturity of the people in the system and of the leadership is crucially important. How much anxiety and tension is flowing through the relationships will profoundly affect the nature of the interactions. One diagnostic indicator of anxiety is how much people are blaming others. Let us turn our attention to communication.

Communication under pressure

Communication should be based on mutual respect and openness. The character of communication between people comes under particular pressure during a conflict. Yet, not only should difference and conflict be seen as an essential aspect of any human community, they should be valued as an opportunity for everyone to learn and grow. To realize this opportunity to grow, the church needs to be committed to certain ground rules that should govern how individuals relate to each other. In any disagreement, the participants must avoid direct criticism or blame of the other. Everyone should take responsibility for their own behaviour. This means that we pay attention to our emotions and choose carefully what feelings to voice in a relationship. A shared resolve to pursue self-awareness is integral to any church seeking to learn through conflict.

Good communication makes for a good community

Good communication is integral to a healthy community. Anything that can be done to develop the speaking and listening skills of individuals will increase the capacity of people to relate well to each other. The leader's role is to model good communication. You must speak constructively and listen attentively. Furthermore, you must be ready to teach on this important topic. In all your interactions, and especially in meetings, you will have opportunities to help people learn to express themselves in ways which help to sustain good relationships and foster mutual understanding.

Good communication defined

Good communication is marked by three features. It is open: as much as possible, within the bounds of mutual respect and confidentiality, communication should engender transparency. Only for clear reasons should information be withheld. Secondly, it is direct: we avoid going through an intermediary. Whereas indirect communication distances people from each other, direct communication strengthens relationships. Thirdly, it should be honest. Although honesty sometimes has to be tempered, we should certainly shun dishonesty. Deception undermines relationships and is destructive of the community's life.

With these three markers of healthy communication put in place, let us now look at some particular obstacles to effective communication, and how to tackle them.

Be specific

Help the speaker to focus on specific events and incidents instead of making sweeping generalizations:

> "She always makes life difficult for me."
>> "*Tell me about an occasion when this happened.*"

> "The sermons have been very poor recently."
>> "*What specifically haven't you liked?*"

Listen—don't interrupt

Let the speaker have his or her say. When someone interrupts, you can, in the first place, ignore them, but if they persist, you will have to make it clear that they must defer to the current speaker. At the same time, you can stress that there will be an opportunity for them to be heard: *"Bill, I'd like to hear your thoughts, but for now let's listen to Mary's opinion."*

Revealing the underlying point of tension

When you are faced with someone blaming or attacking someone else, do not collude with or challenge them, at least at first. Rather, attempt to help them to identify the source of the tension.

> "He's so inconsiderate, he's always late."
>> *"Being on time is clearly important to you."*

> "She's lying. There is no truth in what she's saying."
>> *"You seem to see things completely differently."*

Speaking only for yourself

When someone seeks to include other people on their side of a conflict, keep the focus on their own feelings and reactions. The goal is to keep the communication direct; you are to insist that they stick to expressing their own views. Discourage them from speaking for other people. Whether they are fairly representing them or misrepresenting them—and you do not usually know either way—your task is to encourage them to own and share their point of view.

> "Nobody in the church likes that family."
>> *"Could you tell me more about why you dislike them?"*

> "Phil and Anne have also been verbally attacked by him."
>> *"Tell me about when you have found him aggressive."*

Letting others speak for themselves

When an individual interprets someone else's opinion, you should deter them and defend the right of everyone to speak for themselves.

"I think that Steve is trying to say that this change is far too radical, and that we are throwing the baby out with the bathwater."

"I'd like to let Steve continue, so that he can let us know what he thinks."

Encouraging everyone to participate who would like to do so

Especially when there are some dominant voices, it can be liberating for the less confident to be offered a particular opportunity to speak.

"What about those who've not spoken yet? Are there any comments and thoughts you'd like to share? I'd like to hear your take on this issue."

Disclosing statements framed as a question

When someone effectively makes their point under the guise of a question, do not answer the question but reflect back the implicit statement. By so doing, offer them an opportunity to say more.

"Don't you agree that it's just downright irresponsible to have a building project when our finances are so stretched?"

"Sounds like you feel this is irresponsible. Tell me what you think."

Avoiding being drawn into an argument on one side or the other

When a protagonist seeks to enlist you on their side of the conflict, resist. Instead, turn the focus on to them, their feelings about and their side of the argument. By guarding against being drawn into taking sides, you keep a useful neutrality which means that you could, if need be, mediate in the dispute.

"Don't you believe what she did was totally irresponsible?"

"Obviously, you believe it was irresponsible. Can you tell me more about it?"

"Wouldn't you be livid, if he had done that to you?"
  "I'm interested in hearing more about your anger."

Staying calm under attack

When someone starts to blame you, do not get defensive or launch a counterattack. Your goal is to maintain a good relationship and to remain in conversation. Do not defend yourself or attack them. Rather stay calm; focus on hearing and understanding what is troubling your critic. Be curious about their thinking. Ask questions to explore their point of view.

"Well, I can see that you're taking her side."
  "Sounds like you feel that I'm being unfair. Can you explain to me why?"

"You're throwing your weight around again. You always want to get your own way."
  "So you feel that I'm exercising too much control. How could we do things differently?"

Clarify and explain if appropriate.

"My task is to lead this process: I have been given the authority to facilitate this consultation. I am not here to influence the outcome but to help you, the whole group, to reach your decision."

If you do feel rattled and unsure how to respond, you can simply be honest about your feelings. To avoid the confrontation escalating into a personal clash between you and your antagonist, you can draw others into the conversation. In broadening the exchanges by including others, you diffuse some of the tension.

"I feel upset and unsure how to respond. I'm committed to respecting everyone's view. Hence I don't want to dismiss what you say. I wonder how others feel about the point that has been made."

Speaking from the heart

Rightly, there is a lot of emphasis in Christian circles on listening. Various courses and books highlight what a gift it is to be heard and understood. There is less stress placed on authentic speaking. Yet, for any meaningful conversation, there needs to be thoughtful speaking, as well as active listening. Talking honestly, and at any depth, is not easy; it means taking a risk. To reveal something of who you are, what you think and feel is to make yourself vulnerable. However, it is only by taking this risk that relationships can develop and deepen. This kind of speaking I have labelled as "speaking from the heart". Introducing the thinking of the French philosopher Emmanuel Levinas (1906–95), John Wild of Yale University argues that in response to the "questioning glance" of the other, a real response, a responsible answer must be given. This means that I must be ready to put my world into words and to offer it to the other. There can be no free interchange without something to give. Responsible communication depends on an initial act of generosity, a giving of my world to them with all its dubious assumptions and arbitrary features. They are then exposed to the questions of the other, and an escape from egotism become possible.[19]

Authentic communication depends on individuals taking the risk of revealing what they think and feel. "Speaking from the heart" makes conversations meaningful, fosters mutual understanding and engenders community.

In many exchanges, we tend to talk about anything and anyone but ourselves. This is safer. Sharing something of your own thoughts and feelings is risky. However, although you do make yourself vulnerable, you also make it possible for a closer relationship to develop. You create an opportunity for genuine intimacy. On the other hand, you can arrive at a false closeness through talking about someone else you have in common. By speaking negatively about them, you side together against them. This collusion brings you nearer to each other, but it is based on the exclusion of the third person who is absent. In so far as they are distanced, pushed away, you feel nearer to each other. This is accentuated by a shared sense of superiority. This can feel cosy, but there is an essential falseness about it.

Rather than seeking closeness, you might want to distance yourself from your conversational partner. One way to guarantee getting some space is to go on the attack. This can be the result of some provocation. You might be angered by something that they have done or not done. Their failings, in your view, warrant a dressing down. There is an honesty and straightforwardness about this kind of full frontal assault. However, your motives could be less clear cut. Attack can be the best form of defence. In order to divert attention from your own failings, you blame someone else for what has gone wrong, or even worse, criticize their character and their motives.

Talking about someone behind their back or being directly disapproving are not ways of speaking from the heart. There is a lack of honesty and openness. You are not revealing what is happening with you. Instead, you are excluding or attacking and both these approaches show defensiveness and put up barriers. They make authentic intimacy harder.

When you hear someone talking about someone else, your task is to turn the focus back to the speaker and to encourage self-disclosure.

> **Demanding:** "When are they going to start showing me the respect I deserve?"
> *"I'd like to know when you felt they started showing disrespect. What happened?"*
>
> **Blaming:** "It's their entire fault. If only they had been ready on time."
> *"Tell me about the impact of what happened on you"* or
> *"What would you like to see happen?"*
>
> **Mind-reading:** "You're trying to mess this event up for everyone."
> *"I'd be interested to know why you think that I'm trying to mess it up."*

By marked contrast, speaking from the heart is about keeping others informed about your thoughts and feelings. By offering your own experience, you set an example for others to follow. Everyone is encouraged to share more of themselves, whereby relationships are taken to a deeper level. In so far as we desire to draw close to someone, we must approach others with a willingness to share what we are thinking and feeling.

Speaking from the heart is about making statements that reveal what is going on inside us. It is about telling others our feelings, our needs, our preferences and our reactions to what is happening. These means taking the risk of starting with the first person pronoun; some examples follow.

> **Feelings:** "I feel upset by what happened at the meeting last night."

> **Needs:** "I'm not a last-minute person, and I can't work at speed, so I need you to get me the information at least a day in advance".

> **Reactions:** "When we discuss things so late at night, I don't sleep well."

> **Preferences:** "I like it when we find time once a week to talk together properly".

Whereas these statements convey a clear message to your conversational partner, you are not speaking about what they have done or not done primarily. Instead, the prime focus is on how you have responded. You are disclosing what you feel and how you have been affected. This presents the other person with an opportunity to understand you and your perspective better, and to respond. The relationship can deepen through such an exchange, since, through clear and honest communication, you offer a good model of how it is done. If they, in turn, reciprocate, then you have both taken steps towards greater mutual understanding.

This kind of speaking requires self-awareness: you need to know what you are thinking and feeling. "What exactly do I feel?" and "How is this affecting me?" are two questions that can help self-reflection, and get you in touch with what is happening to you. You need to exercise some discrimination here. There is a need to work out what is fundamentally about who you are, and what might be coming from other sources. The more you practise the discipline of regular self-reflection, the better you will be able to tell apart what you have absorbed from the people around you—their reaction—from your own authentic response to what has happened. Once you have reached this conclusion, you then need the courage to share what you think, even if it is markedly different from the prevailing view. Being honest and open makes you vulnerable, especially when what you say challenges what others have already said; it can feel risky—after all you do not know what the reaction is going to be.

Clearly, the capacity to speak from the heart is cultivated by the discipline of self-reflection. Taking time and thought to get in touch with how you are feeling and to observe what is happening to you demands commitment. It is a discipline that is rewarding, and you will notice the fruit of it. As a result, you become more self-aware. This greater self-knowledge will impact on all your interactions and relationships. When you grow and develop, everyone around you benefits.

Another feature of centred speaking is a determination to speak only for yourself: you do not seek to bolster your position by pretending to speak for others too. Your sentences start with "I" not "We"—unless, of course, you have been delegated to speak for a group! Additionally, you avoid generalizations; instead you talk about specific times and places. A readiness to take responsibility for your own behaviour and words, born out of a readiness to change and grow, is another characteristic of speaking from the heart. You know that you need to learn and be transformed; you cannot make changing someone else your goal. Trying to do so can make you demanding and leave you frustrated! Instead, let the change in you prompt others to do likewise. As you develop, everyone experiences the change. They are challenged to do likewise, to learn to "speak from the heart".

Being a good role model

In order to facilitate good communication in your church, you may need to do some specific teaching on it. It is essential that you model good communication yourself, and certainly, if you do not, you will undermine your teaching on this topic. This is far from easy, especially when under pressure. If you want your church to mature, then you must be open, direct and honest in your communications and seek to speak from the heart. Committing yourself to good communication demands emotional and spiritual discipline; only in so far as you understand yourself, your values and feelings can you hope to communicate from the centre of who you are. Seeking greater self-awareness through reflection, spiritual disciplines, including prayer, and seeking feedback from friends and colleague are integral to becoming a good communicator.

Whenever you are in dialogue with others, attentive listening should characterize how you relate to others. In this way you help others to speak from their centre. If you are giving careful consideration to them, you enable others to take the risk of saying what they think and feel.

In your leadership role, you must also be on your guard. You must look out for bad communication, and do what you can to modify it or to challenge it directly. This requires you to stay calm, and to have the requisite skills and the courage to put them to use. By taking the sting out of destructive statements, you can protect the church from their harmful consequences. You help to keep the community healthy, and moving towards maturity.

When you are chairing meetings, you have a particular responsibility and power to foster good communication. In a meeting, centred speaking and deep listening are the signs of a mature body, whose members have learned to relate to each other attentively. As the leader, you can set the standards and have them formally agreed. Then you must defend them. While upholding the agreed norms demands vigilance and strength, it is important. The rewards are great. Within reach is a shared and growing, mutual understanding, alongside a deeper and sharper awareness of each other. Authentic encounters, elusive and precious, are more likely. Through these personal exchanges, we can experience something of God's immanence.

When what you are going to say will be difficult for the other person to hear, it is important to speak about yourself, your view, your feelings, and the impact on you, not to blame or accuse. This is the mature approach as it is about taking responsibility for your opinions and feelings. It also reduces the risk of the other person becoming defensive, and the potential for destructive conflict.

"I felt annoyed when you changed the venue from the hall to the church because of all the hard work I'd put into getting the hall ready."

"It's very frustrating for me when you get the draft to me late, as it gives me less time to check it before it is distributed."

Say what you would prefer. Rather than withholding information about your own desires or stating them aggressively, it is better to state clearly and calmly your own likes and dislikes. The additional advantage of this candour is that it implicitly invites others to be equally honest.

"My preference is . . . "

"What I'd like to see is . . . "

"It would be helpful to me if you could . . . "

Clarify your intentions. If people know what you are trying to achieve, then they can choose to help you succeed or not. Either way, it obviates any misunderstanding about the goal.

"I'm hoping that we can finish this meeting by 10 p.m."

"What I want is for us to enjoy working together."

"My intention is for us to be a strong, capable team."

Empowering others

The way in which you interact with and respond to others can have a significant impact on their ability to "speak from the heart". You can empower people to discover what they think or feel. You can encourage them to give voice to their thoughts and feelings. On the other hand, when you, by inattention, discourage others from discovering and articulating their own insights and emotions, you undermine their sense of worth.

You effectively assert yourself over and against them. If you act as though you are superior, you make them feel inferior. Here are five responses to your conversational partner that disempower them.

> **Advising:** Telling the speaker how to solve their problem rather than helping them to explore it for themselves. "You should change the day on which your group meets."

> **Judging:** Criticizing the speaker. "That's no way to react!"

> **Diagnosing:** Making claims about the speaker's situation. "What's really bothering you is that you're feeling left out."

> **Probing:** Asking for further information out of curiosity or posing a leading question which thinly veils an accusation. "Why did you do that?" "Have you considered saying sorry yourself?"

> **Cajoling:** Although the intention is to reassure, the speaker might well experience this kind of response as distancing and even as a rebuff. "Don't worry about it. You'll be fine." "Pull yourself together. In a few weeks, it'll all be over."

Instead, a good leader seeks to empower others by giving them their full attention and listening patiently.

Most people are enabled to draw upon their own inner resources, previous experiences, knowledge and insights through the supportive presence of someone else. Paying proper attention to another individual means putting aside your own ideas, opinions and preferences, in order to listen. This requires internal recognition of your thoughts and feelings. Otherwise, your own reactions are likely to preoccupy you, or to distract and interfere with your engagement with the other person. This means that you need to note what is happening inside you, whilst keeping your distance from whatever is stirring there. Your level of self-awareness is defined by your ability to see your internal landscape but not become absorbed by it. To become more present to those you encounter, you need to give some time and energy to deepen your own self-awareness.

When, in conversation with someone, we discover their anxiety, pain or uncertainty, we can feel uncomfortable. This discomfort means that we can be tempted to curtail the exchange at this level and make either a premature rush to solutions or bring the dialogue to an end. While offering advice or suggesting a way forward to someone might seem to be helpful, it can put a block on their own grappling with the issue and hinder them from finding their own answers. Besides hampering their thoughts, this drive to seek a resolution can disempower. Well-meaning advice can debilitate. At its worst, it can lead to dependency, grounded in the belief that you are the expert.

Enhancing co-operative communication with others

Co-operation demands both the willingness to articulate our own position and to engage respectfully with the opinions of others. We need to be able both to assert ourselves and to encourage the expression of different points of view. Only then can we avoid the risks of, on one hand, not making our proper contribution to the discussion and, on the other, undermining the contribution of others. There are some underlying skills that a leader can develop in order to enhance co-operative communications.

Paraphrasing

Paraphrasing is summarizing in your own words the significant aspects of what someone has said. By paraphrasing you demonstrate that you have listened, and it offers a straightforward method of checking and clarifying that you have understood. It affirms the worth of the speaker and, encourages them to say more. In heated exchanges, it slows down the pace and reduces the intensity of the interaction; when under attack, it can reduce your defensiveness and give you some time to formulate a considered response.

When paraphrasing, remember that you're trying to understand the speaker's perspective, so keep the focus on them. This means that your responses will be about what they have said. "So you felt . . .", "You believe that . . .", "When she left the room, you were feeling abandoned". While it is better, generally, to restate what you have heard in your words, it can be important to reflect back specifically words which refer to strong feelings. Otherwise, the speaker might feel that a carefully chosen word that captures exactly how they felt has been missed. Similarly, when paraphrasing it is helpful to mirror some of the emotional intensity as you encapsulate what you've heard. An attempt at paraphrasing may begin like this:-

> "So you were really fearful to be asked at such short notice . . . "

> "You thought that I was being unfair when . . . "

> "Let me just check that I understand you. You're saying that you want to come off the cleaning team as soon as possible."

Being receptive

Even if you are being castigated, you should be ready to invite further information and comment. Only when you have a comprehensive grasp of the case being made, are you in a position to respond intelligently.

> "Say more about . . . "

> "Could you give me a specific example . . . "

> "I'm interested in what you have in mind. Can you tell me what you envisage?"

Listening for harmony

Co-operation is strengthened when points of agreement are recognized and underlined.

> "I agree with you that . . . "

> "I share your excitement about the possibilities . . . "

"I see that we have the same goals . . . "

Planning the conversation

For an important conversation, it is productive to spend some time at the outset agreeing its process and purpose. This removes the risk of being at cross-purposes about the reason for and structure of the encounter.

For example, for a more informal encounter; "Anne, I would like to make some suggestions about the music for the service on Sunday. We can agree together what should be included. Which evening this week would be best for you?"

For a more formal meeting, more time will need to be spent on establishing a common mind on the purpose and process, during which there should be many opportunities for the participants to shape the outcome.

1. Agree on purpose

   Explain your purpose:
   "Today I'd like us to discuss who we might add to our team."

   Check whether there is a dissenting view:
   "Does anyone have a different understanding?"

2. Jointly design a process

   "Now we've got agreement on the purpose, I want to propose a process for the meeting and to see what you think of it."

   Advocate a process and share reasoning:
   "I suggest we think through what kind of person we need on the team before we begin to think of names. I want us to try to reach a consensus decision about who we should ask. Yet, we do need two new members to help with the general workload, so, if need be, I'll have to decide, taking your views into account, of course."

Check whether there are any suggested revisions to the process:
"Can anyone see how my proposal can be improved? Or maybe there is a better process we can adopt?"

Reach agreement about the process:
"Do we have agreement about the process?"

3. Begin by discussing the content of the conversation

"OK, now we've agreed the process, let's begin by discussing what kind of person we need on the team, in terms of skill and personality."

Nurturing and communication

At the heart of long-term care for the church family is the task of training members in good communication. By modelling high quality communication, the leader can set an example to everyone. Also, when the need arises, the leader can explain what it means to speak and listen in a way which demonstrates respect and appreciation. For example, when the leader is chairing a meeting, they can state that one of the process goals is to encourage more people to participate in the discussions. By seeking to pay attention to the views of more people in formal meetings, this practice should influence the church's wider life. As you make it clear that it is a goal and demonstrate it, others learn to help others to find their voice in their other interactions. Here is a possible list of rules commensurate with the aims of increasing participation—in a church group or meeting, for example a Parochial Church Council meeting:

1. No one is allowed to speak without receiving permission from the group leader.
2. The leader has the right to defer the right to speak to those who have not made a contribution yet, rather than by the order in which the requests to talk are made.

3. The leader is allowed to slow down the pace of the discussion by pausing between comments, in order to encourage wider participation: some people need more time to digest which has been said and to formulate a response.

When a meeting is called in the name of Christ and submits to his authority, he is in the midst, and the community can rely on the guidance of the Holy Spirit. In recognition that Christ is the instigator of our actions and the shaper of our corporate life, each meeting should begin with a Bible reading and a prayer. Our common desire is that our discussion and decisions should be, and should clearly be seen to be, in response to God's initiative.

The effectiveness of the meetings, as a means of co-operating with the Holy Spirit in discovering God's will depends upon the following conditions:

1. Each member should try to see the matter under discussion in the setting of the whole of life, in the light of the common purpose, and avoid pressing a merely personal point.
2. Everyone should be open to hear what others have to say.
3. Participants should speak their mind simply and directly.
4. No one should remain silent because they fear the consequences of what they have to say.

Co-operation is fundamental to community life

A curious, questioning response turns communication into dialogue. In community, dialogue and discussion should be about a shared quest for truth. It is foundational that we reason together. Recognizing our own fallibility, we know the value of working together to reach decisions. A forum where wisdom can be shared and issues tackled is reassuring for the members of the community. When decisions are made collectively, common life becomes coherent and cohesive. Learning to collaborate, valuing each individual's contribution and arriving at an outcome everyone can support depends on effective communication. Individuals need to know how to say clearly what they think and to listen carefully to other views, especially when they are different from their own. Your task as leader is to teach and exemplify good communication. Then the community will flourish.

CHAPTER 7

Coping with Difficult
Individuals and Groups

When facing difficult people and tense situations, you should try to remain curious. Do not jump to conclusions; bide your time and try to work out what exactly is happening. By asking questions of those involved, you signal your commitment to engage and understand. Through staying inquisitive, you are connected with the issue and the people but this enquiring disposition gives you a certain distance. In turn this gives you space and time to analyse. As you probe and tease out what is driving the situation, you can stay calm. Paying attention to your own response first means that you are better placed to help deal with the problematic individual and the taxing issue.

Dealing with people who invest themselves in an issue

In church life, there are frequently issues that ostensibly are trivial and should be easy to resolve but which turn out to be explosive. This is often because the individuals concerned have a strong emotional investment in the outcome. Where a flower display should be placed in the church building might seem a non-contentious question, until you discover that someone likes a floral display in a particular spot, because it is near where their recently deceased spouse used to sit. Whether alcoholic drinks are served at a farewell party seems a relatively straightforward question, until you discover that this decision is usually made by the Social Events Planning Team, chaired by Mrs Smith, whose husband is an alcoholic.

These examples should make us wary of making swift judgements and snap decisions. Additionally, once aware of how much is invested in a particular issue, the leader needs to allocate the time and energy needed to find a resolution. Whilst avoiding being held to ransom by the underlying powerful emotions, the leader must first understand the background. Only when they have a sure grasp of the backstory can they move on to consider the decision-making process. They might find this frustrating ("Isn't it ridiculous to spend so long talking about the flowers, or fussing over another minor decision in the church's life?"), but taking the matter slowly will prove better in the long run, in addition to the worthwhile pastoral work involved and the further confidence and trust in their leadership that will be gained.

Advising those who are being emotionally pursued

A mother, a life-long Roman Catholic, keeps insisting that her adult son should stop going to his local Baptist church and return to the church in which he grew up. She is adamant and persistent. In every conversation, this subject features. The son has tried every conceivable response to encourage her to drop the issue but to no avail. What should you advise him? You could advocate that he refuses to talk to her and to see her, unless she agrees not to mention his churchgoing pattern again. Angry confrontation might be another suggestion. Yet, both these approaches are unlikely to be successful, because behind his mother's dogged pursuit of this matter is anxiety, and if her son were to cut himself off from her or to tackle the matter with a robust challenge to her behaviour, her anxiety would simply increase. As a result, she is likely to redouble her efforts to persuade him to revert to her denomination, to chase him more ardently. A wiser option for the son would be to put more effort into the relationship, instead of defending himself. This extra attention will reassure his mother that she is still important to him and that his attending a different church is not tantamount to rejecting her. When he has put your suggestion into practice by returning home frequently and taking more interest in her past and current life, the matter of his churchgoing habits should slowly fade into the background.

Parental figures in the church community

In most church communities, there are people who are viewed and operate as parents. They are well-established, respected individuals who have a disproportionate effect on the corporate life. The wise leader needs to take them into account in their strategic thinking. Affiliating with a "mother" or "father" could be a significant step forward in terms of strengthening the leader's position, in deepening their influence and in furthering their goals. There are three fundamental and mutually reinforcing methods to ally you to someone else: affirmation, sympathy and identification. Affirming them with appreciation and praise swiftly builds the relationship. Responding to any expressions of feeling with understanding fixes an emotional connection. Finding and highlighting similarities between yourself and them helps to create a rapport.

Sometimes in a church community, there can be rival parental figures; they can be uninterested in or distant to each other or actively antagonistic, looking for opportunities to fight. Finding ways to bring these powerful people, who usually represent a constituency, together, is a worthwhile exercise and, if successful, could have a dramatic bearing on the health of the church.

Simply inviting people to be physically together in the same space is a very straightforward way of giving people the chance to move closer together emotionally: there is a direct correlation between being physically and emotionally close. If you can also encourage them to play and laugh together, this will greatly increase the likelihood that good connections will be formed.

Over-functioning and under-functioning

There is a joke which poses the question "in what way is the local church like a football match?" The answer: at a football match, there are 22 people rushing around exhausted and 20,000 people watching them do it. Whereas the figures may be different for your nearest church, I suspect the point is still well made. In churches, in families and in any group, it is possible that some people will be over-functioning, doing more than they should, and others who are under-functioning, doing less than they should.

Both dysfunctions have their origins in different reactions to anxiety: typically over-functioners are too ready to take on anxiety that legitimately belongs to others, whereas those under-functioning are likely to want to avoid anxiety that might derive from their own position in the system. It is also worth noting that excessive busyness on the part of over-functioners also serves to distribute anxiety through the system.

Needless to say, this situation is good neither for those who are too busy nor for those who are too passive. Those overly active are likely to be overdoing it to the detriment of themselves and the work that they are doing. Shirking their commitments, those who are relatively inactive remain irresponsible. Clearly, there is an unhelpful reciprocity sustaining this situation. The way to prevent this arrangement developing, or to break it if it is an established pattern, is to define clearly everyone's responsibilities. Alongside articulated and agreed detailed descriptions of their respective roles, a monitoring process will have to be established and implemented. Otherwise, there will be tendency to slip into unhealthy patterns.

Of course, the question that comes to mind is "Which came first, the chicken or the egg?" How did this unhealthy dynamic arise? Is it down to the over-functioner or the under-functioner?

What the over-functioners need to ask themselves is whether the rest of the family is under-functioning as an adaptive response to their behaviour. They need to be confronted with the hard truth that it is inappropriate and debilitating to do for other people what they can do themselves, whatever they may say. No one can make anyone else more responsible. Yet over-functioners can be encouraged to adapt their behaviour, by refusing to take on tasks or roles that are not theirs. In order to make this change, the over-functioner needs to contain the anxiety generated when someone does not do their job or does not meet the over-functioner's standards.

Under-functioners need to be challenged to make their contribution. Their self-depiction as inadequate, hopeless or with no choices should not be taken at face value. Taking their proper responsibility and fulfilling the role assigned to them on the basis of their gifts is integral to being a mature participant in community life. They must be encouraged to become more consistently involved—to step up to the plate and hit a home run!

By making a criterion of the success of our pastoral care whether the recipient is comforted or encouraged, then we may be left feeling inadequate ourselves. In turn, we may decide to avoid pastoral situations because of the uncomfortable emotions that they arouse in us.

Instead, our responsibility is to be there. Our presence expresses our sense of connection. We cannot be accountable for what someone else feels; our need to make them feel better intrudes, reducing our level of attention and militating against an authentic caring engagement on our part.

In any case, pastoral care is more than "making them feel better". If that becomes our goal in the encounter, we are in danger of taking responsibility for how the other person feels, which is akin to over-functioning. Rather, good pastoral care is primarily about paying close attention to the individual, their situation, feelings and hopes. By listening carefully, you are in solidarity with them and that feels supportive. Together you can then focus on whether there is anything that they can and need to do differently. As a Christian minister, you are seeing if there is scope for growth in faith, hope and love, the theological virtues. That means that when it is appropriate you'll offer to pray either with them or afterwards, whichever they prefer.

Secrets

The existence of a significant secret adversely affects the church family. A secret divides the church into two factions: those who know, the in-crowd, and those who do not, the outsiders. This division estranges those on different sides of the divide, and for those on the same side generates a tenuous companionship. Those who do not know the secret have an incomplete picture, because for them a piece of information is missing. The presence of a secret puts a strain on everyone, infecting the whole church community with anxiety.

Even though gossip might seem a rather petty feature of church life, it does undermine relationships across the church. At its worst, cliques and tensions result. Your task is to deter gossip.

Secrets create triangles where two people are close and the third individual is excluded. Two are in on the secret; one is not. Whilst the secret is kept, these relationships are fixed. Until the secret is revealed, the barrier between those who know and those who do not keeps the two sides apart. Although those on the outside might even be unaware that there is a secret, they can sense the emotional distance caused by it. The coldness and rigidity of relationships is an indicator that there may be a secret that is impeding the church's interpersonal dynamics. Static relationships mean that there is less scope for development. Only by disclosing the secret can there be movement. When it is brought out into the open, the secret is stripped of its power. The usual fluidity and openness of healthy relationships are restored. Your ability to lead is renewed and individuals are freed to respond to your challenge to grow. As interpersonal dynamics are given new energy, relationships can deepen authentically again.

Emotional triangles

In your interactions, you are likely to come across these two types of emotional triangles. The first consists of three people, two who are present and talking to each other, and a third who is absent. For example: the church secretary and treasurer complaining together about the inadequacy of the church's leader. The second is two people and an issue that is the subject of their own conversation. For example: a wife comes to the leader to share her concern about her husband's drinking habit.

When you encounter either of these two situations, you should not collude. You cannot accept the emotional triangles. You need to challenge the presentation of the problem. Your focus should be those in front of you. By relating directly to those with whom you are talking and refusing to talk about those who are not there, you get out of the triangle. In the first case, you address the experience of the two people and their mutual relationship. In the second, you pay attention to the other individual and what actions they can take.

However, triangles are also integral to how most people cope with anxiety. By talking to a third party about someone they find difficult, the tension they feel is relieved. Even so, the role of the leader is to avoid triangles, to model the more mature approach of direct communication, and to be open to developmental feedback. By being accessible and ready to engage with feedback, you set an example. Alongside being a calm, non-anxious presence, you play your part in reducing anxiety in the church. Then there is less need for others to manage their anxiety by triangulating.

One of the features of emotional triangles is that anxiety moves around the triangle. Ensuring the anxiety is located where it belongs in the triangle is a key to making some progress. For example, if you sense that the tension between the church treasurer and the church secretary is manifesting itself in their irritability with you as the leader, then you try to help them to focus on the source of their anxiety and to address the difficulties between them. Being cross with you is a way of avoiding the demanding task of working on their relationship.

Triangles also conceal conflicts: differences are not addressed directly; rather they are discussed with others in secret. This is unhealthy for church life. When there is any kind of crisis causing the anxiety level to rise, triangles proliferate. As a leader, you need to become attuned to the presence of a triangle. Triangles are likely when things do not seem to add up. When you sense that something is not being said or that the account of what has happened appears incomplete, there is probably a triangular relationship somewhere. You should then ask yourself who else and what else could be involved.

When you find yourself being drawn into a triangle, you resist by insisting on direct communication: you will not talk about someone who is not there. If, as soon as the church secretary begins their gripe about the church treasurer, you ask, "Have you spoken to the treasurer about these matters?" you would have signalled that you were not prepared to be caught up in a triangle. Pushing back and holding on to the importance of direct communication is the way to break it; you have "de-triangulated".

When you are consulted about a situation that involves two people and an issue, you should again encourage direct communication between the two people concerned. For example, if a wife tells you about her husband's excessive drinking, you should not latch on to the issue, although some exploration of it would be reasonable. Instead, you should concentrate on their relationship. Your goal is to help them talk together about the wife's concern regarding her husband's drinking. In fact, you should deter her from telling you too much and encourage her to talk directly to her husband about it. Otherwise a false closeness is established, which over the long term could undermine the marriage, as opposed to strengthening it. There is a caveat: you need to ask whether the wife is concerned about how the husband might react to any attempt by her to open up the issue of his drinking, to any attempt by his wife to challenge his drinking habits, however gently.

Strong leadership is about keeping out of triangles, staying connected with everyone whilst true to yourself. By talking about someone else, you keep a comfortable distance from the person with whom we are conversing. Yet, triangles are really a means of avoiding deep emotional connections.

As triangles, actual or potential, are always lurking not too far away, you need to be on your guard. For instance, you should not talk about the treasurer to the secretary. If you want to be trusted and to be an example to others, you must avoid talking about someone behind their back, with rare exceptions. Talking to people directly must be the modus operandi of anyone in leadership.

How readily you are prepared to talk directly with people and share your feelings and values will depend on whether these personal exchanges happened in your family of origin. If you struggle to talk at this level, then doing some work on your relationship with members of your birth family can help you. Seeking to deepen each relationship should be your aim. By talking one-to-one with each member of the family in which you grew up, and initiating more significant conversations, you will find that you are enabled to relate similarly to others outside the family. This does not, of course, preclude chatting about sport and politics, but for the relationship to deepen you should take the risk of talking more personally. Besides strengthening the relationship, relating directly in your family setting empowers one to do so at work, in church and elsewhere.

De-triangulation

It is only the people in a relationship who can change it. Trying to interfere in a relationship from the outside is completely counterproductive and frustrating. Relationships can only be changed directly from the inside. What a leader can do is to help those in the relationship to reflect and consider how they might act and think differently.

When confronted with a relational triangle, the leader's goal must be to encourage and enable the participants to relate to each other directly, otherwise the stress causing the triangulation becomes lodged with the most responsible of the three participants. If the triangle is maintained, the conflict is not resolved. Any attempts to resolve it through the intervention of an outsider can only move the anxiety around the triangle. For example, should you be drawn into the conflict between a warring couple, you are likely to get stuck hearing both sides vent to you, but negligible, if any, progress will be made towards a resolution of their conflict. Your task is to encourage and enable the couple to talk to each other. If this is too difficult initially, you can meet with them individually to prepare the way for a face-to-face encounter. In these conversations, you set out to understand their underlying feelings before identifying the issues. Asking each of them to articulate how they want the relationship to be different helps them to get beyond the current impasse. By picturing how they want to relate to each other, hope is renewed and fresh energy is brought to the process. When they do decide that they are ready meet together, you can offer to be simply present or to mediate.

Allowing yourself to be drawn into a triangle might look like an attractive prospect in the short term. It seems less challenging than working with each individual and seeking to bring them together. There is also something seductive about being a confidant. Be very wary of the false sense of intimacy generated by someone sharing at this emotional level. Being asked to help has an attraction all of its own anyway. A husband, newly married, comes to confide in the female minister about his marital difficulties. He describes his wife as "selfish and uncaring" and begins to cry. What should she do? She needs to respond sympathetically, but also needs to guard against commiserating overly with him. If she prolongs the conversation or sees him again, she could find herself hooked into a triangle which would be fraught with dangers for both of them. The right thing is to see husband and wife together. This avoids an inappropriately close relationship developing, as well as signalling her commitment to both of them. Should the minister discover that the difficulties in their marriage are entrenched and realize that she is out of her depth, then there could be a need for someone with greater expertise and experience to help the couple. Nevertheless, initially, offering to facilitate a conversation between the couple is good start on the journey to an improved marriage.

When caught up in a triangle, make sure that you encourage direct communication on all of its three sides. A key element is to urge the person in front of you to consider what to do about the other relationships in the triangle. To use the same example, if a wife confides in you that her marriage is in difficulty, you can help her to reflect on her relationship with her husband. You can ask her, "What does she want to be different? What does she want to say to him?" Given the tension in their marriage, you must reassure her that she can tackle the difficulties. Your task is to help her get ready to engage with her husband about the problems as she sees them. This is achieved through questions that empower her to take a stand. She has control of her behaviour, not his, and that is where the focus needs to be in your conversation. Once she sets her mind to act differently, the relationship will change. An opportunity for the marriage to improve is opened up. Again, this example assumes that it is safe for the wife to broach the issues that she has identified with her husband. If the husband is verbally abusive or physically violent, then this becomes a Safeguarding issue and demands a different course of action.

Always remember that you cannot change the relationship between two people—only they can. If you try to intervene, you will probably make things worse. This is even more likely if you take sides: you then become part of the problem. You place the one you support in a dependent position, and the other will feel under attack.

Here are some more examples of how to de-triangulate—an example of two people and an issue—a husband, wife and the wife's spending habit.

> In a marriage, the wife's spending was almost uncontrollable. She could not resist buying things and had run up huge debts on her credit cards. Her husband got more and more worried about her behaviour. In spite of his attempts to convince her to stop, she blithely went on frittering their money away. At this stage, the anxiety is firmly lodged with the husband. Taking a step back and analysing the triangle, he decided on a different course of action: he set his face to deconstruct the triangle by removing himself. He disentangled their finances, closing down all joint bank accounts, leaving them with only their own individual accounts. He then told his wife that she must take responsibility for her own spending and that he was not going to bail her out, if she began to sink. As a result, the anxiety is firmly and correctly lodged with the wife. Within three weeks, she had sought some help to change her addictive behaviour.

Another example: Adam, Ben and Chris—friends and enemies!

> Ben and Chris had been friends but had fallen out and were no longer speaking to each other. A mutual friend, Adam, felt he could not stand by and do nothing. He went to Ben to find out what the problem was. Ben had a long list of complaints about Chris. Adam then went to Chris to reel off the many accusations Ben had against Chris. Not surprisingly, Chris became angry with Adam and Ben, and began to tell his side of the story. Adam acted as an intermediary for a few weeks, but he was not sleeping and his efforts appeared to have made no difference. The anxiety about the breakdown in the relationship was residing with Adam, and he was feeling its burden. Adam decided to put into practice a different approach. He went to Ben and Chris to tell them independently that he would remain a friend to each of them, but he would not take responsibility for their friendship with

each other. He also made it clear that he was prepared to help them think through what they needed to do to be reconciled, if that is what they wanted to do. The anxiety had been placed between Ben and Chris, where it belonged. Adam made a point of regularly being in touch with each of them by phone, email and by popping around. Within a few weeks, Ben and Chris were talking and their friendship was restored.

In both of these examples, there was a genuine problem: in one case, a shopping compulsion and, in the other, a broken friendship. Breaking the deadlock was not possible through engaging with the content. Instead, by changing the emotional processes and by altering the relationships, those who need to address the presenting issue are confronted directly with it. Those who have the ability and primary responsibility to find a resolution have the onus placed on them to act.

Anxious churches

Anxious churches feel "stuck": "stuck together" and "stuck where they are". When a church feels under pressure, its members become insular. When there are tensions within a church, the fault-lines are accentuated, and it is likely to fragment. Individuals gather into like-minded groupings. As cliques are formed the corporate life, the sense of togetherness, is undermined. The result is often a church characterized by parochialism or riven by cliques. From the outside this looks unattractive. Yet, if you are on the inside an inward-looking church or a cosy clique can feel safe and comfortable. Values and expectations are shared, and there is a clear sense of identity.

Meeting people who are different from us, whether they are a newcomer or a stranger, or someone with a clashing point of view, can unsettle us. However, unless we are disturbed and challenged, we will not grow. Any grouping that shuts itself off and disassociates itself from its context and other agencies will stultify. Safe it might be, but it is in danger of stagnating. Spiritual death follows. The answer is to help people feel safe. Insularity is a fearful reaction to a perceived threat. Insomuch as those around us or the wider world look intimidating, we cling to those like us. To counteract the anxiety, the leader needs to offer reassurance and stay non-anxious. As the levels of stress reduce, there is scope for change; rigid patterns can shift and new ones emerge. Your role is to help everyone feel safe, so that they can let go, and enjoy interacting and learning from those unlike themselves.

A shared lack of confidence results in people clinging together. This leads to muddle and confusion. No one knows their own boundaries—where they begin and where they end—or their responsibilities. Clarity is lost. In this context, a blame culture swiftly develops and flourishes. At its centre is the false premise that other people are responsible for our behaviour; they are not. Pushed to its limits, this mind-set leads to an abdication of responsibility for our emotional response, by asserting that other people are "in charge" of our reactions. This produces profound anxiety. We, and our circumstances, seem out of control. Not surprisingly, any perceived threat triggers a strong negative response. When a stranger appears, the barriers up; defence is paramount. An anxiety-ridden church will find it hard to be hospitable to strangers.

Differentiation, fusion, togetherness and aloneness

In analysing churches, it is worth considering these two questions. Are the individuals encouraged to differentiate, to think independently, or is conformity prized with the danger that individuality is lost? Does the church foster togetherness where close relationships are the norm or is there coldness, an emotional distance between members, which leaves the individuals feeling separate, alone?

When individuals are so close to each other, and uniformity is the goal rather than unity, then no one has the capacity to function autonomously. "Fused togetherness" is a shorthand. This kind of community would hold that "togetherness is sameness". Predictably and significantly, when all think alike, no one thinks very much.

By contrast, when individual isolation is combined with fusion, this is caused by the combination of an aversion to closeness and a drive for conformity. In this situation, everyone seeks to maintain a sense of self by staying at a distance from each other. This phenomenon indicates the presence of some very powerful individuals. Underlying this way of interacting is the attitude: "the only way that I can be myself is to be away from those who are emotionally powerful for me".

"Together with differentiation" is what communities should be seeking. In this context, individuals are encouraged to think for themselves before coming together to reach a collective decision. This openness to others is combined with an appropriate distance that allows each individual to hold their own point of view. Whereas the better-differentiated individual will not be striving to be distinct and separate from the rest of the group, they know that there is a space to "stand out from the crowd". They will be deterred by the "loneliness" that results. This situation if it arose could be labelled "differentiated isolation".

Patterns of reactivity

In response to anxiety, churches often take the cowardly path, seeking to avoid the difficult issues and flee from the ensuing conflict because of the inevitable discomfort. There are four distinct reactions, although they are forms of denial.

"Compliance" is a label for what is essentially a deceptive attitude. The compliant individual appears co-operative. They say that they agree with what is being asked of them but are, in fact, resistant. This leads to them carrying out their role poorly or not at all. It is hard, at least initially, to detect this covert sabotage. Typically, it is only after some time that this destructive pattern of behaviour is spotted.

Outright rebellion is overt and obvious. People who react strongly and in opposition to others do so to create what is for them a comfortable emotional distance.

Power struggles are essentially ongoing battles for ascendancy. Two sides compete for control. Both want to define what they will and will not do. Both want to dictate what the other should do. Everyone feels angry and frustrated. Besides stirring up these draining emotions, this ongoing dynamic on both sides means that attention and energy are channelled towards winning. While there may appear to be interludes where the interaction has stopped, invariably both parties are constantly focused on each other. This behaviour is characterized by self-justification, posturing and pronouncements about the antagonist.

Simple and straightforward emotional distance is swiftly recognized. If someone has a weak sense of self, others present a distinct threat, especially those who are very different. This kind of person can only manage relationships on their own terms. If they cannot get their way, they will withdraw. In so far as someone is pressing for emotional closeness to be based on being alike, they are revealing a tenuous sense of self. They can easily feel out of control and uncomfortable. When this happens, the only way to retain a sense of their own identity is to withdraw, if not physically then emotionally. In order to develop a strong identity, the individual needs to decide on their values, and form their own opinions, and then take the risk of sharing them. This can be particularly challenging if the person to whom we are relating is powerful emotionally. This developmental work gathers momentum as the individual goes repeatedly through their process of deciding what they think and telling others. This will give confidence in engaging with people who are different from them, and make it more likely that a range of opinions will be heard on any topic under discussion. A further outworking is that they can enter more easily into mutually beneficial friendships and be less directive in their current relationships.

CHAPTER 8

Building Teams and Community

Building a team takes time! Persistence and discipline are needed. This is a worthwhile project, for a well-functioning team is more than the sum of its parts. An effective team achieves great things.

We can learn much about what makes a great team by considering what undermines the effectiveness of a team. In his book *Five Dysfunctions of a Team*, Patrick Lencioni identifies five interrelated features of a team that is not doing well:

1. An absence of trust revealed in an unwillingness to own up to mistakes and to share weaknesses.
2. A fear of conflict seen in an artificial harmony and an incapacity to engage in a painstaking and passionate debate about ideas.
3. Lack of commitment characterized by an ambiguity about decisions and goals. Without healthy conflict and a proper airing of different views, team members are not in a position to commit to a way forward.
4. Avoidance of accountability indicated by reluctance for team members to challenge each other. Without a firm commitment to a clear plan for the future, even the most ardent people hesitate to point out actions and behaviours that seem counterproductive to the good of the team.
5. Inattention to results signified by individuals prioritizing their own status and ego above the common good of the team. When the team members are loath to hold each other accountable, this dysfunction can thrive. Individual needs (for example, career development or recognition), or even the needs of their division, are put above the collective goals of the team.[20]

Building trust

Truly cohesive teams trust one another. If team members are confident that their peers are committed to the success of the team and not driven by self-interest, then competitiveness is replaced by co-operation. Furthermore, then they can take the risk of owning up to their mistakes and acknowledging their weaknesses. This is countercultural, as typically it pays to be competitive with our peers and protective of our reputations.

A lack of genuine debate is a tell-tale sign of an absence of trust; conversely, every effective team engages in vigorous discussion. In teams where there is distrust, disagreement is hidden, beneath the surface, unexpressed. This is unhealthy, and the team will perform poorly. In strong teams, the team members are actively engaged with each other and personally invested in achieving their goals. Any concerns are raised, and when difficult issues are discussed everyone is committed to sorting them out.

Trust does not happen by accident. It needs commitment. Therefore the team members need to be prepared to invest in the team. They need to agree that they are going to learn to trust each other. This demands a commitment to be together and to work together. There is no substitute for shared experience and collaborating together on shared tasks; these are the essentials for trust to develop. Being together and working together deepens the relationships between individuals and fosters a sense of team. The leader has a vital role to play. Your integrity is vital. You must be trustworthy. You set the pattern. By being reliable, you model what it means to be a good team member. You set the team ethos. Eventually, and this is one of the great truths of leadership, the team will reflect back to you your own essential qualities.

You need to get to know each team member, their personalities and their attributes. If you are to lead the team effectively, you need to know the members of the team. Take the time to build a relationship with each individual. This ongoing task is integral to your leadership; do not neglect it. Your investment in these relationships generates a reciprocal commitment to the team and its goals.

There are several exercises to help you and the rest of the team to get to know each other. While these structured practices can seem artificial and feel somewhat laboured, they do enable trust to deepen. Asking each individual to share something of their personal histories gives everyone an insight into how other team members have been shaped by their life experience. Also, by revealing something deeper, everyone takes the risk of trusting the team. The trust gradually grows as small steps of trust are taken. Thereby, it makes sense to choose some relatively safe topics at the start of this process. Here is a suggested list of questions to ask people to consider.

- What is your home town?
- If you have siblings, can you tell us something about them?
- What were your childhood hobbies?
- What was your biggest challenge growing up?
- What was your first job?

A more daring and demanding exercise, that builds trust and helps everyone to understand their role within the team, is to ask each individual to identify their contribution to the team, and what they need to do to improve. Besides helping to strengthen relationships, this exercise enables the team to have a greater shared understanding of its strengths and weaknesses and what it needs to do to get better. Another way is for the team to look together at each individual through one of personality and behavioural preference profiles, for example the Myers-Briggs personality profile. This defines each individual according to traits and preference. It reveals ways in which team members are alike and how they are dissimilar. This non-judgemental analysis can lead into a discussion of each individual's preferred ways of working. By looking at the combined results, you are given an overall picture of the team, revealing its strengths and weaknesses.

To fulfil the aim of building trust, everyone has to overcome their need for invulnerability; there is no short cut here. To begin to establish this level of openness, it is essential that the team leader takes the risk of revealing more about themselves and, in particular, their weaknesses. Unless the leader takes the initiative, other members are unlikely to share at this deeper level. Once the leader has risked a degree of vulnerability, the team should, hopefully, be prepared to go deeper. For example, if you ask every individual to spend five minutes or so deciding what they believe is their biggest strength and weakness in terms of their contribution to the team and its work, you should be the first to share with the team. Everyone will take their cue from you. If you show some trust in the team, others will do likewise.

Engaging in unfiltered conflict around ideas

Trust is the prerequisite if debates are to be rigorous. Without it, people will not engage in open and constructive conflict, never mind ideological debate. Mutual suspicion, or worse, shared distrust, is bound to undermine progress and mar how the team functions. Often, the team can seem to be working well, yet on closer examination, simmering tensions and hidden disagreements can be just below the surface. A lack of energy and commitment are indicative of this malaise. Sarcastic remarks and passive aggressive behaviour or failing to do what has been agreed point to an underlying discord. Destructive conflict saps energy and undermines the team. Generated by competiveness, this argy-bargy jeopardizes teamwork.

By building trust, productive conflict becomes possible because team members do not hesitate to engage in intense debate. Arguments about the nature of a current problem, or about the possible solutions and their relative merits, can then be productive. Constructive conflict centres on the team's task and on achieving the desired outcomes.

Whereas a harmonious team is unquestionably a "good thing", it cannot be made a higher priority than the need for proper debate. Prioritizing harmony detracts from the greater goal of creating an ethos which values appropriate conflict. Individuals should not hold back their opinions and honest reservations because they feel compelled to maintain harmony. If so, then unity is mistakenly thought to be same as uniformity. In fact, the risk is that the uniformity masks the underlying disunity. An authentic unity is based on recognition of the differences between people. Concealing them undermines unity. On the other hand, when unanimity emerges, as a result of issues having been tackled and areas of conflict resolved, then that is to be celebrated.

This quote from Sir David Brailsford of the Team Sky Cycling team from 22 July 2013, in which he talks about the possibility of having Bradley Wiggins and Christopher Froome, both Tour de France winners, in the same team, underlines this point tellingly:

> People talk about having team unity and team harmony. I don't buy that at all. Most of the best teams I've been with, they're not harmonious environments.
>
> This is not a harmonious environment. This is a gritty environment where people are pushing really hard.
>
> What you need is goal harmony, and there's a big difference between the two.
>
> You can't rule anything out. Once you start ruling things out, saying, 'No he can't do this, and he can't do that' . . . We're not in the game of ruling things out; we're in the game of ruling things in.[21]

How to foster an ability and willingness to engage in healthy conflict

One of the leader's tasks is to tell the team that the right kind of conflict is fruitful and that teams are less effective if they avoid it.

The leader should be keen to go digging for the issues that lie below the surface which people are reluctant to discuss. You should seize the opportunities to bring into collective focus sensitive issues and to ensure that the team members work through them. You should make sure that the team stays with the conflict until it is resolved and, again, draw out the collective wisdom of the group, enabling the team to reach the best decision. When you see that people are struggling and finding the tension uncomfortable, you should remind everyone that what they are doing is necessary.

However, you should avoid intervening too soon! When the team begins to engage in meaningful and productive conflict, the leader must resist the urge to intervene. Rather the leader should let the discussion run its course, allowing the scope for a resolution to occur naturally, even though this might feel uncomfortable. By holding back, you enable the team to develop its ability to work together through difficult issues.

After the conflict is resolved, the leader should reinforce the point by emphasizing that the preceding conflict has been good for the team. For example, if there has been a challenging and tense meeting which nevertheless has moved the team forward, then the leader might simply express that "building a team is not easy". The leader can also underline the importance of what is happening when the process feels uncomfortable: "It is very important that we have these vigorous debates. Though they might feel difficult, they are essential if we are to examine the options rigorously and properly."

Encouraging conflicts may be uncomfortable, but do it anyway!

Fighting about the issues is the right kind of fighting. Without it, the resulting decisions will be weaker and have flaky support. To shirk this collective responsibility is to refuse to strive for the best. When the discussion involves deeply-held convictions, then the clash might well feel disturbing. Learning to cope with a level of interpersonal discomfiture is an essential requirement for every team member.

Fostering authentic commitment to the church's decisions

If people are to commit wholeheartedly to a plan or a decision, they have to be convinced that their view has been heard. Without the opportunity for everyone to express their opinions, any reservations remain hidden and questions hang unanswered in the air. Having not been properly engaged from the outset, people feel disconnected. They then withhold their support for the subsequent course of action. By contrast, a process which ensures that everyone's opinion is expressed and heard, even if there are different and conflicting viewpoints, means everyone feels engaged in making the decision. As a result, the whole church is much more likely to rally behind some agreed course of action. If this open, transparent and engaging approach is integrated into church life, then the church will pursue its goals effectively. That is why this is so important. If the church cannot learn to engage in productive conflict, then it is doomed not to reach its potential. Apart from the odd recalcitrant person, most people do not need to get what they want come what may. However, most people do expect that their views will be heard and considered, and that they will receive a response.

The same is true for teams within the church. Having engaged in open and fruitful conflict, whereby the team members' expertise and experience have had a full impact, a team can commit to a decision, knowing that it is the best that they could have made.

Although there can never be a guarantee that the decision is right, the maxim that "any decision is better than none" is worth heeding. To postpone a decision can result in a sense of paralysis with energy draining away; instead, implement the decision providing there has been genuine debate and clarity about the outcome, even if there has been a sizeable minority opposed. There will be a stronger commitment than would result from any attempt to reach a consensus: those who have voiced doubts and those who have been solidly and strongly in favour will back the decision taken with more resolve than if some broad, lukewarm consensus is reached, which has no one's wholehearted support.

If there is a lot of anxiety about an issue, then discussing contingency plans and reflecting on worst-case scenarios can help reduce the tension. As you help the team to explore what would happen "if it all went wrong", anxiety is reduced. Then the team's thinking is more rational and astute.

Some decisions are about shaping a process for consultation or implementation. In these cases, it is critical that the result should be a clearly defined process with specific deadlines for each stage.

At the end of the meeting, there should be a review of the decisions taken; this gives an opportunity for further clarification. Additionally, it is important to ensure that everyone understands how these decisions are to be implemented and who has responsibility for what. Making sure that those who need to know of the decisions are to be informed is also part of the rounding-off stage of a meeting.

You cannot let opposition to any proposed change distract you from good processes. When concerns are expressed, you address them. Once they have been taken into account, you cannot let continuing dissent disrupt the agreed plan. Accepting that people have some reservations about a particular course of action may seem tantamount to a readiness to back down. Yet, empathy and a willingness to engage with other points of view does not equate to a change of mind. While listening to the dissenting voices is essential, once the way is agreed, you should not waver. Unless new information comes to light, you should press on.

You must be comfortable with the prospect that any decisions taken may prove to be flawed. Recognition that some outcomes will be unforeseen—"the law of unintended consequences"—might make you reconsider but must not hinder the pursuit of closure on issues. A decision, after the appropriate deliberation, must be reached! Your task is to make sure that the team implements the decision made.

Mutual accountability

Once a decision is made and a clear direction agreed, you must schedule regular meetings at which progress is reviewed. You must foster mutual accountability characterized in the implementation phase. The team ethos must be marked by an expectation that the highest standards in performance and behaviour are maintained and defended by all the team members. Keeping the team at this level is primarily your responsibility but is shared by everyone on the team. Although team members find it difficult to highlight someone's poor performance because of the fraught conversations and interpersonal discomfort that might follow, this reluctance must be overcome. If a team member takes the risk, it will demonstrate a deep commitment to the team and mutual respect, and reinforce the high expectations of each other's performance that should be the norm for any highly motivated team. Otherwise keeping relationships comfortable becomes, by default, a higher priority than the team doing its best. Team members cannot allow the fear of interpersonal tension to override their commitment to the team's success. Everyone must be prepared to confront someone who is not pulling their weight.

This is not easy! Trust and respect make it possible

Some people are difficult to hold to account. The reasons vary. Whereas some can appear, though deceptively, compliant, others are straightforwardly defensive or intimidating. Challenging another team member about how they are spending their time or whether they are making enough progress is a testing task. Rather than providing a strong negative reaction, it will be viewed as helpful if the team ethos is characterized by mutual trust. If the questioning is known to be prompted by a concern for the team's efficiency, and not by competitiveness, then it will be received in the spirit it is intended. The basic working assumption for every team member should be that the others are competent and are trying their best. From this position, when questions are asked, they should prompt the recipient to engage openly and curiously rather than defensively. If open communication can be sustained and the barriers stay down, then productive mutual learning can result.

The leader patrols the territory, insisting the standards are maintained

You must be vigilant, looking out for behaviour that undermines the team's performance. When an individual's ego rears its head or someone demonstrates a lack of trust, you must bring this to everyone's attention and underline that these attitudes are unacceptable. A key question to each individual is: "Are you making this team better, or are you contributing to its dysfunction?"

It is part of your role to spell out expectations about mutual accountability and also to judge in any dispute between members about what is acceptable. The leaders must also be ready to let the team know that they are falling beneath the required standards. You should encourage conflict around ideas, push for clear commitments and expect everyone to hold each other to account.

If team members are to hold each other to account, there must be a clear set of shared expectations about appropriate attitudes and behaviours. The team needs to specify overall aims, shared values and individual responsibilities. Your task is to keep these constantly before the team; they must shape everything that is said and done. It is imperative that team members should apply the agreed criteria, and assess their own and each other's contribution.

When the team is successful, celebrate. It is good to mark achievements, and it also reinforces the set of common expectations. Rewarding success signals the central importance of getting results. Keeping a tight focus on the team's aims gives it an ongoing sense of purpose and makes its individual members highly motivated.

The team's goals need to be defined and must include specific short-term objectives, as well as long-term targets. Ambitious goals will stretch the team and draw out a high quality performance. Seeking only to survive or maintain the status quo is not enough, and likely to prove counter-productive. Devoid of vision, the team's energy is going to ebb away.

The team is accountable beyond itself; its aims should, therefore, be known by those it represents and those it serves. You need to ensure that these stakeholders are kept informed and to provide the opportunity for hard questions to be asked. The leader needs to ensure that the results are clear to ensure that the team's performance is transparent. Any achievement by the team should be acclaimed, and any action which contributes to the team's success should be highlighted. The leader needs to keep the team's aims before it and monitor progress. "How are we doing?" is to be your constant refrain.

If the leader tolerates actions which undermine the team's effectiveness, then they are culpable. Who is more to blame when a team member's stroppy attitude and inept contribution reduce the team's output by 50%? The team member or the leader? The leader, for not confronting the poor performer!

Defining the goals

"If everything is important, then nothing is." Your goals must be SMART or SMARTER.

Specific: The goal must be clearly defined and completely understood. This is achieved by paying attention to the questions: Who? Where? When? If your goal statement is vague, you will find it hard to achieve because it will be hard to define success.

Measurable: You must be able to track progress and everyone must be able to know whether or not the goal has been achieved. Good definitions of the goal tackle these questions: How much or how many? How will I know when I achieve the goal?

Agreed: Your goal must be relevant to and agreed with all parties; all stakeholders should be consulted and be resolutely on board before the venture begins.

Realistic: While it can be a challenging, even stretching, goal, it must be attainable. Setting targets that are beyond reach is drastically demotivating and depressing. Ensure that the actions you need to take to achieve your goal are those you can do and control. Is this goal achievable?

Time-bound: Goals must have a deadline. A good goal statement will answer the question: When will I achieve my goal? Without deadlines, it is easy to put goals off and leave them to die. As well as a deadline, it is a good idea to set some short-term milestones along the way to help you measure progress.

Ethical: Goals must include a commitment to act with integrity, clarity and, whenever possible, transparency.

Recorded: Record your goal and progress towards it. Written goals are visible and have a greater chance of being completed successfully. Recording is necessary for planning, monitoring and reviewing progress. Is your goal written down?

Keep the focus on being the best church possible

The church's vision must be formative in every aspect of its life and shape its future. Given its history, its context, its identity and informed by its vision, the church must endeavour to be the best it can be. The starting point for any church's drive to develop is worship and prayer. Becoming more dependent on God is integral to any realization of a church's vision. Furthermore, the church must be confident that the vision she is pursuing has arisen out a prayerful process and comes from God. Throughout the ongoing course of initiatives, changes and projects, the church needs to undertake a journey towards God. Prayer and action need to inseparable, and should feed each other.

In any team, there will be a division of responsibilities and delegation of tasks. Alongside every member working to the best of their ability, everyone must be committed to the success of everyone else. It is not acceptable to have individuals standing back and taking no interest in what another team member is doing. If someone is struggling to fulfil their role, this affects the team's performance and should matter to everyone. This mutual concern should lead to the team members' support of one another. When the team sees that someone needs help to improve some aspect of their work, everyone should rally round to offer emotional support and any relevant advice, and, if necessary, pitch in to help.

Whatever a team member's loyalties and responsibilities within the organization, each of them must regard their commitment to the team as paramount. For example, departmental heads at a meeting of the senior management team of an organization should put aside their sectional interests for the benefit of the team. Although "helping the team win" and "advancing your career" are not mutually exclusive, for each team member the former should be more important than the latter.

In a business context, the danger is that the individuals on the team pursue their own self-interest, boosting their own career prospects, for example, to the detriment of the overall results of the company. Personal recognition and attention are put ahead of collective success for the team. This is unacceptable. Fostering a united commitment to the well-being and aims of the team is fundamental to your role as leader. Individuals must subvert their personal ambition to the goals of the team. To draw on a sporting analogy, the role of the coach of any sports team is to create the best team possible, not to further the career of individual athletes.

In business, there will be several clear results—easy to measure—that will signal success or failure. Likewise, in sport, winning or losing is the primary marker of how the team is faring. In church life it is less clear how to discern whether the Christian community is doing well or badly. The most obvious indicator, because it is relatively easy to measure, is the number of people who attend services or who play some part in the church's life. However, while tracking the numbers is an indicator of levels of participation, there are many other characteristics of a Christian community that is functioning well, though they are only accessible through subjective judgements and anecdote. This is problematic, because, unless the outcomes sought can be defined and recognized, it is hard to interpret whether progress is being made. Without a clear articulation of the aims and some awareness of whether they are being achieved, it is hard to develop any sense of momentum. Moreover, there is a risk that energy will become diffused and the church will struggle to realize its potential. The feedback offered by strangers and newcomers provides insight into the warmth of the welcome and the spiritual temperature of the church. You can ask people for their observations directly in conversation or more formally through a questionnaire. You must also pay attention to what you see. Notice and note the impression left on those who come into contact with the church, and listen out for what people say.

Common goals and values

Although it might be hard to identify some quantifiable outcomes, a team within a church—a building project team or a team that plans the monthly all-age service—can agree some aims. These must be kept at the forefront of the members' minds, otherwise there is a risk that once agreed, they are, effectively, shelved and have minimal bearing on everyday activity. The ideal is that they shape and inform the team's decisions.

Being true to yourself

In Christian leadership, there is no scope for "playing politics". If you are tempted to seek to manipulate people's reaction to you, resist. Otherwise you undermine your own integrity and this will rob your ministry of authenticity. Moreover, your relationships will be marred, as you cease to treat people with respect, and they are reduced to a means to your own ends. If you conceal your intentions in order to elicit the response you want, then you are being disingenuous. While tailoring your words and actions to the audience is essential if you are taking your context seriously, when it means that you are being deceptive about your real plans, this is morally wrong and counterproductive in the long term.

A case study[22]

The Vision for Saracens Rugby Union Football Club is "to be the most hard working, innovative and caring rugby organization in the world".

This is, to say the least, ambitious. Whereas the adjectives "hard-working" and "innovative" are likely to be prized by any forward-looking, aspirational organization, "caring" is not often associated with the cut and thrust of competitive sport.

This radical vision was a feature of what was described by the CEO in 2009 as a "Saracens Revolution". Allied to targets about business and sporting success was an emphasis on the character of the players and club. Brendan Venter, the Director of Rugby at the time, considered that strong relationships and individual development were integral to the progress of the club. "You can't think about winning all the time. I'm far more interested in my players, along with me, improving as people. That's basically the only thing that really matters." He also said, "If we win everything there is to win, but we've broken relationships, we've lost the plot."

The club is to be a community characterized by mutual care. "Making memories" is an aim which reveals an eye to history and the long view, besides expressing an expectation of loyalty. Commitment to each other is one of the aspects of the culture defined in the club's vision statement. We will . . .

- Be a trusted group of friends who work extraordinarily hard for the club and each other;
- Innovate by pushing the accepted boundaries on and off the field;
- Care for every player and staff member, and their families, as individuals;
- Develop a club culture based on a work ethic, discipline, honesty, and humility;
- Sustain this culture by planning succession from within at every level;
- Critically reflect on our own pursuits of personal excellence;
- Be relentlessly positive and energized at all times.

Most of the markers would not be out of place in a church, but the last might be. Although there are biblical injunctions to "rejoice always" (1 Thessalonians 5:16) and to "give thanks in all circumstances" (1 Thessalonians 5:18), sadness, anger and frustration are the appropriate responses to disappointment, injustice and plans that have been thwarted. By acknowledging these emotions, a community shows that it is grounded in reality, authentic and not in denial.

The 2017 season saw Saracens win the European Champions Cup for the second year in succession, a colossal achievement. After the semi-final, the club took the players on a thirty-six-hour "bonding trip" to Barcelona.[23] Journalists and sports pundits questioned its value. Mark McCall, the Director of Rugby, responded:

> We believe that over time it's a really strong way of making the relationships they have even closer and even tighter. If you get some short-term pain for long-term gain, then that's OK.
>
> If you watched how our players defended in our 22 last weekend [against Munster]—we made 92 tackles in our 22—you start to get a sense of the togetherness, the connections that exist and the fight that they have.

Those things don't just happen, they happen by spending a lot of time together at the training ground and going through days like this together, but also seeing each other socially. They've worked really hard down the years.

Close-knit relationships are integral to the club's ethos—they are essential to a caring community—and the benefits are seen on the pitch in the heat of the battle.

Saracens did lose the Premiership play-off to Exeter in 2017, a rare defeat. At the end of a titanic match which Exeter edged by two points, Mark McCall's response was gracious.[24] Even just after the match had finished, he, and the players, were able to applaud Exeter's victory and affirm their attributes. The club is accustomed to winning, but its staff and players also know how to lose well. A hard-nosed winning mentality and humility may seem an unlikely combination; nonetheless Saracens demonstrate that they go hand-in-hand. By creating a good, caring club built on the virtues of discipline, honesty, diligence and humility, the foundations are in place for success on the rugby field for the long term. Paying attention to the common life and the culture is vital to the wellbeing of the individuals and the team, and is instrumental in achieving the club's goals. This parallel is instructive for church leaders.

CHAPTER 9

Leading Towards and In Conflict

Conflict and faith

"Making every effort to maintain the unity of the Spirit in the bond of peace." (Ephesians 4:3) A peace manifesto for the church involves commitments about how we think and act in our life together. It does not mean that conflict should be suppressed.

In thought

Conflict should not take us by surprise. On the contrary, it is integral to church life. In the New Testament, there are many references to how to handle tensions and disagreements. Disputes were a formative feature of the life of the early church (Romans 14:1-8, 10-12, 17-19: 15:1-7). Through them the Church has discovered insights into the issue under debate. Indeed, it can be argued that God has shaped the Church and the gospel it proclaims through its internal conflicts. Its own history demands that the Church recognizes that disagreements are woven into its life. By accepting the inevitability and fruitfulness of conflict, the pressure to produce an artificial harmony is reduced. When conflict does occur, there is less likely to be an anxious, reactive response.

A Christian view of conflict should be positive and hopeful. Within any disharmony, there is an opportunity for growth. Despite the difficulties and struggles, there is no space for despair. Instead, we should cultivate a deeper trust and hope (Ephesians 4:15-16). God's intention is that, through profound engagement with each other and with the issues, we grow. Greater self-awareness, a deeper mutual understanding and a more profound grasp of the Christian gospel are on offer. Nevertheless, it is natural that our hopefulness is tempered by hesitancy. In conflict, it can feel that there is much at stake. Yet, it provides a propitious context in which to learn and to discover something new. The Chinese character for crisis captures this duality, as it consists of two symbols, one of which means "danger" and the other "opportunity".

Processes to resolve a conflict should be surrounded with prayer. In turning to God, we acknowledge our dependency. We express too our openness to what may emerge through the conflict. We must guard against any defensive attitudes slipping into our prayer life, whereby we begin to pray for our own success or for the other side to change!

In action

Rather than criticizing behind someone's back, we should go straight to those with whom we disagree. No other approach is healthy for those directly involved or for the church community (Matthew 5:23–24, 18:15–20). The encounter in which the conflict is first addressed should be characterized by gentleness and humility. Laying out the problem in simple and straightforward terms is the first task.

In a conflict, it is incumbent on both sides to listen carefully. Each individual should attempt to summarize what they have heard, giving the other person the opportunity to correct any misunderstandings. Applying this careful method, while it can feel a shade ponderous, fosters a sense of mutuality. It reflects and helps us to realize the goal of understanding each other. The reference in the prayer written in the early twentieth century, but commonly known as the Prayer of St Francis, to the primacy of understanding the other is apposite: "May I not so much seek . . . to be understood as to understand."

Jesus' words in the Sermon on the Mount are salutary too: "Do not judge or you will be judged" (Matthew 7:1).Your aim in any conflict is to remain calm, open and transparent by guarding against reacting defensively. You should be slow to make judgements. Wait until you have a sure grasp of what is happening before you reach any conclusions.

You should be predisposed to work through disagreements. Reaching a constructive resolution is the outcome you want. The first step in this process is to identify the issues. Then list the underlying "interests": these are defined as the values that mean the issue matters. Your aim should be to engage with the issues, looking for mutually acceptable solutions. A satisfactory conclusion embraced by both sides can only be found if due attention is paid to the "interests" that each side is looking to defend. Therefore, only when you have drawn out all the issues and every "interest", should you begin to generate some possible ways forward. Each option must be evaluated carefully against the aspirations of all those involved. Does it meet the "interests" of both sides? Working together in developing a joint solution can be an arduous and time-consuming process. Yet, careful, deliberate negotiation is essential to finding a workable agreement. Inasmuch as the participants are prepared to work at it, to accept what is possible and let go of any preconceived ideas about an ideal outcome, a mutually satisfactory resolution becomes more likely.

In life

Hold tightly to your Christian convictions and be determined to seek a mutual solution. However heated the conflict, do not lose sight of your common commitment to Jesus Christ and the primary calling of love—be steadfast in love (Colossians 3:12–15).

If an impasse is reached, then it is wise to seek outside help from skilled conflict resolution experts. While we should begin by looking to reach a resolution within the local church, the gifts and training in mediation available in the wider church should be used if necessary. One of the organizations that could be approached is Bridge Builders, an agency established to seek to transform the way conflict is handled in the Church, which offers trained mediators.[25]

When an agreement cannot be reached and reconciliation is proving elusive, then turning over the decision to others in the congregation or the broader church could be appropriate. This requires both sides to exercise considerable trust in the wider Christian community.[26] What this means in practice depends on the scale of the dispute. With one-to-one or conflicts within a small group, this may mean allowing others within the church to arbitrate. In congregational disputes, this may mean allowing others to arbitrate or to devise a constitutional decision-making process by which all are committed to abide.

Being the Body of Christ

It is biblical and in line with our solidarity with our brothers and sisters to strive for a fair and mutually acceptable outcome to any conflict. This avowed goal resonates with and gives expression to the paramount values of peace and justice. The apostle Paul argues that taking the conflict outside the church in any way vitiates the bonds of love within the church. The direst path to take is to the law courts. Paul specifically abjures this drastic step in his first letter to the Corinthians (1 Corinthians 6:1–6).

Finding Christ's way in the conflict

Awe and reverence before God

In conflicts, there is a temptation to blame God for the difficulty we are experiencing. Why has God allowed this to happen? Why doesn't God make it clear? Why doesn't God vindicate my cause? Whatever our complaint, we cannot blame God. However strong our argument against God appears, the notion of calling God to account is fundamentally absurd. Even if we can imagine a heavenly court, who would sit in judgement and what language would be used? In God's presence, the only appropriate response is amazement and silence. At the end of the book of Job, the eponymous figure, on encountering God, puts aside his complaints and arguments, and "repents in dust and ashes" (Job 40:6).

The need for wisdom

Sadly, wisdom seems to be an all-too-rare personal attribute. In debate, victory is sought more commonly than wisdom. Rather, most discourses are shaped by the struggle for advantage, where success is defined as asserting your position over and against the competing perspectives.

God's wisdom leads us to view other people, and especially those who are different from us, with respect. We should recognize what makes anyone to whom we relate distinct to us. When we notice how someone is unlike us, this can feel threatening. We must, however, resist the urge to become defensive, which can, in turn, lead us to reject those who challenge our easy assumptions, our way of seeing the world. In any genuine encounter with another, we move from a familiar and comfortable setting where we feel in control to a strange and disturbing relationship which reminds us of how much we do not know. Through this new person, our world is enlarged, and our understanding of reality is deepened. Commensurately and most importantly, this means we move closer to God, for the stronger our grasp of reality, the better our understanding of the divine.

The reality of all social interaction is that we always, to some extent, remain strange and mysterious to one another. Understanding someone completely is beyond us. Indeed, we tend to find that the more we know someone, the more aware we are of what we do not know. Every revelation opens up a further mystery. Therefore, the closer we get to someone, the more conscious we are of our differences. This incongruity is the frustration and the fascination of human interaction. Yet, we must live with this sense of distance, and accept and enjoy our differences. We must resist the urge to ignore our dissimilarities or engineer an artificial unity. In the mystery of the other, we intuit something of the mystery of God.

Seeing life from the outsider's perspective

In line with an understanding of Christ as victim or outsider, the Church is to see things from the viewpoint of those excluded. We are called to go beyond our customary circle, to seek out the stranger, to step out of our comfort zone. Standing in this unfamiliar place, we gain new insight into God's mission and God's Church. We discover what it might mean to include those who hitherto have been left out. We learn how we need to change to reflect the inclusivity of God's love. We find out what it means to make space, to accommodate those who are outside. This is a stretching, a crucifying obligation. Yet, it is one we cannot shirk, for the imperative to be inclusive is part of the *raison d'être* of God's Church: we are to be a model for the world to emulate. For the Church to be truly catholic, she must embrace the whole of creation. In this limitless inclusion, the Church reflects the boundless love of God for the whole of creation. People of every background are under the benign gaze of God and are the subject of God's benevolent grace.

Seeing life solely from our own perspective brings exclusion and perpetual conflict

Looking out at the world only from our own point of view, along with our tendency to compete, means that we are likely to see those different from us as our enemies: though bound together by this rivalry, we find that we want what they want (and we want them not to have it when we do), and so the resulting conflicts are fought in a hall of mirrors! Those who threaten us are exactly like us in our desire for supremacy.

However, we also desire at some level to get beyond this endless round of competitive encounters. Our weariness with battling for victory leads to a search for a deeper truth. A more profound engagement with reality, we hope, will set us free from seeing life as a struggle for superiority. Once we are aware that our current interpretation of the world is provisional, our quest is to get beyond the limitations of our distorted and partial perception. This search is bound to be persistently frustrating—this is a stretching way to live. It depends on a resolute determination to refuse the lure of a settled satisfaction with the status quo.

Truthful living

It is my conviction that God meets us in the reality, the truth of our situation. In "Burnt Norton", the first of his *Four Quartets*, T. S. Eliot said that "humankind cannot bear very much reality". Yet, it is through accepting the depth and actuality of this moment, this place, this set of memories, this situation that we can co-operate most fully with what God is doing. By contrast, God is elusive in the illusions we sometimes inhabit and the many deceptions we practise.

Truthful living means "being at home" with ourselves. Aware that we are loved and valued as we are, we can patiently let God work with us. Our need for transformation must not be denied, and there should no room for complacency. Knowing that we are precious to God, we can let God continue to mould and shape us. Our fundamental outlook is one of contentment allied to a steady, patient hope in the Holy Spirit's gentle formative role in our lives.

Frequently in the Gospels, we hear the command, "Do not be afraid." This injunction—to "let go of our anxiety"—is founded on the truth that we can trust God. We can release any nagging fear when we can see that Julian of Norwich's vision of the End in Chapter 27 of her *Revelations of Divine Love* can in the ambiguity of the present reassure us that "all shall be well, and all shall be well, and all manner of thing shall be well".

Paying patient, loving attention to the other makes demands on us. We must learn how to be truly present with others. Besides that, we have our own contribution to make. Each of us is set in a particular context. From a Christian perspective, the life we have is a gift. Our obligation is to respond to what comes to us. We are to share our viewpoint. By giving and expressing ourselves, we make our contribution to our network of relationships.

While we are to open ourselves up to others and the world around us, we need also to retain our own sense of identity. We must resist being engulfed by how others present themselves. Paradoxically, however, it is only through our interaction with others that we discover who we are. To say what we think should be a consistent feature in our dealings with other people. Otherwise we impoverish ourselves and the communities to which we belong.

Taking the risk of speaking to someone is to commit oneself. What you say and how you say it defines you in the eyes of others. By so doing, you rule out the other options; you limit yourself. This sacrificial action makes it possible that there could be an exchange of views, out of which something new and innovative might arise. To enter into dialogue is to grasp an opportunity for shared enrichment.

Although we should ensure that we play our part in any situation, we must be wary of seeking to overshadow others or deny them the contribution that they have to make. This deleterious mode of behaving is defined as self-assertion. Striking the right balance here is a subtle task; it demands discernment. We are seeking to be strong without being dominating.

Respecting difference

Respecting difference is based on the truth of God's overarching love for all people. This all-embracing love is exemplified in God's Noahic covenant (Genesis 8:20–22) with all humankind. God's love and mercy for creation and for humanity as the pinnacle of the created order underpins our thinking about how to relate to others who are different from us. Tolerance is not sufficient; even respect falls short of what God intends. A favourable disposition, a desire for the best for those with whom we relate, should characterize all our relationships. This approach, encompassing our attitude and actions, comes under pressure when we interact with those who disturb and unsettle us, and even more so when we encounter those who oppose us.

Our challenge is to retain our loyalty to the faith tradition to which we adhere, whilst making space for those who adhere to a different tradition, or see themselves as our enemies. In the terms of system analysis, being self-differentiated does not mean that we cannot form strong emotional connections with others. The call is to embrace those who sing a strange song, mark a different drumbeat, tell a contrasting story. Finding differences intriguing and enriching enables us to have open, creative and stretching relationships with those who might otherwise be strangers at best and enemies at worst.

Knowing Jesus

Grace

The resurrection of Jesus is a wonderfully gratuitous and disturbing event. Confounding and shocking though it was, this cataclysmic event was consonant with the rest of Jesus' life in its otherness. Jesus disconcerted all he met, even his own disciples, and the resurrection was the climactic expression of how Jesus transcended expectations. His challenge to the contemporary cultural norms, particularly those of the religious establishment, stirred up opposition to him. By flouting the current norms of good behaviour, and especially the expectations of a religious teacher, a rabbi, he attracted the attention of the religious authorities. The resulting swirl of attention, opprobrium from his religious opponents and enthusiastic popularity from those who embraced this charismatic wonder-worker, brought a notoriety that threatened the political status quo. A combination of a conspiracy by his religious enemies and expediency by the Roman rulers resulted in his crucifixion.

Forgiveness

Jesus' prayer on the cross, "Father, forgive them, they know not what they do" (Luke 23:34) bears fruit in his Risen Presence. We see in the post-resurrection encounters that there is no harking back to the past, no mention of revenge, no lingering bitterness; rather God's forgiveness is offered. In Jesus' presence, we are summoned to move beyond our human tit-for-tat, to receive healing for the wounds of the past and journey into God's future where Jesus waits for us.

Mission

The resurrection is the centre from which any talk of knowing Jesus or having a personal relationship with him flows, and in addition it is the most important criterion for such knowledge. This means that we need to view our own Christian experience through the lens of the events of Good Friday and Easter Sunday, which epitomize and fulfil his whole life. For the raising of Jesus was the gracious giving back of his whole life, including his death. Counter-intuitively, the resurrection life of Jesus incorporates his death: he is the crucified and risen Lord. Hence, the Risen Jesus is "the crucified one". Our understanding of the Church's participation in God's continuing mission is shaped by this insight. Sharing in God's ongoing work, the Church participates in Christ's death and resurrection. Dying for the Church is marked by sacrifice and surrender. These wounds of Christian mission prefigure resurrection and glory.

The primacy of the vulnerable

The "poor in spirit", "those who mourn", "the meek", "those who hunger and thirst for righteousness", "those who are merciful", "the pure in heart", "peacemakers", "those who are persecuted for righteousness' sake", those defined by the Beatitudes (Matthew 5.1–12) share a common vulnerability. Those who are on the edge, the victims of abuses of power, are by definition vulnerable. A longing, a hope that life might be better than it is, arises out of their sense of weakness. This yearning opens them up to God and propels them towards God's Kingdom. These victims of the power and violence of the world come to Jesus. They respond to his message of grace and transformation with open hands and eager hearts.

Jesus abjures violence and condemns the abuse of power. He teaches his disciples how to respond to those who inflict violence on us, those who reduce us to the status of victim by their brutality, and those we might naturally label as "our enemies". In his Sermon on the Mount, Jesus says:

> You have heard that it was said, 'An eye for an eye and a tooth for a tooth' but I say to you do not resist the evildoer. But if anyone strikes you on the right cheek, turn the other also; and if anyone wants to sue you and take your coat, give your cloak as well; and if anyone forces you to go one mile, go also the second mile. Give to everyone who begs from you, and do not refuse anyone who wants to borrow from you.
>
> *Matthew 5:38–42*

By refusing to meet hostility with aggression, you resist those who seek to pursue their agenda through coercion. Your response is not shaped by the provocation. You are not reactive. You retain your integrity and stay grounded in your own values; in doing so you stand determinedly against your aggressor. Rather than react in kind or allow your behaviour to be in any way influenced by what has been done to you, you remain determinedly self-defined. You know your values and you stick to them. You decline the role of antagonist.

Recognizing the nature of the conflict

It must be borne in mind as we consider conflict that the drive for reconciliation cannot be an absolute principle. Although arguments between two individuals, in most circumstances, can be sorted out by mediation, reconciliation is sometimes not possible. In fact, when one side is clearly in the wrong or where there is an undeniable injustice or evil is at work, it would be absurd to try to broker a resolution. Rather, the wrong, injustice or evil must be identified and denounced. The truth must be proclaimed. A challenge to the status quo must be issued. This has an application in interpersonal dynamics as well on a larger scale. I know from my training and experience as a harassment adviser that conflict resolution is not appropriate if there is clear evidence of bullying and harassment. If that is the situation, then the victim needs protection and the perpetrator needs to be held to account.

When a conflict is rooted in an injustice, then you cannot remain neutral: to do so is, effectively, to take sides, to align yourself with the oppressor. For example, the outrage of Apartheid in South Africa did not call for mediators but protesters and prophets! Only when state discrimination along racial lines had been abandoned could the task of reconciliation begin. Following the first non-racial democratic elections in 1994, the Truth and Reconciliation Commission was set up and President Nelson Mandela appointed Archbishop Desmond Tutu as the chair. Not to stand alongside the downtrodden is to align yourself with those who hold power. In the fight for justice, your passivity aligns you with those perpetuating oppression. If you seek even to reduce the tension and take the heat out of the conflict as a precursor to resolving the dispute, you run the risk of giving the impression that the basic injustice is somehow acceptable. Of course, it is not. When the status quo maintains unjust structures and relationships, it must be challenged.

The proclivity of Christians to seek harmony, to find the *via media*, in any clash, is understandable. Strong co-operative relationships are central to a Christian understanding of a healthy community. Therefore, when there is a dispute and people are at loggerheads, it is not surprising that a speedy resolution is sought and reconciliation between warring parties attempted. Yet, in the face of injustice and oppression, the call to seek justice must be paramount. Insomuch as there cannot be authentic reconciliation without justice, justice must come first. In Christian circles sustained tension is likely to be particularly uncomfortable; the Church is predisposed to seek harmony and to shirk the challenge of making a genuine peace. The emotional discomfort generated by conflict can distort people's thinking. A darker influence might be a lack of compassion for those who suffer from an injustice. Much worse, there could be an unconscious or deliberate support for the oppressor. Christians are shaped by the prevailing culture, as well as their faith. Ideally, they view their culture through the lens of their faith rather than the other way around, but we must recognize that none of us can escape the influence of the dominant values of our context. Absorbing prejudice and even being drawn into a loyalty to the side of the oppressor can be the disturbing result. An aversion to confrontation or a reluctance to face the harsh realities of injustice may be further reasons why, instead of taking a prophetic stand against the powers-that-be, an attempt is made to reconcile. It must always be borne in mind that the quest is for transformation not a false peace.

In conclusion, in grave and dire conflicts arising out of an imbalance of power and inequity, neutrality is illusory and wrong. Instead, the Christian responsibility is to pursue robustly the righting of wrong, to challenge injustice and to fight evil. As the prayer goes, "Holy Spirit, comfort the disturbed, and disturb the comfortable." We cannot be comfortable when there is injustice; the dissonance between how things are and how they should be drives us to seek change.

The primacy of the quest for justice and truth over a false and superficial peace

Jesus made a distinction between the peace that God wants and the peace the world sometimes seeks (John 14:27). In God's Kingdom, truth and justice cannot be compromised. Falsehoods and injustice must be uncovered and put right. Those with a vested interest in the status quo must be challenged and if that means conflict, so be it. By turning over the money changers' table, Jesus proclaims his outrage at the misappropriation of the pilgrims' money. This is a powerful example of

Jesus confronting the authorities (Mark 11:1–19). Rather than preserving peace and unity at all costs, truth and justice must be pursued relentlessly, even at the cost of fomenting conflict and stirring up dissension.

Before we can determine an appropriate response, the nature of the conflict confronting us must be discerned. If there is a clear moral choice at stake, we must side with those who are in the right and oppose those who are in the wrong.

If both sides are basically right and working for the common good, then it is important to collaborate with them in order to overcome the obstacles that impede them from co-operating to achieve their common goals. On the other hand, if we discover that both sides are wrong and acting oppressively, then we must challenge them. Otherwise, we could be drawn into to mitigating a conflict, whereby we collude in maintaining an injustice!

Structural conflict

The roots of some conflicts are in the structures in which they are set, in which case, rather than thinking in terms of individuals being right or wrong, we must understand the dispute in structural terms. If a society is unjust, then any conflict must be understood in relation to the fundamental relationship of oppressor and oppressed. We realize that the conflict is not about the individuals but about the structures. Regardless of the behaviour or attitudes of the individuals, the cause of the oppressed is right and just, whereas the cause of the oppressor is wrong and unjust. Hence, not to side with the oppressed in their fight for justice is to side with the oppressor.

Loving our enemies

When Jesus commands us to love our enemies, this does not mean that we pretend that they are our friends, nor does it imply that we must avoid confrontation and conflict with them at all costs.

If we are committed to justice, then those who defend the unjust status quo are by definition on the opposite side to us, and could be labelled as "enemies". To set them free from the system in which they are oppressors can be regarded as a loving act. Christians should be engaged in deliberate action to further the cause of justice without falling into the trap of hating those who are the beneficiaries of the injustice. We have an obligation to be in solidarity with the poor and oppressed, whilst being equally passionate about the well-being of those in positions of power.

In countries scarred by grave injustice, taking sides in the conflict is obligatory; judging from a distance is not enough. Choices have to be made; neutrality is not a viable standpoint. For example, when under financial pressures, a government might consider slashing the overseas budget to cut taxes to stimulate economic growth. In weighing up the relative needs of those in a prosperous western country and those in dire poverty in the other two-thirds of the world, there is no contest. Similarly, the debate around the renewal of Trident nuclear missiles brings into sharp focus the issue of nuclear weapons per se, and whether, given other priorities, this is necessary expenditure. Surely, it can be argued, we can spend this money on better causes at home and abroad. Our task is not to find a "balance" or to find a middle way whereby we reconcile the competing interests. On the contrary, we must protest, acting and speaking prophetically on behalf of those in desperate need.

Handling conflict

The best way to manage conflict is to treat it as something normal and bring it out into the open, where it can be handled fairly and constructively.

When differences of opinion emerge, some people will choose to withdraw, whereas others will engage. As leader you need to maintain an open and friendly relationship with everyone, regardless of their reaction. Your key role is to remain connected with those who make complaints or accusations. By increasing contact time with them you staying non-anxious, gives them the opportunity to calm down and remain connected.

You need to be consistent and resilient. Conducting yourself in an exemplary way and keeping your principles is so important in managing conflict. By avoiding defensiveness and refraining from attacking, you will be able to maintain an open relationship with protagonist and antagonist alike.

Throughout the conflict resolution process, you need to be clear about your current position while being prepared to reconsider it. This conveys to others the right combination of strength and openness that, hopefully, others will adopt.

The leader sets the tone, the atmosphere of the community. By giving permission for others to be themselves, you give everyone the scope to express their individuality. As your self-awareness deepens and you become more prepared to share yourself, you, by your example, invite others to do likewise. Your own growth spurs others on to explore and discover who they are, to know why they think what they think and to offer their point of view to the community.

This attitude also allows disagreements to surface. Explicit conflict is, of course, healthier than a concealed dispute. As contentious issues surface and are tackled, you need to be able to control your emotions. Self-control starts with a willingness to take responsibility for your own emotions. Sometimes it will be wise for you to delay a response to a situation or proposal. Taking time in this way allows you to avoid reacting to any provocation precipitously and to reach a measured decision.

Being an effective leader in the face of conflict

Staying rooted in God

Your capacity to deal well with conflict is directly related to your ability to stay calm, which in turn is linked to your relationship with God. Adhering to some spiritual disciplines is good practice, whether contemplative or meditative prayer or another way of praying that suits you; the essential feature is that you have a plan for staying grounded in God and fostering a deepening relationship with God. It is worth noting that some people find working with a spiritual director invaluable in exploring and developing their response to God.

Inviting and modelling self-definition

Whenever there is a conflict in one of your relationships, it is important to discriminate between what you are contributing to the conflict and what comes from your interlocutor. No one else can distinguish between what is yours and what is not. This task is yours alone, and it must be done.

In the heat of an argument, the temptation is to react to the other on their terms. Instead, you need to breathe, take your time and respond on your own terms. Whilst listening and paying attention to your opponents, you should model for everyone how to exercise self-control and articulate your view. In openly stating your feelings, goals, values, preferences and roles, you invite others to do likewise. Instead of reacting to opponents, defining oneself becomes the norm. As a result a healthy, more mature church develops.

Be a calm presence and stay connected, especially with those with whom you disagree

Welcoming and exploring differences

Create ongoing structures that invite dialogue, feedback and evaluation. Be wary of a decision that seems to "fly through" uncontested. Seek determinedly to draw out other points of view to discover the full range of opinion, and stress how vigorous debate leads to better decisions. Moreover, set an example by even presenting views contrary to your own, whereby you will underline the value of different perspectives.

Establishing conflict as normal and productive

Expect conflict. Be open about its presence. Name it. Explore it. Invite it. Build on it. Relish it. Conflict is the stuff of growth and change and progress. Learn from it and help others to learn from it too. See it as an opportunity to learn new truths about yourself, others and God.

Do not judge

When conflict arises, it is imperative that the leader remains non-defensive and non-reactive. Symptoms of a self-protective attitude are name-calling and making threats. An open and responsive approach, on the other hand, involves a steadfast commitment to avoid making judgements about your adversaries or the strength of their arguments.

In the Sermon on the Mount, Jesus instructs his disciples:

> Do not judge, so that you may not be judged. For with the judgment you make you will be judged, and the measure you give will be the measure you get. Why do you see the speck in your neighbour's eye, but do not notice the log in your own eye? Or how can you say to your neighbour, 'Let me take the speck out of your eye,' while the log is in your own eye? You hypocrite, first take the log out of your own eye, and then you will see clearly to take the speck out of your neighbour's eye.
>
> *Matthew 7:1–5*

Here Jesus offers a searching attack on those who are swift to condemn others but are blind to their own failings. This hypocrisy is bound to draw sharp criticism from others. Yet, Jesus' point is that their critique of others' behaviour will echo God's prior judgement of their attitude. The theological principle that Christians are called to act towards others as God relates to them is inverted: if you condemn, you will be condemned. This reciprocity also applies notably with regard to forgiveness: if you withhold forgiveness, you will not be forgiven.

The illustration above, drawn maybe from a carpenter's workshop, clarifies that the fault is not in recognizing your neighbour's fault but in not scrutinizing one's own attitude and behaviour as rigorously. By neglecting to undergo self-examination, you are less acute in your judgements of others. Your own faults distort your perspective. Conversely, if you do open yourselves to reflect on your own attitudes and behaviour in the light of God's searing truth, and make repentance integral to your discipleship, then you are more likely to be able to offer developmental feedback to others sensitively and insightfully.

Underlying Jesus' teaching is the truth that we criticize others rapidly but are loath to analyse ourselves or to accept other people's critique of us. Indeed, pointing the finger judgementally at someone else deflects attention from ourselves, and can be a form of self-defence; when the focus is on someone else, it cannot be on us!

Under pressure, the tendency to judge others and to be less self-reflective is exacerbated. Therefore, it is vital that in the midst of conflict, the leader remains calm; they can then play their role in keeping the anxiety levels low and the debate rational. By exemplifying an approach that is respectful and courteous, and by engaging with the arguments, you foster this modus operandi for the whole church. As a result, the quality of debate is better; relationships between people remain cordial and the outcomes are improved.

Keeping decision-making processes exploratory

Throughout a process that seeks a significant decision in the church's life, invite feedback and suggestions. Receive them non-defensively, listen carefully and accurately summarize the concerns before responding. Endeavour to set any problem to be solved as a collaborative task. By working together to find a solution, you get the benefit of everyone's input. Mutual accountability and responsibility for the work, two of your goals, are integrated and implemented. In all your interactions, especially when they might be strained by strong resistance or outright opposition, show respect. Be absolutely committed to sustaining good relationships with all who are involved.

A salutary example

St Michael House in Coventry aims to help people to engage in conflict fruitfully and to learn, when necessary, to disagree whilst maintaining mutual respect.[27] Here is the statement from November 2011 of the House's aims and ways of working.

St Michael's House is a practical expression of Coventry Cathedral's commitment as a world centre for reconciliation to be a place where people come to address difficult and contested issues through honest, open and informed conversation and dialogue. How we occupy shared space with those who differ from us is as important as the matter under discussion. The following protocols should govern conversations convened by St Michael's House. Participants will be invited to give their consent to working within these guidelines.

Protocol One: Respect for the Space

- We seek to create a safe space where all feel welcome and respected.
- We seek to be an inclusive space, where all views are heard and diversity encouraged.
- We offer space which is private but not secret.

Protocol Two: Shape the Conversation

We invite participants to give careful attention to each other and therefore:

- Listen actively to those speaking.
- Acknowledge what others say before moving on to have our say.
- Separate people from the problem, the personality from the argument.
- Tell our stories to share about ourselves.

We commit to a process in which we:

- Accept how we and others feel and the legitimacy of our feelings.
- Become mutual and interdependent participants.

- Concern ourselves with shared interests and not defined positions.
- Develop sensitivity to the views and perceptions of others.

We acknowledge our responsibility to:

- Recognize others have a stake in the outcome.
- Remain open to the future we must share.
- Retain our curiosity in the other person.

Protocol Three: Share the Learning

We encourage participants, when possible, to openly share knowledge and understanding gained from being part of this space. We expect participants to be free to use any information received, but neither the identity nor affiliation of the speaker, nor that of any other participant, may be revealed. We require that participants refrain from exploiting others with whom they have shared this space by misuse of what has been learnt.

But the wisdom from above is first pure, then peaceable, gentle, willing to yield, full of mercy and good fruits, without a trace of partiality or hypocrisy. And a harvest of righteousness is sown in peace for those who make peace. James the Apostle.

CHAPTER 10

Being Prepared to Have Difficult Conversations

"It shall not be so among you . . . "

Mark 10:43

As a leader, your duty to challenge patterns of behaviour that are detrimental to the health of the church is daunting. Telling someone that you are concerned about their actions is risky. Offering this kind of feedback, best described as developmental, can prompt a strong reaction, even a fierce backlash. Do not be put off, though. If you choose to withhold your observations, you put the vision of a cohesive, loving community in jeopardy. Out of concern for everyone's welfare, you tell the truth. You do so in the hope that the culprit may choose to change.

Besides your role in shaping a safe, healthy community, you are also motivated to confront problem behaviour by your commitment to open and honest relationships. Taking the time and making the effort to express your concerns signify the value you place on strong relationships and on each individual. Integral to fruitful and helpful engagements with others is your determination to maintain your integrity. This entails being honest, although your honesty should be tempered by compassion. This way of relating is nurturing, providing the genuine possibility of growth for you and the other person. An instructive parallel can be drawn between the equation "confrontation plus love brings growth" and the theological dynamic of judgement and grace leading to salvation. In the honesty and truth of the best human interactions, we see mirrored how God's judgement—radical and honest—challenges us clearly to grow towards Christian maturity.

Integrity

The goal of Christian maturity is that our exterior life should be consistent with our core values. This requires integrity and transparency. An integrated life means that there is a consonance between the way we live and how we aspire to live. A transparent life means that people can see through our behaviour our interior life, our values and our hopes. When our lives are integrated and transparent, then we can be described as "living authentically".

Speaking maturely

Part of speaking wisely is matching up how we go about expressing what we want to say with the content of our communication. For example, if we wish to communicate a message, we should make a statement; if we want to receive a message, we need to frame a question. While rhetorical questions can serve a purpose in oratory, they should be reserved for our sermons or speeches, because in conversation they distance us from your conversational partner. In our dialogues with others, the aim is to be simple and straightforward. Therefore, guard against using questions as a substitute for making a statement; rather speak honestly and directly.

When we are trying to develop and maintain good relationships, speaking candidly can trigger a defensive reaction, even an angry response. When our clarity stirs up strong emotions, this can, at least initially, disturb us. In addition to helping calm the situation, seeking to be curious and to ask questions about how the other person's perspective maintains the relationship and stops the feelings escalating. However, some questions are better than others. For instance, be wary of using the question "why?", as it can feel threatening. It might appear judgemental, aimed at eliciting a response by which a person or their motives can be evaluated or judged. "What?" or "how?" can be more readily used to find out what will build up an individual or develop a relationship. "What do you think?" or "How do you see it?" are two questions, for example, that are neutral and give the other person an opportunity to explain their own position. Moreover, this kind of question helps that other person to let go of their defensive attitude and strong feelings, and reconnect with us.

Understanding anger

When faced with an angry individual, remember that beneath the strong feelings, there are concealed expectations. Underlying every angry statement, there are hidden demands. Again, the irate protagonist might be unable to articulate those demands but they are there.

Do not be swayed by their anger—remain calm. Address their behaviour. Hold them to account. If their behaviour is unacceptable, say so. Refuse to be intimidated, but do not be drawn into a personal duel of attack and counterattack. Instead, focus on their difficult behaviour whatever it might be: standing too close, raising their voice, interrupting, for instance. Then you can stay in the conversation, whilst you maintain your integrity and high standards of behaviour. By focusing not on the person but on their behaviour, you can seek to stay in relationship with the other as you stand up for yourself.

Dealing with angry feedback begins with acknowledging the other's emotions and complaint. For example, let's imagine that you've arrived late for a meeting. At the end, the convenor calls you to one side and castigates you. You could respond with "I understand that you are angry that I was not here when the meeting began. I'm sorry."

Then you can ask how you can put it right, after which you get the response, "I am grateful for your apology, but if you could redouble your efforts to be here punctually, I'd appreciate it. Your presence and contribution are so important to the success of our meetings."

The next step is to make an offer based on what you have heard. You state your position: "I see that you are content with a verbal apology. Thank you. Today I misjudged the time the journey would take because there was a traffic jam en route. I usually leave about 30 minutes to get here. I'll allow 45 minutes in future. I regard these meetings as a high priority. I value your role as convenor and your willingness to hold me to account. How does that sound?"

Once you have explained your position, you should check that it is satisfactory to the other person, in this case, the reply could be something like this, "That sounds great. Thank you for engaging with my concern so generously."

I-Statements

I-statements are laudable. They are honest, clear and confessional. Here are some fundamental statements using the first person personal pronoun that define a constructive disposition towards others:-

- "I differ from you." (To differ is not to reject.)
- "I disagree with you." (To disagree is not to attack.)
- "I will challenge you to change." (To challenge is to compliment.)
- "I will invite change." (To change is to grow.)

Holding each other to account is an aspect of caring for each other

Developmental feedback is a gift: it offers the other person an opportunity to grow. However, confrontation only works where there is a shared sense of solidarity. By making all conversations caring and supportive, you shape a culture where difficult conversations can be integral to the way in which people relate to each other. Again, a community that is characterized by mutual acceptance frees everyone to be more honest without ever being insensitive.

Authentic relationships include difficult conversations

If you are to foster authentic relationships in your church, you must learn to speak simply and listen empathetically. Moreover, these skills are prerequisites for constructive confrontation. When giving what should be labelled "developmental feedback"—rather than "negative" feedback or any other term which is pejorative—you should focus initially on your observations, not your conclusions. Your first task is to describe what you have seen without making any judgements. If the focus shifts to apportioning blame, then the conversation can become adversarial. Once the recipient of the feedback has recognized the need to change, then seek to help them to find ways forward. Rather than offering advice and answers, proffer ideas, information and possibilities. Throughout the process, favour the questions "What?" and "How?" over "Why?"

How to have difficult conversations

In order to be trusted, you must take the risk of trusting. To receive trust from others, you must show that you trust them. This requires you to open yourself up. If your vulnerability is respected, prized, and reciprocated, then mutual trust develops. With a basis of trust established, challenging conversations become more likely and have greater impact. Jesus promises to be with his disciples when they practise the art of loving confrontation (Matthew 18:20).

Plan ahead

Think through how you will approach the person, what you will say, how the person might respond. While it is helpful to consider possible ways in which the conversation might develop, you should not overly prepare. Otherwise it is likely to make you more anxious and less able to engage in a relaxed and responsive manner.

Choose a safe location

You want the person you are planning to confront to feel as safe as possible; do not do so in front of other people or across a desk. Find somewhere where the other person feels at home; an informal, preferably neutral setting should be chosen.

Ask permission

Most people will respond well to a request for a meeting, particularly if you allow them to choose the time and place. By contrast, asking to talk about "the issue now" can be seen as provocative. The best approach, most likely to induce a co-operative response, is to inform the person that there is an important matter which you would like to discuss with them and then ask when and where they would like to get together. They might decide that here and now is fine, but, even if that is the case, they would still have appreciated that you had let them decide the timing and location.

Be straightforward about the issues

Do not prevaricate; go directly to the issue that concerns you. If you try any other route, it can be seen as manipulative and bordering on the dishonest. While you need to be specific and clear about what needs to change, you need to respect the other person and affirm the importance of your relationship with them. Contrary to how confrontation is commonly understood, there is not a contradiction between being tough on the issue and committed to the person. In fact, challenging someone carefully is an indication of a deep commitment to them. Given the emotional energy required, you are more likely to confront someone who is significant to you.

Be honest about your own preferences

When we confront, we invariably want someone to change their behaviour. It is important to be clear about what exactly you want to be different. If someone is, for example, talking about you critically to your colleagues, you might express your preference and the change you want to see like this: "I would prefer, in the future, if you would come to me personally when you think that I've done something wrong. I've found that I respond best when I'm spoken to directly in a one-to-one meeting."

Be prepared to listen

Once you have shared your concerns, you must be prepared to listen to the other person's point of view. You can invite them to respond to what you have said: "Now I want to hear your perspective. What do you think of how I see things?"

Let people hold you to account

When someone confronts you, resist the urge to defend yourself. To avoid this impulsive reaction, strive to listen carefully to the person's concern. Paraphrasing their key points displays that you are paying attention to what is being said. Before continuing, you begin your summary of their position with "I want to make sure that I understand your concern . . . is this right?"

Something to be learnt

When you ask to have what will be a difficult conversation with someone, you put yourself in a vulnerable position. You put yourself on the line. They might, of course, be reluctant, or even refuse to meet. If they do agree to meet, then they might hold back from a proper exchange. Indeed, once the process begins, it might, at least at some stage, seem out of control. The path the conversation takes is unpredictable. The goal is that, in the exchange, new insights may be gained and a deeper relationship result.

A stumbling block when holding people to account

If your own comfort is a higher priority than telling the truth, then you will tend to balk at confronting people. However, unless leaders are prepared to challenge errant behaviour and obstructive attitudes, individuals, teams and organizations under their oversight will underachieve. The outcome of this inner conflict will determine the effectiveness of your leadership and, in turn, the effectiveness of your team.

Start small

If we begin to address the minor discrepancies between your expectations and the prevailing behavioural norms, this will give you an easy opportunity to practise this approach and build your confidence. By tackling these minor issues, you might, thereby, avoid having to deal with major issues. Do not be put off by claims that certain matters are trivial and not worthy of attention.

Tackle the issue close to the event

Act swiftly after you spot a problem. Ask for a meeting and specify the agenda; be direct; for example, "I want to talk with you about the delay in the project."

Creating structural tension

Whenever we work with teams, it is vital to focus on two critical states: things as they are and things as you want them to be, the actual and desired situations. The gap between the two generates a dissonance, whereby a creative impetus for change is generated. The drive for progress continues while this unresolved tension remains. Energy can be unleashed and a steely determination maintained, if the focus continues to be on what is still left to be done to reach the shared goal. Alongside celebrating steps forward, highlighting the continuing dissonance between the reality and the vision gives ongoing momentum and a continuing sense of progress.

Honesty pays in the short and long term

Be simple and straightforward in your communication. If you are, people pay more attention to what you say, both when you call someone to account but also when you compliment them. Affirmation, if you take time to give it proper weight and significance, can have an immensely positive value.

Truth within the team

Teams, even more than individuals, can be conflict-averse. Even so, dealing with reality is integral to any attempt to make the team more effective. For example, if individuals do not make the team's goals a priority over any of their own aspirations, this should be addressed. Equally, the mentality that regards someone else's troubles as not their problem ("Your part of the boat is sinking!") is not acceptable.

If necessary, ask the team to help identify the issue. For example, you may intuitively sense that there is some disharmony in one of your teams, or that there is an underlying issue that everyone is afraid to raise. Do not ignore the awareness, however vague and hazy, that there is a problem. Rather, at the first opportunity, say whatever your intuition is telling you, notwithstanding how vague it might seem. You might introduce your observation with "Now, I'm not able to put my finger on exactly what I'm sensing, but . . . ."

A learning context provides the right setting to issue the challenge to change

The purpose of any difficult conversation with an individual or within a team is to see what can be learnt by those directly involved for the benefit of the team as a whole. It is worth remembering that what is learnt by the team might be valuable learning for the organization too. A learning culture sets the tone and offers the right atmosphere in which current performance or attitudes can be challenged, and also means that any lessons gleaned for the organization are more likely to be readily received and implemented. The question "What are we learning?" should be a constant reference point for every individual, team and the organization as a whole. You should seek to create a learning ethos that embeds the principle that learning is a priority. When it is the norm to take every opportunity to learn, your team and the organization have the means to develop and improve.

Singing from the same hymn sheet

Any agency that is doing meaningful work that respects its members and is able to learn is well placed to build a shared ethos and vision, a common culture. Generating a culture demands sustained good practice; only a sustained consistency embeds the right attitudes and behaviour. As everyone works in the same way to the same ends, a gathering momentum is generated. This is a gradual process, demanding determination and a consistent approach over the long term. When there is the right alignment within an organization, there is a powerful internal unity and an enjoyable working atmosphere. In its relationships with outside bodies, it is clear and committed. Furthermore, it is better at realizing its goal; it is more effective.

A process for holding people to account

Acknowledging together the present reality is the first step. There then needs to be some analysis which will include an exploration of people's thinking about how the current situation has been reached. Once there is agreement about how the problems have arisen, work on the way forward can begin; a plan outlining what needs to be done can be constructed. After this strategy has been agreed and implementation has begun, there must be a process of regular review to check progress.

Act sooner rather than later

It is better to face the difficult issues when they are relatively small and insignificant. Delaying an encounter is counterproductive, as the situation will exacerbate and will then require a more demanding confrontation later.

Step 1: Deciding what to do

When you become aware that there is a difference between what you expected and what has happened, then you have to decide what to do. If you reach the conclusion that some action must be taken, then you need to bring the issue out into the open. This step is equivalent to saying, "Let's take a look at reality together and see if we can agree." You must, at this point, get agreement about the facts. For example, "The work was due on 14 June. Do you agree?" We should not shy away from highlighting this kind of discrepancy. We need to be those who set and defend an ethos where the truth is sought and told.

Step 2: The journey to this point—how did we get here?

Ascertaining how the present problem arose is a key stage in formulating a plan to ensure that it does not recur. A series of questions can elicit the required information. "What happened?", "What decisions were made?", "What was the outcome of those decisions?" Part of this essential process is working out the thinking that lay behind any decisions.

In reflecting on an individual's contribution to the current crisis, it is helpful to remember that there are two distinct phases of any action: the design (what was intended, and the execution) and how the plan was put into practice. A thorough and precise exploration of the story will help to identify and understand the critical decisions.

Spend as much time as it takes to help the team acknowledge the current situation and agree together a description of the present reality. To make sure everyone agrees, work on refining the description until everyone can answer this question in the affirmative: "Does this statement accurately reflect reality?"

Arriving at a shared description is often a struggle. There can be vested interests to challenge, fears of the resulting implications to calm, and defensive attitudes to manage. You will need to note but not be waylaid by the emotions aroused. They are not to be the focus; there is a task to be done. People can defer confronting reality by concentrating on how they feel: this is ultimately futile, for at some point reality confronts us! This is a ploy to deflect attention away from the onerous work of defining the current situation. Be warned: how someone feels is not related to how well they acknowledge reality. You cannot concede ground here; you must relentlessly pursue a general acceptance of reality. Without it, it is impossible to move forward.

This kind of exercise is simplified if there is clarity about who sets the expected standards and what they are.

Step 3: Working together to produce an action plan that is clear and agreed

Once there is a shared understanding of the issues and joint commitment to tackle them, the focus shifts to how that is to be done. The task is to collaborate on putting together an action plan. Following this meeting, the next steps must be specific with no room for misunderstanding. Once this detailed plan has been drawn up and has everyone's support, the leader should ask the participants to reflect and check that they feel comfortable and committed to the outcome. If they do, then there should be some formal signal that everyone is in agreement. This can be achieved by a show of hands or by asking all those present to sign the agreement. No one should leave the meeting harbouring unexpressed doubts or reservations. Otherwise, the agreement could unravel, and the leader would have to go back to the drawing board!

Step 4: Creating a feedback system

You need to establish a mentoring relationship with your team based on a shared ambition "to learn and to improve". The culture you are seeking to create can be summed up in a few pithy statements. "We can tell the truth. We can learn. We can improve professionally. This organization has room for learning." The overarching goal is to have great workers turning in great work.

CHAPTER 11

Learning to Mediate

Mediation: an overview

Mediation is a process, facilitated by a third party, whereby disputants discuss the issues causing conflict and seek to find mutually satisfactory resolutions. Typically, and certainly in church circles, the process is a voluntary one, and the parties usually agree on the mediator. The mediator's role is to assist the parties in identifying their needs and interests, to help them generate options and reach agreement.

For mediation to work, the participants need to identify their needs—what must be addressed—and their interests—what are they seeking to defend. Through careful listening and dialogue, there is a potential for the individuals involved to learn about themselves and each other, and, as a result, for relationships to be deepened. While the goal of conflict resolution is to tackle the contentious issue, there is also an opportunity for the individuals to grow and for their relationships to deepen.

While it is presented as a linear process, most mediation will cycle through various stages a number of times before making progress. Mediators should regard the logical, sequential steps as an ideal, defining the general direction of travel. It is key that those facilitating the process respond to those involved in the conflict, paying attention to their sticking points and moving forward at a comfortable pace for both participants.

Introduction by the mediators

In the welcome and introduction, try to set an informal but focused tone. To help the participants to be grounded, ready to listen and talk honestly, and to release anxiety, you may consider a number of options: spiritual or cultural rituals, prayer, silence and readings. The appropriate use of humour, when it is likely to feel stressful, can release some tension, and help the parties to relax a little.

Then state the purpose of the encounter and affirm both parties for their willingness to use mediation.

1. Welcome and introductions:

   "I am grateful that you have both made meeting a priority and have been able to make it today. I am Joe Bloggs, the Rector of the parish."

2. State the purpose of the meeting:

   "I am here to help you to resolve your conflict about how the local cemetery is managed. In particular, we are here to focus on the issue of gravestones and the action taken by the Town Council. Thank you, Mr East, for coming today to represent the local residents, and to Mr West for being here on behalf of the Town Council in your role as Town Clerk."

3. Incorporate some gathering ritual that helps the participants to reflect and to approach the mediation calmly and hopefully:

   "As you are both Christians, I thought that I would read a short passage from the Bible about God helping us in difficulties. Then I'll leave a short silence before praying for the Holy Spirit to guide us and give us wisdom as we look for a mutually acceptable outcome to this dispute."

4. Outline the process that is to unfold:

   "Each of you will describe the situation from your perspective. At the end of each of your accounts, I will try to summarize and create a list of the issues that we need to address. Once we have agreed that we have a comprehensive list, we'll then systematically look at each of those issues in turn. As we explore these issues, we'll be seeking either to reach some agreement about the next steps or, if possible, some resolution. What we are striving to find is an agreed way forward."

5. Describe the mediator's role:

"My task is to help you talk to each other constructively, in order to find a solution that works for you both. I am not here to adjudicate, to apportion blame or to tell you what to do. My role is simply to guide you through this process which gives you an opportunity to collaborate and discover a way beyond the current impasse."

6. Get agreement on ground rules:

"Ahead of the start, I should like us to agree some ground rules. Let's talk about confidentiality first. What is said, unless it infringes someone's safety and wellbeing, will be kept confidential. If we can guarantee that what is shared here stays in the room, then that gives us the freedom to be honest with each other. Are you both happy to sign up to this rule? Thank you. The second rule is that we agree to listen to each other, respectfully and without interruption. Again, is that OK with you both? Thank you."

Storytelling

There are a number of goals for this stage in the process. Paramount—and this is the key to the success or otherwise of what follows—is building trust and rapport. As the mediator, you are to model empathy and respect, regardless of your own internal reactions to what is being said. When there are marked differences between your values and the conduct of the protagonists, strong emotions are likely to be stirred up in you. You need to keep these hidden by trying to understand and to see each person's account from their perspective. You must then seek to summarize each person's story in turn, checking and revising, until you have an agreed summary.

Besides looking to capture each participant's narrative, you are listening for commonalities. You should note and record issues that surface in both versions and the feelings that both express. Beneath the stated issues, there are other issues—what is at stake—which each participant is seeking to defend or pursue.

Alongside searching for a sound understanding of what has happened, you aim to develop trust between you and the participants. These two aims can be in conflict. If you make gathering the information accurately your top priority, you are likely to ask a host of checking and clarifying questions. This is likely to irritate the speaker, and to create an atmosphere of interrogation; it can seem as though you are more interested in eliciting the facts than in the person telling the story. Therefore, allow the speaker to finish their account before asking any burning questions, and then keep these to a minimum. There will be an opportunity to gain further clarification in the later stages of the process.

When trust is low, questions, even open ones, can be problematic. Rather than using a question, a simple enquiring statement can be just as good. Instead of "Who is Mr South?" you could try, "Say more about Mr South." A simple declaration that you have not quite grasped something can prompt further conversation, for example, "I don't understand what happened to upset you." The verbs "describe", "clarify", "expand" all invite further explanation and are useful in drawing people out, encouraging them to talk. These statements signal your desire for an open, constructive exchange.

Whenever there is mistrust, there is likely to be heightened anxiety. As a result, as the first person tells their story, the other party will probably want to contest, even refute, what is being said. There will be a strong temptation for them to interrupt. You must not allow this to happen; rather you must withstand the pressure. You must remain calm and brook no argument about the ground rule, "no interruptions". Unless you take a stand the first time there is an interruption, it will become harder the next time, and rapidly you can lose control. Moreover, both parties will lose confidence in you and the process. However, it is helpful, indeed vital, that the party who is listening is able to record their concerns. A pen and a pad can be given them to write down anything and especially the points that they would like to challenge. You should also assure them that they will get their chance to put their side of the story. When the interruption comes, you might say something like this: "Excuse me. I'd like to remind you of the rule that we agreed at the beginning that we would listen to each other and not interrupt. Do log your points on the pad provided, so that you don't forget them. You'll get your opportunity to respond by telling your story. Thank you." Then turning to the other party, you can say, "Now do continue."

If you sense, as one party tells their story, that the other one is getting riled by what is being said, then referencing that emotion can help to calm the situation. "I know you disagree, and I want to hear your views as well."

The overriding priority for you is to listen. Progress will only be made if you offer support and encouragement to each participant. Your personal interest in each individual enables them to begin to broach a resolution and to take the risky step of moving from what are often highly defended and entrenched positions. While your concentration and attention are essential, you do not have to log everything that is said. What is lost in gathering information is gained in the level of trust engendered. Noting the significant words and themes of each account is necessary, however; the task is to encapsulate the critical issues and strongest feelings from both stories.

Toward the end of this stage, you should affirm both participants. "Thank you for sharing your stories and listening well to each other."

Concluding with some kind of summary of what you have heard builds confidence by making it clear that you have understood the issues and heard the feelings expressed:

> "There are a number of issues. You share a concern about 'respect for the dead', and the grieving relatives. We'll identify all the issues on the flip chart presently. I also notice that you both feel strongly about this matter. You share a common sense of hurt about what has happened, and Mr East feels 'angry' and 'sad', whereas Mr West expressed 'dismay' and 'shock'. I suggest that we move on to explore the issues together in more depth and detail."

Identification of the issues

Completing a comprehensive list of the issues is a vital stage, essential to the work that is to follow. The task is to finish with an exhaustive list that both parties acknowledge as a joint record. Otherwise, the next steps will be undermined, as other issues surface and obstruct progress. Therefore, reaching agreement is essential, and the time allocated to this phase should not be stinted. There is no short cut: as you seek to agree that you have expressed each and every issue in a way that is acceptable to both participants, you may need to check and clarify several times.

Here are three golden rules to follow as you put together this foundational list of issues:

1. Issues about the relationships are as important as those derived from the content of a dispute. They have a valid place on the list. For example:

   "Respect for each other" should be included alongside "the danger the unstable gravestones posed to visitors to the cemetery".

2. The language used to describe the issues should be neutral rather than inflammatory or biased!

   "Mr West's grumpy attitude" should be replaced, for instance, with "How we relate to each other."

3. In order to avoid a long and overly detailed list, the issues should be stated simply and generally. By keeping the number of issues low, hopefully no more than five, you make the ensuing task more manageable. For example, "safety of those using the cemetery" includes "the likelihood that a gravestone will collapse", "the risk of people tripping on them" and "the danger of them breaking, when they fall". The last three particular examples can be subsumed in the overall heading.

Until you have complete agreement about the issues and how they are described, and that the list is comprehensive, continue to check and revise until you do. Once you have an affirmative response to the question, "If we successfully tackled these issues, would that resolve the problem for you?", then you can move to the problem-solving stage.

Notwithstanding all the warnings about ensuring that you have an exhaustive list before continuing, it must be recognized that other issues might surface later in the process, in which case add them to the list!

The problem-solving and healing stage

This stage requires the mediator to be adept at switching from negotiating substantive issues to addressing tensions in the participants' relationship. Making the judgement about when to focus on personal hurts and when to give attention to the issues that have caused the conflict requires wisdom and comes with experience. As you acquire greater knowledge, you will become more adept at spotting when the antagonism between the participants makes progress on their dispute so unlikely that it must be tackled first. Skills you have acquired will help you to decide the timing of these changes to the focus of the exchanges.

You need to begin with an issue. There are different options as to how to choose the first one. Starting with the easiest first is a good idea when things are tense and trust is low. Solving one of the issues early in the process helps to build momentum and lifts everyone's confidence that a way forward can be found. In so far as there is a pressing issue at the forefront of both parties' minds which is preoccupying them to the extent that it precludes any proper engagement with anything else, then there is no alternative but to begin with it. In all cases, you are looking for the participants to agree about which issue to address initially.

Once you have chosen an issue, ask each of the parties to explain their understanding of it. Encourage them to state why this issue is important to them. These reasons reveal the underlying interests at stake. As these concerns and interests are identified, acknowledge them and capture them in a list:

> "You have both identified the safety of those using the cemetery as an issue, I'd now like to hear from you both about how this matters to you, and what you would like to see happen next."

After you've explored both parties' understanding of the issue and how their concerns can be met, you then invite them to think about how the issue might be resolved satisfactorily. Generating different options should be a free and creative process; you want as many as possible. By avoiding any judgement about the usefulness of these ideas, you foster a relaxed and free-flowing exchange. In addition, your role is to help both parties to stay positive and to state what they want. You keep focused on their desired outcomes, defined according to their own concerns and interests and not in opposition to each other.

Throughout this phase you are looking for commonalities—shared concerns or interests—as these help to build the relationship between the parties and are likely to be basis of the resolution of the issues. While there is bound to be some reference to the past and the grievance that has triggered the conflict, you need to shift the participants' attention to the future:

> "You both want those using the cemetery to be safe. Mr East is very cross that a mourner had a gravestone fall on her foot whilst attending a grave, and he does not want that to happen again. Mr West, you share that same concern, and you are equally troubled by what happened to Mrs Smith, and I know that you have apologized to her and sought to make amends. I guess that we want to try to agree to look to the future. We need to find a way of ensuring everyone's future safety. One idea that was met by nods from you both was the possibility of a quarterly check on the gravestones by the town council's head of maintenance, a 'wobble test' so to speak."

Once you have secured agreement on how an issue should be tackled, be sure to get a definitive and specific statement of what has been agreed. A precise and detailed plan results in both parties being confident and clear about the next steps:

"If you are both content with that approach, perhaps Mr West can copy Mr East into the letter to the Head of Maintenance in which the dates of the quarterly inspections for the foreseeable future can be listed. How does that sound? If you are both happy with this approach which I have encapsulated on the board here, I'll include it in my summary of this meeting, which I will subsequently send you both."

Alongside addressing the issues, you aim to help both parties understand each other and be on better terms. Therefore you take note when strong statements are made and acknowledge any hurt feelings that have been expressed. Mutual recognition of the pain and anguish caused by the conflict is integral to finding a resolution and some measure of reconciliation. Empathy is the precursor of compassion, and compassion precedes forgiveness.

In terms of mutual understanding, it is helpful to move from general statements about feelings to emotional responses to specific events:

"Mr East, you said that the way Mr West treated you hurt and upset you, and left you feeling cross. I'd find it helpful if you could give me a specific example."

When exploring the feelings generated by the dispute, you want to encourage each participant to take responsibility for their own feelings and to share them. You need to watch that they do not use the opportunity to express their emotions as another chance to blame the other party:

"When you tell us how you feel, I'd be grateful if you'd begin with an 'I' not a 'You', Mr East. Just now, you said, 'He made me so cross when he spoke to me on the 'phone. He was so brusque, offhand, and even dismissive.' Can you think of another way of putting it that centres on how you felt, not on what Mr West did?"

To foster mutual understanding, you can ask each party to paraphrase what they have heard the other one say, and to check that they have grasped what has been said:

> "Mr West, I'd like to ask you to put in your words what you have heard Mr East say. Then Mr East, I'd like you to tell Mr West what he's got right and what he's missed."

Paraphrasing each other's statements fosters a shared understanding of perspectives and feelings. By inviting both sides to articulate the other's position, you give an opportunity for clarification and a direct exchange between the two participants. Any face-to-face communication that is calm and enquiring helps to restore the relationship. As the encounter develops, and if it is carefully managed by the mediator, the relationship should become easier and less volatile, and trust, which has probably been undermined, returns. When you sense that the time is right, you can step out of the role of intermediary and pave the way for direct exchanges between the two parties:

> "Mr West, I wonder if you could tell Mr East directly, what you just told me."

After feelings have been properly aired, you should begin to think about how you can secure some movement in their relationship. Your goals are straightforward: you want to resolve the conflict and restore the relationship. Asking both participants to indicate their needs, in order to let go of their feelings, is a good starting-point. You might take the slightly more risky step of inviting them each to say something that they think would help the other to let go of their negative feelings. To assist them, you could proffer some suggestions:

> "Mr West, you might want to offer an apology, state your regret, make some commitment about the future or anything which comes from the heart which you think would be helpful for Mr East to hear."

Understandably some feelings and attitudes might be deeply entrenched, in which case do not rush the participants. On the contrary, you must give each of them the time and space to hold on to their feelings as long as they need. Ironically, if you, as the mediator, state that they can hold on to their emotions for as long as they want, this reminder gives them the leeway to let go of a grudge or the space to release blocked emotions.

Agreement and resolution

Successful mediation leads to agreement about what needs to happen next. Given that conflict typically engenders strong emotions, and the trust that is established in mediation can be fragile, it is important that any commitments are logged carefully and specifically. This builds confidence in the process and between the participants. The resulting list of agreed actions should stipulate who is agreeing to what, where, when and how. It is easy at the end of mediation, after what might have been an arduous and tense conversation, to feel some relief at a satisfactory conclusion and to lose sight of the crucial importance of this final stage. The final comprehensive agreement must be composed and checked. Otherwise the value of the mediation achieved may be lost afterwards, and you may find that all the good work has been undone.

It pays to be specific and clear about deadlines. Ambiguity is a recipe for disaster! Avoid words which are open to interpretation, such as "soon", "frequent" or "reasonable". Use specific words, dates and times. For instance, "Mr West will write a letter in which he apologizes for his rudeness to Mr East. He will put it through his door at 19 Fraser Lane, Godalming by Tuesday 3 February 2020." The mediator can use some humour about the attention to detail but must ensure that every aspect of the agreement is specified and logged.

The agreement should refer only to actions to be carried out by the participants. It should not be dependent on someone else's actions; if it is, then there is a risk that the agreement could break down because of the failure of a third party to act. Besides listing carefully each step that has been agreed, any significant exchanges that have helped the parties move towards a resolution should be recorded. Acknowledgements of responsibility and statements of apology, forgiveness and affirmation are worth recording. For example, "Mr East apologized for how he described Mr West as a 'cantankerous buffoon' to a local journalist. He acknowledged that this was grossly unfair. Furthermore, he affirmed that Mr West was fair-minded and reasonable, and was doing a good job as

Town Clerk." Capturing these significant steps that have helped restore the relationship contributes to a full, rounded and valuable summary.

Before concluding, time should be spent on guiding the disputants to agree how they will handle any problems that arise between them in the future. You might also schedule a rounding-off meeting to confirm that all the agreed steps have been taken. The purpose of this meeting is simply to check that both sides have adhered to the agreement. If that is not the case, then there is more work to be done in order to reach a final and conclusive resolution.

When you think that you have an exhaustive agreement, you need to check that this is the case. "Does this agreement as it stands cover all the issues? Are you prepared to commit yourself to it? You'll see that I've written up a date when I'll be in touch with you both to review progress—is that OK with you both? That's great."

The final act is to confirm the agreement. Signing a document which is then copied or sending both parties a copy of what has been agreed afterwards are two possible approaches. The former is preferable because it can be done there and then, avoiding any subsequent disagreement. It is essential that both parties have and retain a copy of the agreement. You hope that each of the participants regard it as binding and honour it. Beyond the meeting, it is good if you hold them to account at some set future date. Having this check as part of the ongoing process signifies you continue commitment to the outcome. Moreover, your engagement with both parties at a later date is reassuring and gives them added confidence for the longer term.

Listening principles

An ability to listen, and to listen well, is also crucial.

1. Listen respectfully.
2. Listen lightly for the words and tightly for the meaning.
3. Remain curious and open, rather than assuming and judging.
4. Listening is an act of will more than an act of skill.

Leaders in trouble

When it comes to mediating, there are two ways in which leaders can get it wrong. They can be too authoritarian or not self-defined enough. In the former case, the leader runs the risk of stifling full, honest exchanges, whereas in the latter case people do not know where you stand.

Ethics of mediation

The relationship between those at odds is the most important thing. If a conflict has developed into a crisis, then the protagonists will have begun to feel vulnerable and become self-absorbed. But they can re-engage with the contentious issue if they feel that someone has listened and understood their situation and empowered them to play their part in reaching a resolution. It is the mediator's goal to facilitate this empowerment and change of attitude. Throughout the mediator must be impartial; their only interest is to achieve a fair and favourable outcome for all concerned.

Having difficult conversations

To avoid unnecessary conflict, it is wise to agree the purpose and process of a conversation at the outset. If you are initiating the dialogue, then explain your intention and explain your understanding of the process. Then you check whether each party has any concerns and, if so, what they are. Once these have been addressed, if necessary, you can hopefully start with an agreed purpose and a way forward.

Centred speaking and listening facilitate open and honest communication. Similarly, you can disable others by not listening. Our body language can indicate swiftly that we are not prepared or able to listen. After all, most of our communication is non-verbal, for example our tone of voice or our posture. We can also disable others by what we say. Here are some examples.

Advising—telling the speaker how to solve their problem:

- "Why don't you . . . .?"
- "Maybe you should . . . "
- "If I were you, I'd . . . ."

Judging—negatively evaluating the speaker and/or their problem:

- "Don't be so awkward about it."
- "That's not very constructive."
- "I think that you're the one that's got to face up to problems."

Analysing/Diagnosing—telling the other about their motives or situation:

- "What's truly bothering you . . . "
- "Your insecurities are distorting your thinking."
- "Maybe he reminds you of your father."

Questioning—probing for more information about the other's problem. Sometimes the line of questioning can imply a judgement:

- "Why did you do that?"
- "Was that a kind thing to do?"
- "Have you considered biting your lip and saying nothing?"

Reassuring/minimizing—trying to make the speaker feel better by minimizing their experience:

- "Don't worry about it."
- "You did your best. Stop fretting."
- "Don't look so glum. Soon it'll all feel like history."

You empower the participants through the quality of your "presence"; this can be defined as your readiness to give each one your attention. As this means setting aside your reactions to each individual and what is said, this requires an inner vigilance. In so far as you notice how you are responding, you can observe what you are experiencing without being distracted by your internal dialogue. The subject of your careful attention is thus enabled to connect with their own ideas and inner resources, rather than depending on you. By listening generously to them, you give them the space and time to reach a considered decision that is authentically theirs. By contrast, genuine progress is hampered if you direct the conversation too hastily towards finding the solution. If you try to rush to a conclusion, the received message is likely to be something like this: "You do not know this situation better than I do and are less likely to be able to arrive at the right answers than I am." Short-cutting the essential stage of "seeking to empathize and understand" is likely to engender resistance. Then any advice you offer runs the risk of being rejected regardless of its merit, simply because you have not taken enough time to engage with the participants, to understand and, by so doing, liberate their own ability to find a resolution. Even worse, by undermining their autonomy, you are inviting dependency. This is unhealthy.

Reframing opportunities

Reframing is about responding to the speaker's provocative statement in a way which validates their experience whilst helping them to articulate their point more constructively.

From general to specific

The aim here is to help the speaker to focus more clearly on specific actions of events which underlie their presenting feelings or opinions:

> "He's the most difficult employee I've ever had."
>> "*Tell me in which ways you see him as being difficult.*"

> "I just don't like it."
>> "*What particularly bothers you?*"

Identifying underlying feelings

The aim here is to identify and acknowledge the feelings that underlie the words of the speaker:

> "I can't believe that they would sack me without any consultation."
> *"Sounds like you're feeling betrayed."*

> "I'm trying to do my best but I have so many people giving me conflicting advice."
> *"That must be really frustrating."*

Laundering/neutralizing attacks

The purpose is to validate the intensity of the feelings by recognizing and articulating the undergirding concerns:

> "She doesn't care about the music group. She keeps missing our practices."
> *"Ensuring the music group works well is important to you, isn't it?"*

> "He's cavalier and insensitive. We're doing too much new music and doing it badly."
> *"Singing well in church on a Sunday matters to you, doesn't it?"*

Identifying hidden offers/points of agreement/commonalities

It is helpful to acknowledge and build on hints of progress or positive movement:

> "They expect me to do all this work, but I've never had any training."
> *"So if you had adequate training, you believe you could handle the work."*

> "If he played his part, then I'm sure that we could make things better."
> *"What specific things does he need to do?"*

Responding to triangulating attempts

Try to validate the speaker but avoid being drawn into a triangle:

> "Don't you believe that he should have known better?"
> *"Clearly you believe he should have known better."*

> "Wouldn't you be livid if she did that to you?"
> *"I'm interested in hearing about your anger."*

Responding to speaking for others

It is important to try to intervene when a party tries to speak for others:

> "People are saying that we need to have more prayer meetings."
> *"Can you let me know what you think?"*

> "John and Mary have had the same problem believing his stories."
> *"Say more about the stories with which you have struggled."*

Responding to clashing stories

Try to bring clarity to a situation or to reach agreement on how to proceed from here:

> "I wasn't even there."
> *"I'm confused; you say you weren't there, but a while ago you talked about seeing Fred."*

> "She keeps saying I knew about the money, but I didn't."
> *"Say more about what you do know."*

Responding to blaming statements

Seek to avoid defensiveness or counterattack by responding to underlying fears or concerns:

"Well, you've got it in for me, no doubt about it."

"It seems that you don't think that I am being fair to you."

You're power mad. What's your agenda?"

"So you think that I am not handling this process well. How could we improve on what we're doing?"

Conclusion

Within the church, the leader has a role to spot when people fall out and a responsibility to help resolve disputes. Mediation skills enable them to play their part in facilitating the resolution of conflicts. When tension between people has escalated to the extent that their relationship has begun to fracture, misunderstandings are harder to clear up and attempts to sort things out more likely to fail. In these circumstances, there could be a need for a more formal mediation process. By your readiness to help resolve conflict, you model a commitment to engage with contentious issues and interpersonal tension. Besides facing these difficult aspects of church life head on, you signal to everyone that these situations are manageable. As a result, when dissension springs up, the church's anxiety level is reduced, and there is a shared sense that the presenting issue will be addressed. It will be known that you will not shy away from calling a meeting to talk through the conflict in the hope of finding a mutually acceptable resolution or, at least, a common willingness to disagree amicably.

These mediation skills could also be of use to the wider community. If it is known that you are an accomplished practitioner, then you might be invited to help in other contexts. For example, you might be asked to mediate between neighbours or in a civic setting. Tackling conflict well is a goal both within the church and beyond, and the church leader can be at the forefront of a societal drive to help people settle disagreements and be reconciled to each other.

CHAPTER 12

Collaborating Wisely

In his book *The Provocative Church*, Graham Tomlin argues that the church must be engaged in its local community and wider society, because the ministry of Jesus inaugurated God's Kingdom of justice and peace. Churches need to ask about how they can play their part in God's work of healing and transforming our world. They should start by considering what local issue they can tackle with the resources they have.

> Is it loneliness, homelessness, boredom, the environment, poverty or aimlessness? Naturally, few churches can address all the social problems surrounding them, but with prayer, discernment, a little research and energy, most churches alight on some ministry in their local area that can become a powerful sign that God is concerned for his creation and has not given up on it.[28]

Conversely, if the church pursues goals that it does not also seek for wider society, the church is attenuated. Disconnected from her context, the church becomes an irrelevance, pious, maybe, but certainly ignored. Distinct but separate, the church is reduced to a sect, an abstraction. For the church, there can be no interest that is not an aspiration for the community at large. For the church, there is no good apart from the common good. Thereby, churches should be seeking, wherever it is wise to do so, to collaborate with each other in the pursuit of shared goals. In addition, opportunities should be grasped to work fruitfully with other agencies beyond the church in the service of the common good.

Being good at collaboration

"Being good at collaboration" is an increasingly prized quality sought in leaders. Correlatively, greater collaboration is seen as the answer to decreasing resources in the public sector, business and the church. With a reducing number of "professionals" and diminishing congregations, frequently "collaboration" is held up as the means whereby the church can maintain itself and seek to engage in more mission activity. "Collaboration" as the answer to the current crisis has been repeated so often that it seems to have become a kind of mantra, and certainly it is so rarely subjected to hard scrutiny that it seems to have an almost mythical aura. Although the motivation to get more out of existing assets, in order to provide services, and for the church to maintain its ministry and mission, is laudable, there is far too much store set by the benefits of collaboration. Crises cloud our judgement. Denial means we are loath to accept the hard facts. Do not believe the hype! Pointing this out, however, makes you feel like the child in Hans Christian Anderson's story of the Emperor's new clothes who exclaimed, "But he's not wearing anything at all."

When we look at our experience of collaboration, we are all too conscious of occasions when it has not been worthwhile. Those involved could not agree on what had to be done or how to do it. The meetings took an inordinate length of time, and despite one or two good outcomes, they did not justify the time and effort spent on shaping and implementing the project.

In some ways when Martin T. Hansen states in his book *Collaboration* that "poor collaboration is worse than no collaboration at all",[29] he is stating something that we know in our gut already. By contrast—and again we should not be surprised to learn this—besides good collaboration being effective, it is essential in complex organizations if they are to be successful.

Since collaboration as such is not always a "good thing", we must keep in mind that it needs to be mutually beneficial to be worth pursuing. Our goal is not simply "collaboration"; we are seeking "good collaboration".

Therefore, as leaders, we are looking for opportunities for collaboration, but only when it makes sense. The decision about whether to collaborate or not demands careful thought. A judgement must be made. The question is "on what basis?"

There needs to be a proper evaluation of any opportunity to collaborate. If the prevailing culture is characterized by competition and independence, this militates against effective co-operation. Any attempts to work together can be impeded. As a result the drive and energy needed to take advantage of any possible gains will be greater. The church can be prone to parochialism from which arises a fierce independence. Allied to this insularity is competitiveness. "Empire building" can seem like a higher priority in some churches than the wider good of the church. Catholicity is replaced by congregationalism. Both these tendencies make collaboration in the church problematic.

Two other related obstacles lie within the orbit of the leader, and those whose advice they seek. Either they can underestimate the costs that are likely to include more and longer meetings, or they overestimate the benefits.

Typically collaboration requires that considerable time and energy be given to establish solid and constructive working relationships. While the participants might know about each other, their relationships are unlikely to be strong enough to bear the rough and tumble of working together. In addition to getting to know each other, the new team will have to agree the norms which will govern how they relate and how they work together. This takes time, and might not be wholly successful. Continuing misunderstandings and friction could hinder progress and drain energy.

Initially, and given the widespread emphasis on it, collaboration can seem very attractive, and we can imagine huge benefits. The prospect of synergy—the whole being greater than the sum of the parts—can be very alluring. Time savings, energy gains and great results are all appealing. However, it is imperative that the leader is not swayed by what might prove illusory advantages. A hard-headed analysis of the most likely outcomes is essential.

Bad collaboration characterized by lots of friction and poor results is frustrating for everyone and makes collaboration on other projects much less likely.

Besides being able to assess the wisdom or otherwise of collaboration, the effective leader must be able to motivate and enable people to work together when needed.

The first step is to evaluate the opportunities for collaboration. Remember that collaboration is not an end in itself; it is a means to an end. In this assessment phase, concentrate on the probable outcomes generated by working together. These need to be set out alongside the inevitable downside of collaborations: hassles, misunderstanding, the extra time and energy invested, as well as the opportunities lost through focusing your effort on this collaborative venture.

Assuming that you are convinced that there is merit in collaborating, the next task is to tackle the barriers blocking the path. An insular culture, characterized by exclusion, dogmatic attitudes and a determined self-reliance, produces individuals who are predisposed not to co-operate with others. Competitiveness and busyness can also make people reluctant to help and to share what they know. In order to remove these barriers, the leader has to unify people by setting an attractive, attention-grabbing, unifying goal. Alongside casting a vivid vision of the benefits of collaborating, the leader must establish teamwork as a core value and continually stress the importance of collaboration. In terms of the wider context, the church as a whole must seek to identify, promote and affirm opportunities for collaboration.

A compelling unifying goal is one which requires all those you ask to be involved in making it happen. Whilst resonating with each individual or group involved, the goal should be bigger than their own more local and particular aspirations. It must be simple and specific. Finally, hearts should be engaged and stirred by what is going to be done together.

Example

The organization "Street Pastors"[30] has a simple unifying goal—to care for, listen to and help those on their town and city streets late in the night and early in the morning on Friday and Saturday. Volunteers from the local churches are recruited and trained and then work together in teams. In most cases, this would not be possible without ecumenical collaboration, and brings the churches together in a venture beyond their own narrow concerns. Whereas this is clearly a mission initiative, it is not overtly evangelistic. Visibly on the streets caring for people is a practical expression of the Church's engagement with its locality.

Effective teamwork

By definition collaboration is "working together". Therefore, moulding an effective and cohesive team is integral. Besides fostering the team's capacity to co-operate tellingly, the leader must not lose sight each individual's commitment. Teamwork is undermined if any individual does not support of the goal or does not take their responsibilities seriously. There is a risk in a team venture that individuals can shirk. Hiding under the mantle of the team, they can easily conceal their lack of dedication and their inactivity.

In line with the overall goal, each individual needs to have their own goals to pursue. Given particular and meaningful tasks, they should be held accountable by the leader. Individual accountability is fundamental to disciplined collaboration.

The leader should seek to model a high commitment to the team and the unifying goal, alongside an equal dedication to individuals within the team. These twin demands do not require a rugged individualism. Far from it! The leader should be open to giving and receiving help, as this is essentially what collaboration is!

Cultivating collaboration within an organization

The first task is to have a recruitment policy that values those who are predisposed to work collaboratively. Whereas it is possible to change behaviour, it is difficult, and certainly not usually worth the effort, to try to change attitudes. Therefore, when recruiting, the leader needs to find some way to test for this mind-set. This could be asking the candidates for a post to work on a shared task. Alternatively, you could ask them to listen to a presentation from each other in turn, and observe how they engage with each other. Are they interested? Do they seem supportive?

Once in place, each post-holder should have support and proper oversight. Besides encouraging them, the leader should be looking out for behaviour that is not consistent with the drive for disciplined collaboration across the board. If swift and direct feedback does not produce a change, then coaching should be available.

Allied to individual coaching, the organization should recognize and affirm those individuals who are collaborating effectively. This means paying attention both to individual performance and results, and also to whether and how individuals are making a contribution to other parts of and beyond the organization. Working with others in pursuit of the organization's goals, within and outside its formal structures, must be encouraged.

Networking skills

Like collaboration itself, networking is costly. It takes time and effort to nurture relationships. For networking to be worth it, it must generate some clear benefits that justify the personal investment involved.

At their best, networks are a means whereby the leaders can identify opportunities. By linking up with others, you might find an idea, an expert or even a collaborative partner. In addition, you can discover and utilize resources that you would not have had otherwise, for example, people, money and buildings.

There are some governing principles relating to networking. Go beyond your immediate context to building relationships. While you need a balance of internal and external relationships, you are more likely to have too few contacts outside your locality. It is much easier and less effort to build a relationship in a more familiar setting. Yet there are likely to be greater gains if you venture to make new relationships outside your comfort zone. In a church context, there are a number of networks, ecumenical, civic, and church, both local and wider, that are worth considering.

In terms of developing a network, you are always looking to increase the diversity of your connections. The greater the range of your associations, the more benefits are likely to be accrued for you and your organization. Hence, given a choice, it would make more sense to spend time getting to know the Chair of the parish council in a rural setting better than someone else in your church.

Networking is a bridge into other worlds in which we do not usually walk. Therefore, in order to obtain access to as many new domains as possible, focus primarily on a range of different contacts rather than the depth of each relationship. Again, this is about using your time wisely.

The exception is when you need to work across boundaries on complex issues. Only strong and trusting bonds between people enable a team to handle sophisticated and nuanced information. Without the closer relationship, the team will not rise to the challenge. Therefore, in this case, special attention needs to be given to team-building from the outset. The team's work in getting to know each other will pay off.

Being a collaborative leader

The starting point for embracing a collaborative leadership style is to subvert your own preferences in service of the biggest goals on offer. In the first place, this is about your own commitment to your church. The ideal is for the church's goal to be your own, such that you can say, "I love this job. I love this church. My own aspirations match up with the church's." Yet you are not protective or insular. On the contrary, when there are opportunities to pursue one of the church's goals more effectively by collaborating with others you grasp them. For instance, if a church had as her aim "to serve God's world through prayer and action",[31] and there was talk of establishing a local food bank,[32] then you would want to be involved. Often food banks are hugely collaborative enterprises. In Saffron Walden, the Salvation Army holds the governance for the project. The Methodist Church building is currently being used as a store. Uttlesford District Council has given a grant towards the cost and provided key personnel to facilitate the project. The Citizen's Advice Bureau is a partner, and the volunteers are drawn from a number of churches right across the district. A relentless determination to further the church's agreed goals is a characteristic of the collaborative leader.

If you are determined to be a collaborative leader, recognizing all the benefits for you—you will be more effective and enriched by your work—and for your organization—the benefits of disciplined collaboration will accrue—then you will need to be prepared to take the risk of involving others in your decision-making processes. This demands a high level of self-confidence, and a security in your own ability to see and shift the arguments put forward by proponents of different points of view. Indeed, there is much merit in having as diverse a range of people participating in decision-making.

The leader's task is to ensure that proper attention is paid to each perspective; the working assumption is that everyone's view is valuable and can contribute to the group arriving at the best decision possible. By definition collaborative leaders listen well; they strive to understand what others think and the reasons for their position on the issue under discussion. Integral to good listening is empathy. As you grasp the feelings stirred up by the debate and behind the different perspectives, you'll have a more rounded understanding of the issue. In turn, you will be better informed and better able to steer the group to a wise decision. This ability to empathize finds its clearest expression when the leader can sympathize and appreciate the views and motivation of those opposing them.

By affirming those who dissent and make alternative proposals, the collaborative leader creates a safe space for others to voice their views, however contentious or at odds with others. Holding and shaping a permissive setting in which a vigorous exchange of views can happen is one of the central features of collaborative leaders.

Besides fostering debate, the collaborative leader needs to be wary that the discussion does not go beyond the stage where it is generating wisdom and helping the group make progress. Aware of the risk of endlessly exploring the issue at hand without actually moving ahead, the leader needs to know when to call a halt. This requires decisiveness. At this point, a decision must be made, and having heard the debate, it is the leader's task to summarize the salient points and to ensure that the group comes to a clear, firm and final decision.

Mastery of this inclusive style, when allied to the ability to make a wise and clear decision once the discursive phase has exhausted its usefulness, makes collaborative leadership highly effective. Besides these two prized qualities, the leader must also engineer and defend a high level of individual accountability. It is all too easy in a group setting for individuals to take a back seat, to coast, while letting others do the hard work. Unless the leader stays vigilant, some members may begin to shirk, hoping that their withdrawal from the fray will not be noticed. The leader needs to pay attention to each individual, noticing how they are and their contribution to the common task, and if necessary, signalling that their wholehearted involvement continues to be needed. Demanding that they themselves and everyone else in the group need to be accountable is also integral to collaborative leadership.

A collaborative leader needs to be humble, generous and courageous, driven by outcomes, not by personal success. The gains of successful collaboration are considerable, but it is costly in terms of time, energy and personal commitment. One of the prerequisites of this type of leadership is a willingness to give up control over the agenda. If the leader is reluctant to give up power, this makes them more likely to stick to their own narrow agendas, rather than open up to possibilities that lie beyond their own preoccupations, which might fulfil their own aims but also encompass others too.

Pride can make a leader assert their independence and claim self-sufficiency. This mentality is expressed in the assertive statements, "I don't need anyone's help" and "We can do this on our own." This bold and brash front can often hide deep insecurities. Underlying fears about being exposed, revealed as not as good as may appear, make the leader loath to be in a setting where they are going to be assessed by others.

If your own status and the bolstering of your own self-esteem are primary concerns, then, again, you will be deaf to any overtures to collaborate. Instead, opportunities that highlight your achievements, and make you look impressive in the eyes of others, will be a higher priority.

David Axelrod, President Obama's campaign advisor, rightly divides leaders into two types: those who want to be something, and those who want to do something.[33] Collaborative leaders are those who are not bothered about being someone but about getting something done.

Working effectively, achieving our goals often demands that we work with others, that we collaborate. This is not incidental to leadership but integral to it. After all, one of the defining roles of a leader is uniting people to pursue a shared goal.

Leaders who successfully incarnate the disciplines and avoid the distractions are liberators. They set people free to achieve what would not be possible in any other way. In so doing, they open up the future, and bring new opportunities within reach in the present.

The Holy Spirit, the Go-Between God,[34] unites people across cultural, ethnic and cultural barriers in a communal mission. The Spirit opens up the future, revealing the concealed possibilities in what can often be a highly ambiguous present. Inspiring collaboration is central to the Spirit's work.

Having had an overwhelming experience of the Spirit which they struggled to describe—"there came a sound like the rush of a violent wind" (Acts 2:2)—the first followers of Jesus surged onto the streets of Jerusalem. There they found a multicultural crowd who were baffled by this "sound" and perplexed, because each could hear these disciples of Jesus in their own language as they spoke of "God's deeds of power" (Acts 2:11).

Peter explains what has happened by referring to the works of the prophet Joel,

> In the last days it will be, God declares that I will pour out my Spirit upon all flesh, and your sons and your daughters shall prophesy, and your young men shall see visions, and your old men shall dream dreams.
>
> *Acts 2:17*

When people seek to collaborate on worthwhile goals, the Holy Spirit is there to help—there to empower the leader, there to build trust, there to give insight, there to unite and guide. The leader's task is to discern when and where collaboration makes sense, and, where it does, to unite and lead. The leader's role is to differentiate between pipedreams and realizable dreams, to see where there are blind alleys and where there are open vistas.

In response to those living on the streets in Peterborough, Ed Walker began to think about how churches in the city could best respond to this need. Now the charity 'Hope into Action' is established with a clear sense of purpose. The vision is to galvanize churches to provide the homeless with a home. Its goal of churches offering hospitality to the homeless in 20 towns by 2020 is within reach. Central to its success is collaboration between local churches and the charity.[35]

Having identified homelessness as an issue in its locality, a church gets in touch with Hope into Action who offer support throughout the ensuing process. The next stage is for the church to buy a house to support two or maybe three people in a vulnerable situation, such as ex-offenders returning to the community or those coming out of rehabilitation for addiction. Each church should consider which cause of homelessness on which to focus. This decision needs to be informed by consultation with the statutory authorities, consideration of other third-sector provision and the reasons why people are homeless in their area. Hope into Action provides professional support to the church; in particular, it secures rent or housing benefit, so that the church gets a return on its investment. Besides providing a loving community in which the residents can find supportive relationships, the church offers practical support and prayer.

This collaborative venture enables, as the former Archbishop of Canterbury Rowan Williams declared at the 2016 Hope into Action conference, "people in our churches to recognize that they can actually do something". The charity aims to engage the church in housing the homeless, thereby transforming the church and the lives of the tenants. By providing a home and people who are committed to loving them, the church enables the tenants to embrace change. This is signified by first of all maintaining the tenancy. Other indicators that the setting and support are proving life-enhancing for the tenants are improvements in how they manage their money, better social relationships, not breaking the law, reducing dependency on drugs or alcohol, and taking on some voluntary role through which they can help others.

One of the major contributory factors to homelessness is a relational poverty, a lack of love. Through their active and faithful commitment to the tenants, the members of the church make up this deficit and point them in the direction of the source of love, God. At the 2017 Hope into

Action conference, Ed Walker spoke powerfully of the ethos of the charity that they seek for the church to share:

> So we want mutuality in our relationships, because we see every tenant as equal, precious with innate worth, talents and strengths and gifts. We reflect that by trying to welcome rather than judge, 'listen to' rather than 'speak at', focus on strengths rather than needs or risks, give responsibility, choice and power, rather than support, charity and hand-outs.

The work of Hope into Action is grounded in a collaborative approach, characterized by a clear focus on the wellbeing of the other, in this case the growing number of people sleeping rough on our streets. This commitment to loving, supportive relationships directly with the church and the tenants, and indirectly through the church members with tenants is life-changing. By this clear and specific action, this exemplary charity is in its own terms "fighting injustice and releasing the oppressed".

CHAPTER 13

Forgiveness

Underlying the call to forgive is an understanding of how God relates to us, and how, as a result, we are called to relate to each other. Since we have been embraced by God in Christ, welcomed, accepted and affirmed, we are to respond in the same way to others. The drama of embrace depicted beautifully in the warm and generous welcome of the Father for the returning Prodigal Son in the eponymous parable is to characterize our lives. In our encounters with others, we put aside our labels such as "good" or "evil" or any prejudgements like "enemy" or "friend" and simply identify them as one of us, a frail, fallible human being. In so far as we recognize our common humanity as primary, we can put aside any social mapping or any other classification. On this basis, we give ourselves in welcome; we seek generously to readjust our identities to make space for them and embrace.

This initial response reflects the primacy of grace in our relationship with God. Immutable and indiscriminate, we endeavour to relate generously to everyone. Nevertheless, this predisposition does not preclude addressing any truth that is between us, or seeking justice one from another. Relationships must be built on honesty and integrity. Wrongs need to be acknowledged, and if necessary put right. Debts need to be honoured in being paid or in forgiveness.

Family systems

As part of the leader's involvement in assisting parishioners to face difficulties as they move to a position where they can forgive, and ultimately if appropriate to reconcile, it may be useful to have an understanding of the role family systems may have played in the situation. An analysis of our own family systems and the reactions they cause in us is also a route to a greater understanding of ourselves as people and as leaders. We need to watch that we do not bring our own unresolved emotional issues to bear on the troubles brought to us by others.

Whenever a person realizes that they are reacting strongly to some provocation, this is indicative of some unresolved problem in themselves. Feelings of anxiety, frustration, anger and sympathy that seem to be out of proportion can relate to some aspect of their past and demand some further exploration. Taking time to reflect and consider what might be behind their disproportionate emotional response can contribute to their self-awareness. Any hours or energy invested in understanding yourself better is worthwhile. Indeed, this should be a high priority for anyone in leadership.

The main way to increase involvement and commitment in the church is for the leader to become safe and less anxious. This demands that the leader give attention to their relationships with each member of their family, particularly those in their birth family. By becoming more grounded, whilst also remaining true to themselves in this network of relationships, they are able to function better in the church setting. Especially, as leader you will learn how to be with each church member in a less reactive and more interested, curious way. By maintaining a safe emotional distance, there is space for a healthier and deeper engagement with each individual. Additionally, you can hear people's stories about others as an attempt to manage their own anxiety and vulnerability.

Reaction to family patterns

A person's patterns of interrelating in their birth families have a significant influence on their future behaviour. For example, if their childhood has been characterized by conflict, then there will be a tendency for them to live in reaction to it. Either they will seek to avoid conflict or tend to seek it out. Whatever response they make will be in reaction to those earlier and formative experiences.

Additionally if they grew up in a family where anger and conflict generated anxiety and discomfort, an angry person would stimulate this response in them, and they would find it difficult to be around an angry person. We are, inevitably, shaped by our early experiences. What we have encountered and how we have been in our childhood determines our own gut reactions to people and situations that remind us of these early and telling experiences.

A prerequisite for beginning to redefine oneself in one's family is an appreciation of the individuality of each member and an acceptance of the choices that they have made. As a person begins to behave differently in the family, this will impact on the system and the different relationships within it. Almost inevitably, this will elicit a response and, maybe, a strong one. In the face of this challenge, the person needs to stay firm but non-reactive. They need to stay calm and maintain their redefined self. As a person persists with a strong and more clearly defined sense of self, this will exert some pressure on others to better define themselves. This is healthy and propitious; one person's growth fosters other people's growth.

When a person experiences anxiety in their relationships in their family of origin, this is, frequently, evidence of an unresolved emotional attachment. This is further put to the test by two questions. How often in relating to your parents do you find yourself reverting to teenage behaviour and attitudes? To what extent are you reactive to another family member or to their reactions to your beliefs, values, feelings and actions?

It is human nature to want to distance ourselves from those who cause us anxiety. High anxiety signals discomfort, unease; it is disturbing. In an attempt to make ourselves feel more comfortable, we blame others and, in the face of criticism, become resolutely defensive. This might mean simply refuting an accusation about our behaviour or could even stretch to denying some facet of who we are. Our strong reaction is a smokescreen to others and to ourselves. Rather than face ourselves and the results of our actions, we point the finger at others and repudiate our contribution to the tension, or outright conflict. Our aim in so doing is to hide from our vulnerability.

Systems thinking in a pastoral setting

We must not collude with those who attribute their own problems solely to what other people have done or to changing circumstances. Their interpretation of their situation should be heard compassionately but must be understood as an attempt to relieve their own anxiety. If we know that their story is shaped by a desire for comfort and a sense of security, then we have gained some distance and a sharper perspective. From this position, we can begin to be a resource to them. Our goal is to help them put their grasp of the issues they are facing into a broader context and to acknowledge their own part in the emotional process of the story. We achieve the latter by asking questions about their role in the problem. Probing their own thinking, feeling and behaviour can lead them to useful insights about their contribution to whatever is happening. Beneath the presenting issues may well lie some deeper unresolved emotional issues. Helping them to become more aware of these underlying tensions is a worthwhile aim. This profounder understanding of what they are doing and what emotions from the past or other relationships are arising in the current context can enable them to act in a freer and more thoughtful manner in the here and now.

Unresolved emotional attachments

Developing an ability to diagnose unresolved emotional attachments can greatly assist a leader. Here are some symptoms to recognize.

Destabilizing coalitions

When members in a family system take someone's side or the side of a particular group, then the system's stability is in danger. In short, coalitions hinder self-differentiation and free, unfettered interaction. They shake the system. The cohesion of the system is at risk. If the system cannot withstand the pressure, then it will fracture.

Watch out for fusion

Over-involvement with or distancing from the family are both symptomatic of fusion—the individual has been unable to form a separate identity and to detach from his or her birth family.

The level of openness, the willingness to explore differences and the degree of significant emotional engagement are indicators of maturity. Someone who is open about their views, prepared to encounter contrary opinions to theirs, has a developed, independent, sense of identity. They are an emotionally mature individual.

Cut-off people cannot heal!

If someone is disconnected from a member of their family, if they are effectively cut off, if they do not see or speak to them, then they will bring a disconcerting intensity to their other relationships. The unresolved issues that have led to a severed connection within the family are carried into future relationships. This displaced anxiety loads these subsequent relationships with a heavy burden. Any emotional issues will be approached with heightened sensitivity and draw a more intense response.

Seeking respite through running away!

Although physical distance can reduce the emotional intensity of a relationship, it does not deal with the established pattern of relating to others that, sadly, is carried wherever we go.

Formative birth family experiences

If an individual blames their parents, they are generally going to blame others for their unhappiness. If they were always "wrong" at home and never found approval, then they will probably find themselves depressed and guilty in their relationships beyond the family. In trying to make sense of problematic people, we should try to imagine them in their family of origin. Any insights gleaned that can help us picture them in that setting will enable us to understand them better.

Watch out for your own role

Whenever analysing a difficult situation, it is important to consider thoroughly the immediate context, including your own role. Only once you have made an exhaustive exploration of the known factors and how they interact can you settle on a comprehensive explanation.

Words of encouragement can foster dependency

Giving praise can be a cloak for fostering a self-serving emotional connection. If someone is consistently offering encouragement, it might be because he or she wants to be in a superior position in the relationship. Ostensibly they are in an affirming role, but they are likely to hinder the recipient's self-differentiation and militate against their individual growth in self-awareness. Their ongoing positive feedback hampers the individual's ability to assess their own actions and their autonomy. In short, it is unhealthy and can become, at worse, collusive.

Knowing the limits of your responsibility and avoiding exhaustion

There is a direct and unsurprising link between those who regularly take responsibility for the functioning and wellbeing of others and burn out. If you choose to act like a "rescuer", instead of letting others face the consequences of their behaviour, then you are putting yourself under intense pressure. In order to steer clear of breakdown when you will be no good to anyone must be aware of where the boundary lies that separates your responsibilities from those of other people.

Projection on to a third party

This kind of projection can lead to a number of outcomes, depending on the dynamics of the relationship; if there is an inequality between those relating, then dependency can result. For example, a church might propose to help a community group. As long as the church restricts its activity to those things that the community group is unable to do, this can be a healthy and constructive dynamic. Notwithstanding this, the greatest gift that can be offered is an interest and curiosity that will foster and enable the community group to develop its own strengths and response to the challenges it faces. In order to remain in this engaged and enquiring position, it is necessary to contain any anxiety about the imbalance in the relationship—we are stronger, therefore we should help more—and to resist the resulting desire to intervene to make things better. There could be, in some circumstances, external pressure from outside the relationship or from the group themselves for the church to play a greater role. Whatever the source, this force to be more involved must be withstood. Instead, the church community must stay non-anxious by remaining thoughtful and connected, rather than fleeing the pressures to be more committed. By so doing, the church is in the best place to keep probing and clarifying where its responsibilities lie. Commensurately, it will avoid putting the community group in a constant position of weakness and to be continually looking for support and help.

A much more sinister example of projection on to a third party is scapegoating. Interaction with people who by definition are radically different can often provoke anxiety and discomfort. Sadly, this unease can swiftly lead to rejection and condemnation. This response can be triggered by divergence around racism, sexuality, religion or culture.

Taking the initiative in peacemaking

In the Lord's Prayer the correspondence between receiving God's forgiveness and our own willingness to forgive is clear. "Forgive us our sins as we forgive those who sin against us" manifests this essential connection between how we expect God to relate to us and how we, by implication, should relate to others. Certainly, it seems that we can only seek God's forgiveness if we are essentially predisposed to offer, or at least strive to offer, forgiveness when people transgress against us.

Likewise in worship; we cannot authentically offer a sacrifice of praise and thanksgiving whilst bearing a grudge or being aware that we ought to make amends when we have wronged someone. Jesus teaches, in line with the prophetic tradition, that the validity of worship depends on a commitment to justice and integrity in the rest of our lives. Thereby, if we know that we are at fault, we must seek to put matters right before we worship (Matthew 5:23–24). Jesus' instruction to interrupt worship, in order to be "reconciled to your brother or sister", indicates the urgent and ineluctable call to be a peacemaker.

A reflection on reconciliation

Given the strong and frequent demands in the gospels to forgive, there is a danger that forgiveness can be offered precipitously and superficially. There can be a rush to proffer and receive forgiveness when those involved are not ready to do so. Despite the clarity and simplicity of the injunctions, it must be recognized that forgiveness is not easy; the worse the injury the harder it is.

A hurt or an offence inflicted in an ongoing relationship is particularly hard to bear; the closer and deeper the connection, the more painful the wound. An open and good relationship is characterized by trust and intimacy. Within this safe setting, people are prepared to be vulnerable with each other and to share confidences. Moreover, risk and commitment are two consistent features of a healthy and developing dynamic.

Whatever the nature and depth of the relationship, when one party hurts another, inevitably the one who is wounded will withdraw. The aim is to gain a safe distance. While it might be momentary or last for years, it should be acknowledged that this is a rational and healthy response. Leaving a painful situation in order to get some relief and decide what to do does make sense.

There can be an impulse and an imperative to rush to be reconciled at this stage. Withdrawal can appear and feel immature and, with numerous calls to forgive ringing in one's head, there is a strong motivation to return to the relationship ready to make up. Although a sense of urgency and a strong commitment to sort out the conflict are laudable, they can prove counterproductive. What can result is a hasty but superficial exploration of what went wrong which leads to a false harmony. On the surface, it might look a textbook resolution—forgiveness offered and received—but the underlying hurt has not been properly addressed and the trust between the parties remains impaired. By withdrawing, some space will be created, and making the best use of this distance is vital to open up the opportunity for a heartfelt and profound restoration of the relationship.

The first step for the injured party is to explore and articulate what has happened and how they feel. Admitting the sense of grievance and putting their emotions into words, and ideally sharing their reaction with someone else in order to get some sense of perspective, all contribute to getting to the truth about themselves and insight into the conflict.

Besides being aware of what has happened to trigger the withdrawal, there should be some reflection on how the current situation relates to other conflicts. There might be some resonances with a previous relationship or a reminder of a deeper hurt from the past. The impact of our own personal history can accentuate our emotions and exacerbate our sense of injustice. Self-awareness is crucial if transference and projection are to be taken into account: we can think that we are fighting our vicar, but it is our relationship with our abusive father that is generating the animosity and the heat. A helpful question in this process of self-reflection is "when have I felt this way before?" Telling someone the answer or writing it down can bring further clarification, deepen self-understanding and help to differentiate between emotion that belongs to the past and what arises from the present.

Throughout this phase, the goal is greater self-awareness. If we know how we have been shaped by past traumas and hurts, then we are less likely to be in their grip. Moreover, by telling and retelling these stories of pain and anguish, we diminish their power to influence our present. If they are heard attentively and compassionately, some measure of healing can result.

The next stage is for the one who is hurt to be in a position to recognize their own power to affect the other and to play their part in seeking reconciliation. This must be an authentic, unhurried and free choice. It should be cold and rational, based on a clear assessment of the risk involved and a willingness to take that chance.

For genuine reconciliation to happen, the offender and offended must be ready. Approaching this restoration of the relationship maturely demands an appreciation of the complexity of interpersonal dynamics. In most cases, the responsibility to forgive will not be the sole prerogative of the one who has withdrawn. The other customarily false assumption is that both should share the responsibility equally; they are both at fault and blame belongs in similar measure to each of them. In however fumbling and awkward a way, the inevitable asymmetry should be addressed. Whereas it is bound to be a struggle, a real attempt to understand and express what happened makes genuine and lasting reconciliation more likely.

Forgiveness—a process, not a one-off act

In extreme cases, for example when someone has been abused, the most that can be possible, and it might take years, is forgiveness. Reconciliation will be out of the question for the foreseeable future, and will in all but exceptional circumstances be thoroughly inappropriate; the legacy of pain and the risk of reverting to destructive patterns are too great.

It is essential when deep wounds have been inflicted on someone to recognize that forgiveness results from negotiating several stages. Whereas the focus here is on severe breakdown in relationships, the principles have a universal relevance to any broken relationship.

Remembering the offence and acknowledging its consequences are a vital first step. Listening to the survivor as they talk about what has happened to them helps them to assimilate their experience and to come to terms with their memories. Paying attention to someone in pain, and hearing what may be harrowing accounts of abuse, is demanding. The temptation is to shy away from the anguish, or to avoid the strong emotions –such as anger and hatred—that arise in them and in you. Worse still, at the outset, there can even be a tendency to side with the offender, and to deny that anything untoward has taken place. We must be on our guard against these propensities and resolve to stand with those who are hurting, enabling them to remember. A compassionate and gentle attention that enables them to unfold their story slowly and thoroughly is a healing gift for those who have been victimized.

It is equally imperative that the offender remembers. Their own recovery depends on their willingness to recall and, moreover, to take full responsibility for their actions. Engaging with the damaging impact that they have had on the survivor allows them to enter deeply into what they have done, thereby opening up an opportunity for them to learn and grow themselves.

Once it is established that someone has been wronged, this basic reality should never be undermined by minimizing the offence. Any insinuation that forgiveness equates to accepting or negating the offence must be resolutely challenged. The distinction between how the victim chooses to respond to the abuser and the original offence must be retained; they must not be blurred. Any misuse of power is unacceptable and our hold on this conviction must not slip.

Strong emotions, such as anger, hatred and bitterness, are a natural outcome of abuse or offence. Thus, there should be no blame attached to the victim for experiencing and expressing these feelings. In fact, working through these emotions by giving them full vent, and having someone acknowledge the underlying pain, are necessary precursors to forgiveness and healing.

Healing is a lengthy process, and forgiveness, which is integral to it, also takes time. Whereas trying to expedite this healing journey is likely to hamper progress, it can be fostered by a supportive church community and by skilled interventions from individuals. In order for genuine and lasting healing to result, the survivor needs to experience justice. Alongside proper acknowledgement of the offence, the offender must be seen to have been held to account. Any restitution that the offender can offer should be facilitated; though it might only be symbolic, it would still be of value.

Reconciliation follows forgiveness; this is the irreversible order. Yet, reconciliation may or may not be possible. Although survivors of domestic violence or sexual abuse might be able to let go of the bitterness and hatred, and no longer hold what has been done to them against their tormentor, it might be far from wise to make any attempt to restore the relationship on any kind of footing. The wounds of the past could still be open. The memories continue to plague. Trust could well have been conclusively and definitely undermined. In this case reconciliation would not be possible or advisable.

However, for the offender reconciliation with God is always possible. In knowing God's forgiveness, they can find some release and learn to forgive themselves. Admitting and repenting of their sin opens up the opportunity from their side for reconciliation. Yet they must wait patiently for the victim to be ready for the some renewed contact. They may never be ready. But by letting the healing process takes its slow and tentative course, it may happen. The task is to be open to the gentle, gracious work of the Holy Spirit as you respond to the pain and hurt. Gradually, some faltering steps towards forgiveness might be taken.

The call to peacemaking in the church

By way of conclusion, let us look at Matthew 18:15–20. While the situation Jesus addresses is clearly defined—"if another member of the church sins against you"—the underlying principles apply to all squabbles or disagreements when often it is harder to know who is in the wrong.

The first observation to make is that Jesus assumes that there will be interpersonal conflict in the Christian community. This recognition should give us some freedom in being honest about its existence and should fortify our commitment to engage continuously with conflict. There is no latitude for ignoring it or "brushing it under the carpet". The injunction is unequivocal: tackle it head on!

Initially, it is the prerogative of the antagonist and protagonist to meet and to engage in dialogue about the contentious issue. This kind of encounter can be a daunting prospect which means that arranging to meet demands some courage, although, in this scenario in this passage from Matthew's Gospel, it seems as though the protagonist's agenda is straightforward, to tell the antagonist how he has wronged him. In general, going with an open mind, ready to listen as well as speak, is the required approach. Shared vulnerability and mutual trust are the conditions that are likely to make the exchanges most fruitful. In order for each party to "listen", they must know that they are valued and respected and are going to be heard in due course themselves.

If, for whatever reason, the "one who has sinned against you" does not listen in this initial encounter, and it seems that this will be judged on whether repentance follows or not, then Matthew outlines a staged process. The next step is for the protagonist to return with two or three others; these additional church members corroborate and add weight to the legitimacy of the grievance. In so far as the common goal of all those confronting the one who has provoked the dispute is to seek a mutually satisfactory outcome, then the continuing aim is to ensure good communication and high-quality listening.

If they do not prevail, then, Matthew says, the one who has caused offence is asked to come before the whole church. Then they seek to persuade them to listen, and strive to find a satisfactory resolution. In short, repentance, restitution and reconciliation seem to be what is required.

It is recognized, however, that the offender might continue to remain stubbornly resistant to persuasion, even by the whole church, in which case they are to be treated as a "Gentile or a tax collector". By effectively placing themselves beyond the community's oversight and authority, they have placed themselves at a distance from the church. Their position needs to be acknowledged and to be reflected in the church's relationship to them. What this means in practice is a moot point. Clearly, given the context, the reference to a "Gentile or tax collector" signifies that those who persist in defying the ethos and disciplines of the community must be regarded as having left. Notwithstanding their decision to withdraw, any community trying to abide by Jesus' teaching and follow his example must continue to pray for the outsiders and love them. In practice, this means remaining open to them, keeping in contact and seeking to encourage them to repent and return.

Having set themselves at odds with the community, the offender is also regarded as rebelling against God for the decision of the community has God's authority. Rightly, we should be wary of equating a church community's decisions with God's too readily. Hence, we need to add the caveat that each church must be similarly accountable beyond itself. As individuals can go astray, church communities can also lose their way. By consulting and checking with other churches—and the wider the circle the better—each church mitigates the risk of cultural and other factors distorting its thinking and judgements.

As Christians engage in this difficult process of seeking to resolve someone's sense of grievance, they can be assured of the Father's help and Jesus' presence with them (Matthew 18:19–20). Being a church committed to peacemaking in her internal life is bound to be demanding; openness, vulnerability and courage are required of the participants. Yet, this kind of encounter is not peripheral to the church's life but at its heart.

If injustices are not put right, if injuries are not healed, and if infringements are not admitted, then community life is undermined and the witness of the church jeopardized. The goal is for slights and wrongs to be swiftly admitted, and for forgiveness to be offered and accepted with alacrity. Directly after Jesus outlines this carefully crafted process, Matthew emphasizes the importance of forgiveness through an injunction and a parable of Jesus.

The imperative to forgive is underlined by Jesus' rejection of a numerical approach to the question of forgiveness. Against the backdrop of the teaching of some contemporary rabbis, Peter's proposal that a disciple is required to forgive seven times could appear generous. Yet Jesus refutes this pedantic, scholarly way of answering the question. His citation of seventy-seven times or seventy times seven is designed not to make the counting task more challenging but to undermine this calculating attitude. Martin Luther King encapsulated Jesus' understanding of forgiveness when he said, "Forgiveness is not an occasional act; it is a permanent attitude."[36]

The mandate to live a life characterized by forgiveness is grounded in God's forgiveness of us. "Relating to others in the way God relates to us" is the theological principle that undergirds much of Jesus' ethical teaching. If we are not prepared to offer to others the forgiveness that we have received, then we are liable to face God's judgement. In the parable of the unforgiving servant, the servant is released by the king from a far greater debt than he refuses to expunge for a fellow servant. Given the scale of God's mercy to us, how can we not be merciful and forgive our brothers and sisters? The severity of the punishment for the "unforgiving servant" demonstrates clearly that a readiness to forgive is fundamentally important to Christian discipleship and integral to Christian community.

CHAPTER 14

The Church Leading the World to
Maturity in Love: A Final Reflection

"When I survey the wondrous cross . . . "[37]

"Take up your cross daily," said Jesus Christ (Luke 9:23). The Christian leader is always first and foremost a follower. Costly, self-giving, sacrificial love is the touchstone of Christian discipleship and the hallmark of Christian leadership. For the follower of Jesus, this kind of love is not defined by another collection of words, or packed with meaning through some carefully chosen illustrations. Definitively, it is circumscribed and portrayed by a single historical event, the crucifixion of Jesus. That's why Dietrich Bonhoeffer stated that "when God calls a man, he bids him, 'Come and die.'"[38]

To lead a church to maturity in love will be costly. The demands of this kind of leadership will leave you feeling stretched and remind you of the centrality of the cross for Christian discipleship. Following Jesus in the way of white-hot, purging love is constantly a challenge. Insomuch as you are finding leadership testing, you are staying close to the One you follow. Being tested, and sometimes almost to breaking point, is integral. As you yearn and strive for the church you lead to be slowly and steadily transformed, reflection on the crucifixion will be instructive. Adoration of Christ crucified should be central to your spirituality. His eternal gift of his life is inspirational and sustaining.

Whilst costly, sacrificial and challenging, Christian discipleship which shapes the leadership described in this book, is, perhaps to some paradoxically, freedom. In the words of the Collect for Peace in the *Book of Common Prayer*: "To serve you is perfect freedom." Authentic freedom is about receptivity and responsiveness to the Christ who leads us. Letting go, foregoing the anxious grasping and grabbing that typifies western culture is essential to discipleship and, as such, fundamental to leading a church to maturity.

Authentic freedom is also the fruit of a commitment to peace and a rigorous pursuit of truth. In striving to grasp reality, there needs to be a radical and ongoing engagement and reflection on experience, in order to arrive at and check your own perspective. Besides this careful attention to your own interpretation, you must also attempt to understand other perspectives through focused listening.

Albeit the relentless search for truth is vital, it does have its dangers. Without love, those striving to find out what happened and to discover reality in the here and now can become hard-hearted. Instead of the truth setting people free, it is used to entrap. The commitment to truth must be accompanied by a commitment to embrace others, by the priority of community.

Forgiveness is the boundary between exclusion and embrace. Once the truth is acknowledged, and forgiveness proffered and received, a warm embrace must mark this transition from enemy to friend. Although rendered a victim, Jesus Christ refuses to conform to the values of exclusion, violence and brutality. He is not defined by those who conspire against him, and have him crucified. By stark and telling contrast, Jesus Christ forgives, and even makes space for them in himself, and, consequently, in the divine life. Bewilderingly, the cross signifies excruciating violence and unbearable compassion. Even *in extremis*, Jesus Christ reaches out in a loving embrace. He prays for those who are brutally killing him: "Father, forgive them for they know not what they do" (Luke 23:34). He binds the Beloved Disciple and Mary, his mother, together in mutual love (John 19:26–7). To the bandit crucified with him, who has faith in him, he promises paradise (Luke 23:42–43). These three sayings from the cross herald and demonstrate God's loving embrace of all people in Jesus Christ.

Jesus Christ "opens wide his arms for us on the cross",[39] in order to create a space for us in God's life. Held in this embrace in eternal life, we are bound to create space for others, their longings, hopes and priorities, in our communal life. In short, we are summoned to offer divine hospitality to others, regardless of what they are or what they have done. Even the deceitful and unjust are included in the loving embrace of Jesus Christ on the cross. This should not surprise us, for we talk readily about the "forgiveness of sins" and the "redemption of the world". Perhaps these momentous truths reel off our tongues too easily. Yet, the implications of this new reality created by Jesus Christ still have the capacity to shock and even outrage. When we realize through personal encounter, particularly with those we find difficult and who strain our patience, the challenge of living according to the truths that every sin is forgiven and everyone redeemed, we can find the gospel disturbing. Grace is amazing and disturbing at the same time. In spite of our discomfiture, we too must offer a warm welcome to everyone, and invite them into the mutuality of self-giving, signified by the metaphor of embrace.

Closely allied to freedom is self-knowledge. Wherever our self-awareness is shallow and less than searching, we are likely to be in the grip of emotions and forces beyond our control. There may be an illusion of free will, but in reality we are trapped. What we do not know or understand has an undue influence on us. Individual autonomy, the golden calf of western individualism, is revealed as a false god and an unpredictable one too.

In order for our self-awareness to deepen, we must seek the source of our being from God. Looking beyond ourselves in prayer, we are set free to be ourselves, and given insight to discover who we are. This journey of self-discovery through giving God our attention in prayer has a necessary condition: we must take responsibility for ourselves. We should not seek to explain away our shortcomings or deny our culpability by blaming others. Rather, we are rigorous and honest, and declare simply and unequivocally, "I have sinned". Acknowledging our need of God's grace and forgiveness is a prerequisite for any authentic Christian spirituality. Humility is an essential virtue if progress in prayer is to be made. Contemplative prayer, defined as silent adoration of Christ, helps to cultivate these qualities that underpin our own growth to maturity. By attending to God in the stillness, we deliberately seek to undermine our tendency to self-justification. Rigorous self-scrutiny, accompanied by insights given to us in prayer, begins to militate against our self-interested interpretations of our own actions and those of others. By seeking to be naked before God, to be stripped bare, contemplation is by definition unsettling, unsafe and unrewarding. In making God the sole focus of our prayer, we can offer ourselves, unprotected and unreformed. As we are, with all our foibles and flaws, we present who we are now, in the hope that God will change us. "God loves us as we are but does not leave us as we are."[40]

As we pray contemplatively, our capacity for selfless attention increases and thereby we are able patiently, attentively and simply to adore God. Drawn by God's infinite beauty and our insatiable desire for God—so often distracted from its true goal by the desire for self-gratification—we know the truth in experience, not just in theory, that our love for God only finds fulfilment in self-abandonment.

In God's presence, we can face reality as it is. We confront our self-deceptions, exposed, yet wonderfully forgiven. We can stand in the stark, relentless light of God, the source of life and the ultimate reality.

By being determined to engage with reality as it is, not as we wish it to be, we open ourselves and the world up to genuine transformation. The Christian faith is centred on the Paschal Mystery: cross and resurrection. We must resist the urge, however, to rush from one to the other. Whereas they are inextricably linked—you cannot have one without the other—and they can be understood as one event, we should not merge the two. Conflating Golgotha and the disciples' encounters with the Risen Christ is to hide from the horrors of Good Friday. Instead we must linger crestfallen and distraught with those first followers of Jesus as they watch their leader die. This is a world of meaningless desolation, tragedy and loss. Standing in the darkness, disconsolate and aware of our own weakness, we must endure. From patient, truthful and courageous engagement with reality, transformation can come. It is only by faithfully standing in the barren landscape that we can begin to imagine a rich harvest. Tragedy and transfiguration belong together in God's loving purposes. However, we must give each their proper place and weight, and never seek to justify or explain tragic events by the good that might emerge. Rather, our task is to embrace the awfulness first, and by steady and sustained attention to enable hope and change to come eventually.

This bleak view of the world runs counter to the brash confidence of modernity. The contemporary western world-view, grounded in reductionist, rational thought, is subverted by the striking absurdity of the cross. Besides the incongruity of God's means of redemption, the cross stands as a sharp rebuke to anyone in power.

In his exchange with Jesus Christ, Pontius Pilate asks, "What is truth?" (John 18:38). They clash in a brief and subtle dialogue about kingship, earthly and heavenly kingdoms, and about the nature of truth. Although Jesus is ostensibly on trial, it is Pilate who is judged and found wanting. Jesus orchestrates a counter trial with Pilate in the dock. The clash, characterized by subtlety, paradox and misunderstanding, is the playing out of the universal drama. The power of truth is up against the truth of power. Consistently through the Bible, the prophets are suspicious of the powerful. Their perspective is too easily distorted by self-interest and the drive to defend their position. The poor, oppressed and powerless have an epistemological advantage: they see reality more clearly. Hence, the prophet's calling to "speak truth to power". "Witness", John's Gospel makes clear, is the instrument of truth.[41]

The self-effacing and straightforward task of telling the truth, insomuch as you understand it, is essential to the work of the church. Nonetheless, this exacting responsibility should be exercised humbly. Awareness that we live in a disordered world, and that our thinking by necessity is disordered, keeps us morally alert, sceptical of easy certainties, and properly concentrated on our own failings. Despite these hesitations, and our undeniable subjectivity, truth matters, and bearing witness to it, even at great cost, is integral to the church's role.

The truth of God's love spurs the church in mission. As the apostle Paul proclaimed in his second letter to the church in Corinth, "For the love of Christ urges us on, because we are convinced that one has died for all; therefore all have died. And he died for all, so that those who live might live no longer for themselves, but for him who died and was raised for them" (2 Corinthians 5:14–15). God's self-giving love is the rationale and motivation for the Church's mission. As well as being the driving passion that initiates and sustains missionary endeavour, God's love is the goal of mission. God's love in Jesus Christ forms the Church, and the risen life of Jesus Christ constitutes the Church. Embodied in our flesh and blood is a reality beyond us: the life of Christ. His life takes us out beyond ourselves in love, and with a task to proclaim God's saving love in Jesus Christ. Therefore, mission is integral, definitive of Church. As the German theologian Emil Brunner memorably declared, "'The Church exists by mission, just as fire exists by burning."[42] Only the Church reaching beyond her life to "every tribe and tongue and people and nation" (Revelation 5:9) vindicates her life. Throughout this movement towards the stranger, the Church shows that Jesus is risen indeed. Conversely, the life of Jesus Christ ceases to be available, is rendered inactive amongst us, if we seek to cling on to it for ourselves.

It is striking in Matthew's Gospel that the assurance of the presence of Jesus Christ is given to his disciples when they take the risk of sharing God's reconciling love. When we seek to draw a miscreant back into the life of the church, we are told, " . . . where two or three are gathered in my name, I am there among you" (Matthew 18:20). Sent out into the world to make disciples of all nations, we are told by Jesus Christ to remember "that I am with you, to the end of the age" (Matthew 28:20). In these liminal experiences, we move beyond our own limitations, our preferred boundaries, and that is where we find Jesus Christ waiting for us.

When we participate in mission, we go bearing two gifts. Offering the riches of the gospel, the wealth of God's Kingdom, and the riches of knowing Jesus Christ, we also share our poverty. The gift on offer can only be received by those who are poor. Authentic exchange in mission can only happen when both the giver and recipient understand their relationship as "one beggar telling another beggar where there is bread".[43]

In C. S. Lewis' book *The Lion, the Witch and the Wardrobe*, Jesus Christ is famously and movingly portrayed as a Lion, known as Aslan. Whilst not safe, and certainly wild, Aslan is good, and Aslan is on a mission:

> When he bares his teeth, winter meets its death,
> And when he shakes his mane, we shall have spring again.[44]

Also, Jesus Christ is a lion in hot pursuit, bent on a headlong, all-consuming chase of you and me. Relentlessly, the hunt is unremitting until we are caught.

Vincent Donovan in his wonderful book about cross-cultural mission, *Christianity Rediscovered,*—and in a sense all mission is cross-cultural—speaks of an encounter with a Masai elder who talks to him about the meaning of faith. He describes how faith is like a lion chasing down its prey with eyes and ears absorbed in rapt concentration. Every muscle strains in hot pursuit. Captured, the prey is devoured, and becomes part of the lion. Then he goes on to talk about God's search for us, God's inexorable quest for us. "All the time we think, we are the lion. In the end, the Lion is God."[45]

The purpose of leading the Church to maturity in love is that the entire world may know that God longs for everyone to meet and know Jesus Christ. The Risen Christ comes to you and me to ask the same question that he posed to the disciple Peter on the lake shore almost two thousand years ago, "Do you love me?" In that Resurrection appearance, the Risen Christ summoned his disciples to "come and eat". Through Jesus Christ, God issues to all of us an invitation to enjoy divine hospitality. Everything is ready: all we need to do is "come and eat". Drinking and eating together draws us deeper into God's life, the eternal love of Father, Son and Holy Spirit.

Living together in this Holy Communion, now and for eternity, we reflect God's self-giving, sacrificial love, and enjoy the fruit of the cross, the tree of life.

Bibliography

Alison, James, *Knowing Jesus* (London: SPCK, 1993).

Alison, James, *Living in the End Times* (London: SPCK, 1997).

Alison, James, *The Joy of Being Wrong: Original Sin through Easter Eyes* (London: SPCK, 1998).

Augsburger, David, *Caring Enough to Confront: How to Understand and Express your Deepest Feelings Toward Others* (Ventura, CA: Regal, 1973).

Baille, Gil, *Violence Unveiled* (New York: Crossroad Publishing, 1988).

Bodaken, Bruce and Robert Fritz, *The Managerial Moment of Truth: The Essential Step in Helping People Improve Their Performance* (New York: Free Press, 2006).

Bonhoeffer, Dietrich, *Life Together* (London: SCM Press, 1954).

Bonhoeffer, Dietrich, *The Cost of Discipleship* (New York: Macmillan Publishing Co. Inc., 1963).

Brunner, H. Emil, *The Word and the World* (London: SCM Press, 1931).

Collins, James C, *Good to Great* (London: Random House, 2001).

Collins, James C. and Jerry I. Porras, *Built to Last* (London: Random House, 2000).

Cosgrove, Charles and Dennis Hatfield, *Church Conflict: The Hidden Systems Behind the Fights* (Nashville, TN: Abingdon Press, 1994).

C. Conte, *Advanced Techniques for Counselling and Psychotherapy* (New York: Springer Publishing Company, 2009).

Craig, Yvonne Joan, *Peacemaking for Churches* (London: SPCK, 1999).

CSWG Associates, *A Manual for Eucharistic Living* (Chichester: CSWG Press, 1984).

Donovan, Vincent J., *Christianity Rediscovered* (London: SCM Press, 1982).

Eliot, T. S., *Four Quartets* (Faber and Faber Ltd. London, 1959).

Friedman, Edwin H., *A Failure of Nerve* (New York: Seabury Books, 1999).

Friedman, Edwin H., *Generation to Generation: Family Process in Church and Synagogue* (New York: The Guilford Press, 1985).

Fritz, Robert, and Peter M. Senge, *The Path of Least Resistance for Managers: Designing Organisations to Succeed* (Oakland, CA: Berret-Koehler, 1999).

Galindo, Israel, *The Hidden Lives of Congregations* (Herndon, VA: The Alban Institute, 2004).

Garratt, Bob, *The Fish Rots from the Head, the Crisis in the Boardrooms—Developing the Crucial Skills of the Competent Director* (London: Profile Books, 2003).

Garratt, Bob, *The Learning Organisation* (London: Fontana, 1987).

Gilbert, Roberta, *Extraordinary Relationships* (New York: John Wiley & Sons, 1992).

Girard, Rene, *I See Satan Fall Like Lightning* (Maryknoll, NY: Orbis, 2001).

Grimsley, Alex, *Vital Conversations* (Princes Risborough: Barnes Holland, 2010).

Hansen, Morten, *Collaboration* (Boston, MA: Harvard Business Press, 2009).

Handy, Charles, *Gods of Management* (London: Arrow, 1978).

Handy, Charles, *Understanding Voluntary Organisations* (London: Penguin, 1988).

Heider, John, *Tao of Leadership* (Atlanta, GA: Humanics, 1985).

Herrington, Jim, Robert Creech and Trisha Taylor, *The Leader's Journey: Accepting the Call to Personal and Congregational Transformation* (Hoboken, NJ: Jossey-Bass, 2003).

Hybels, Bill, *Courageous Leadership* (Grand Rapids, MI: Zondervan, 2002).

Inrig, Gary, *Forgiveness* (Grand Rapids, MI: Discovery House, 2005).

Julian of Norwich, *The Revelations of Divine Love* (Glasgow: The University Press, 1973).

Kreider, Alan, Eleanor Kreider and Paulus Widjaja, *A Culture of Peace: God's Vision for the Church* (Intercourse, PA: Good Books, 2005).

Lao Tzu, *Tao Te Ching* (Indianapolis, IN: Hackett, 1993).

Lathrup, Gordon W., *The Pastor: A Spirituality* (Minneapolis M1: Fortress Press, 2001).

Lencioni, Patrick, *The Five Dysfunctions of a Team* (Hoboken, NJ: Jossey-Bass, 2002).

Levinas, Emmanuel, *Totality and Infinity* (Pittsburgh, PA: Duquesne University Press, 1969).

Lewis, C.S., *The Lion, the Witch and Wardrobe* (Chronicles of Narnia) (London Harper Collins, 2009).

McGeechan, Ian, *The Lions* (London: Hodder and Stoughton, 2017).

Myers, Benjamin, *Christ the Stranger: The Theology of Rowan Williams* (London: T & T Clark International, 2012).

Richardson, Ronald, *Becoming a Healthier Pastor: Family Systems, Theory and the Pastor's Own Family* (Minneapolis, MN: Augsburg Fortress, 2005).

Richardson, Ronald, *Creating a Healthier Church: Family Systems Theory and Congregational Life* (Minneapolis, MN: Augsburg Fortress, 1996).

Roger of Taizè, *Parable of Community* (Oxford: Mowbray, 1980).

Runcorn, David, *Fear and Trust: God-centred Leadership* (London: SPCK, 2011).

Ruth, Kibbie Simmons and Karen A. McClintock, *Healthy Disclosure: Solving Communications Quandaries in Congregations* (Herndon, VI: The Alban Institute, 2007).

Scazzero, Peter, *The Emotionally Healthy Church* (Grand Rapids, MI: Zondervan, 2003).

Schwarz, Roger, *The Skilled Facilitator Fieldbook* (Hoboken, NJ: Jossey-Bass, 2005).

Schrock-Shenk, Carolyn (ed.), *Mediation and Facilitation Training Manual* (Akron, PA: Mennonite Conciliation Service, 2000).

Senge, Peter, *The Fifth Discipline* (London: Random House, 2006).

Smith, Alan and Peter Shaw, *The Reflective Leader* (London: Canterbury Press, 2011).

Steinke, Peter L., *Congregational Leadership in Anxious Times* (Herndon, VI: Alban Institute, 2006).

Steinke, Peter L., *Healthy Congregations: A Systems Approach* (Herndon, VI: The Alban Institute, 2006).

Tomlin, Graham, *The Provocative Church* Fourth Edition (London: SPCK, 2014).

Volf, Miroslav, *Exclusion and Embrace* (Nashville, TN: Abingdon Press, 1996).

Volf, Miroslav, *Free of Charge* (Grand Rapids, MI: Zondervan, 2005).

Warren, Robert, *Being Human, Being Church* (London: Marshall Pickering, 1995).

White, Vernon, *Paying Attention to People* (London: SPCK, 1996).

Whitfield, Charles, *Boundaries and Relationships: Knowing, Protecting and Enjoying the Self* (Deerfield Beach, FL: Health Communications Inc., 1994).

Williams, Rowan, *The Truce of God* (London: Fount, 1983).

Williams, Rowan, *Christ on Trial: How the Gospel Unsettles our Judgement* (Grand Rapids, MI: Wm. B. Eerdmans, 2003).

Notes

[1] For further information, see <http://www.bbministries.org.uk>.

[1] Admittedly, it is an inference from the text that the "glory of the Lord" continued its journey away from the Temple to the exiles in Babylon. Yet it seems a reasonable supposition given the overall thrust of the book.

[2] There are many verses that express this concern for the vulnerable, for example Deuteronomy 10:18.

[3] The Greek word *parakletos* is best translated in this context as "advocate" and conveys the sense someone who will act for the defence when Christians are brought to trial.

[4] C. Conte, *Advanced Techniques for Counselling and Psychotherapy* (New York: Springer Publishing Company, 2009), pp. 10–11.

[5] Peter M. Senge, *The Fifth Discipline* (London: Random House, 2006). What follows is an application of "systems thinking" expounded clearly and comprehensively in this book.

[6] An English translation of the Latin *Festine lente*, which literally means "make haste slowly". It served as a motto for the Roman emperors Augustus and Titus.

[7] Quoted in Janet Gabriel Townsend, *Women's Voices from the Rainforest* (London: Routledge, 1995), p. 9.

[8] Peter M. Senge, *The Fifth Discipline* (London: Random House, 2006).p. 316.

[9] *Common Worship* material is © The Archbishops' Council, 2000, and is reproduced by permission. All rights reserved. copyright@churchofengland.org.

[10] Ian McGeechan, *The Lions* (London: Hodder and Stoughton, 2017), p. 80.

[11] Bill O'Brien, quoted in Peter M. Senge, *The Fifth Discipline* (London: Random House, 2006), p. 202.

[12] From an interview with Arun Gandhi by Carmella B'Hahn in 1999 in which he quotes his legendary grandfather.

13   Quoted in Katherine Schori, *Gathering at the Lord's Table: The Meaning of Mission* (Woodstock, VT: Sky Lights Paths Publishing 2012), pp. 92–3.

14   Quoted in Peter M. Senge, *The Fifth Discipline* (London: Random House, 2006), p. 328.

15   Edwin H. Friedman, *A Failure of Nerve* (New York: Seabury Books, 1999), pp. 1–5.

16   Ian McGeechan, *The Lions* (Hodder and Stoughton, London, 2017), p. 180.

17   James M. Kittleson, *Luther the Reformer* (Minneapolis, MN: Augsburg, 1986), p. 161.

18   "Family Systems" thinking: its key insight is to conceive of the individual as formed by the "system" in which they are set.

19   John Wild, Introduction to Emmanuel Levinas, *Totality and Infinity* (Pittsburgh, PA: Duquesne University Press, 1969), p. 14.

20   Patrick Lencioni, *The Five Dysfunctions of a Team* (Hoboken, NJ: Jossey-Bass, 2002, pp. 195–220.

21   Quoted extensively in the media, for example, *Daily Mail*, on 23 July 2013.

22   This information about Saracens Rugby Union Football Club is widely-known but is drawn from an article entitled "Socrates among the Saracens" published on 12 July 2013 at < http://www.philosophyforlife.org/socrates-among-the-saracens/>.

23   Article in the *Daily Telegraph* on 30 April 2017 by Gavin Mairs.

24   Article in the *Guardian* by Robert Kitson on 21 May 2017.

25   For further details see <http://www.bbministries.org.uk>.

26   See Acts 15, where the issue of the circumcision of male Gentile converts is taken to the "Apostles and elders" in Jerusalem by a group led by Paul and Barnabas.

27   For further information, see <http://www.coventrycathedral.org.uk/smh/>.

28   Graham Tomlin, *The Provocative Church* Fourth Edition (London: SPCK, 2014), pp. 133–4.

29   Martin T. Hansen, *Collaboration* (Cambridge, MA: Harvard Business School, 2009), in the foreword.

30   Street Pastors is a nationwide project which has local expression in cities and towns. This project brings churches together to recruit and train volunteers who will be out on the streets over the weekend offering care and support to those who need help of any kind. It was pioneered in London in 2003 and

is run by the Ascension Trust. For further information, see <http://www.streetpastors.org>.

[31] Taken from the vision statement of St Mary the Virgin, Saffron Walden 2012.

[32] Food banks give out food to those who are in crisis and are often under the oversight of the Trussell Trust.

[33] *Guardian*, G2, p. 6, 16 February 2016 in an interview with Ed Pilkington.

[34] See John V. Taylor, *The Go-Between God* (London: SCM Classics, 2010).

[35] For further information, see <http://www.hopeintoaction.org.uk>.

[36] Gary Inrig, *Forgiveness* (Grand Rapids, MI: Discovery House, 2005), p. 127.

[37] Opening line of Isaac Watts' eponymous hymn.

[38] Dietrich Bonhoeffer, *The Cost of Discipleship* (New York: Macmillan Publishing Co., Inc. 1963), p. 99.

[39] Quote from the Eucharistic Prayer Rite B from *Common Worship* (London: Church House Publishing, 2000, p. 188.

[40] Quote from a sermon preached by the Very Revd Mike Kinman at the Cathedral Church of St Louis, USA, on 11 September 2011 at the 10 a.m. service.

[41] The role of the "witness" is woven throughout John's Gospel. For instance, the blind man who is given his sight by Jesus Christ declares when put under pressure to denounce Jesus, "One thing I do know, that though I was blind, now I see" (John 9:25).

[42] H. Emil Brunner, *The Word and the World* (London: SCM Press, 1931) p. 108.

[43] Gordon W. Lathrop, *The Pastor: A Spirituality* (Minneapolis, MI: Fortress Press, 2011), p. 133.

[44] C. S. Lewis, *The Lion, the Witch, and the Wardrobe (Chronicles of Narnia)* (London: Harper Collins, 2009), p. 88. © copyright CS Lewis Pte Ltd 1950.

[45] Vincent Donavan, *Christianity Rediscovered* (London: SCM Press, 1982), p. 63.

Lightning Source UK Ltd.
Milton Keynes UK
UKHW020621070519
342237UK00014B/1070/P